Piaget, Vygotsky and beyond

Jean Piaget and Lev Vygotsky are arguably the two most influential figures in psychological and educational research. Although born in the same year of 1896, it is only over the last decade or so that the work of Vygotsky has rivalled that of Piaget in importance in the Western world.

Piaget, Vygotsky and beyond examines the contribution made by these two seminal figures and assesses their possible influence over future work to be carried out in the next few years leading into the new millennium. Arranged around five themes (educational intervention and teaching, social collaboration and learning, cognitive skills and domain-specificity, the measurement of development and the development of modal understanding), each paper is followed by a discussant's comments.

Piaget, Vygotsky and beyond is a uniquely comprehensive collection, drawing together a wide range of themes in psychology and educational research that would otherwise be dispersed throughout a variety of different publications. It will be useful to advanced scholars and practitioner-researchers in both education and psychology.

Leslie Smith is Senior Lecturer in the Department of Educational Research, Lancaster University. His previous publications include *Jean Piaget: Critical Assessments* (4 vols, 1992) and *Critical Readings on Piaget* (1996). **Julie Dockrell** is Senior Lecturer in Child Development and Learning at the Institute of Education, London University. Her previous publications include a co-authored book with John McShane, *Children's Learning Difficulties: A Cognitive Approach* (Blackwell, 1992). **Peter Tomlinson** is Reader in Education in the School of Education, University of Leeds. His previous publications include *Understanding Mentoring* (Open University Press, 1995).

Piaget, Vygotsky and beyond

Future issues for developmental psychology and education

Edited by Leslie Smith, Julie Dockrell
and Peter Tomlinson

London and New York

First published 1997
by Routledge
11 New Fetter Lane, London EC4P 4EE

Simultaneously published in the USA and Canada
by Routledge
29 West 35th Street, New York, NY 10001

Reprinted 1998

Typeset in Times Ten by Keystroke, Jacaranda Lodge, Wolverhampton
Printed and bound in Great Britain by
Redwood Books, Trowbridge, Wiltshire

British Library Cataloguing in Publication Data
A catalogue record for this book is available from the British Library

Library of Congress Cataloging in Publication Data
A catalog record for this book is available from the Library of Congress

ISBN 0–415–14743–3

Contents

Figures

Tables

Contributors

Michael Beveridge is Professor of Education and Psychology at the University of Bristol.

Trevor G. Bond is Senior Lecturer in the School of Education, James Cook University, Australia.

Peter Bryant is Watts Professor of Psychology at the University of Oxford.

Robin N. Campbell is Lecturer in Developmental Psychology in the Department of Psychology, University of Stirling.

Margaret Chalmers is Lecturer in Psychology in the Department of Psychology, University of Edinburgh.

Julie Dockrell is Senior Lecturer in Child Development and Learning at the Institute of Education, London.

Gerard Duveen is University Lecturer in the Faculty of Social and Political Sciences, University of Cambridge.

Gerry P. T. Finn is Reader in the Department of Educational Studies, University of Strathclyde.

Paul Harris is Reader in Experimental Psychology, Department of Experimental Psychology, University of Oxford.

Deanna Kuhn is Professor of Psychology and Education, Teachers College, Columbia University, USA.

Brendan McGonigle is Reader in Psychology in the Department of Psychology, University of Edinburgh.

Sharon Nelson-Le Gall is based in the Learning Research and Development Center, University of Pittsburgh.

María Núñez is based in the Department of Experimental Psychology, University of Oxford.

Anne-Nelly Perret-Clermont is Professor of Psychology at the University of Neuchâtel, Switzerland.

Lauren B. Resnick is Director of the Learning Research and Development Center and Professor of Psychology at the University of Pittsburgh.

James Ridgway is Reader in the Psychological Aspects of Education in the Department of Psychology, Lancaster University.

Michael Shayer is Professor of Applied Psychology in the Centre for Educational Studies, King's College, London.

Leslie Smith is Senior Lecturer in the Department of Educational Research, Lancaster University.

Kathy Sylva is Reader in Educational Studies in the Department of Educational Studies, University of Oxford.

Peter Tomlinson is Reader in Education in the School of Education, University of Leeds.

Editorial note

Two savants made seminal contributions to developmental psychology and education in the twentieth century. They share the same centenary of birth. To mark this centenary, the Piaget–Vygotsky Centenary Conference was held in Brighton during 11–12 April 1996. The chapters in this book were all first presented as papers at the conference.

We warmly acknowledge the welcome support for this conference on the part of:

- Education Section, British Psychological Society
- Developmental Psychology Section, British Psychological Society
- Standing Conference Committee, British Psychological Society
- Routledge
- British Academy

Leslie Smith
Julie Dockrell
Peter Tomlinson

Introduction

Leslie Smith, Julie Dockrell and Peter Tomlinson

Jean Piaget was born in Neuchâtel on 9 August 1896 and died in Geneva on 16 September 1980. Lev Semyonovich Vygotsky was born in Orsha near Minsk on 5 November 1896 and died in Moscow on 11 June 1934. Their impact on developmental psychology and education has been prodigious throughout the century and looks set to continue well into the next. Two problems face anyone who plans to address, elaborate and evaluate the work of Piaget and Vygotsky. One is that their output was vast in scale and extent (for bibliographies, see Jean Piaget Archives, 1989; Van der Veer and Valsiner, 1991). The other is that their influence is as seminal as it is variegated. Each has set out standard positions which provide constitutive elements in contemporary accounts based on core constructs which merit worthwhile use, development and revision. Thus subtle decisions are required so that reasonable judgements can be made as to what should be retained and what should be revised in the works of Piaget and Vygotsky with regard to perspectives in psychology and education. This has proved to be no easy matter (Chapman, 1988; Daniels, 1993, 1996; Davydov, 1995; Kitchener, 1986; Lloyd and Fernyhough, in press; Lourenco and Machado, 1996; Smith, 1992, 1996a; Vidal, 1994; Wertsch and Tulviste, 1992).

There is sometimes a tendency to interpret the work of Piaget and Vygotsky in a polarised way, as if the work of one had next to nothing in common with that of the other. On this interpretation, there is an exclusive choice to be made between Piaget, or Vygotsky, but not both. Any such interpretation would have the consequence that developmental psychology and education could have nothing in common, when viewed from a Piagetian as opposed to a Vygotskian perspective. In contrast to this exclusive interpretation of 'Piaget or Vygotsky', there is a more inclusive interpretation in that some ideas are unique to Piaget's work, some ideas are unique to Vygotsky's, whilst other ideas are in their common possession. It will be worthwhile to elaborate this interpretation before previewing the chapters in this volume.

The argument for an inclusive interpretation of 'Piaget or Vygotsky' has two steps, one analogical and the other epistemological. The analogy is based on mountain scrambles. One way to climb a mountain is to walk up an easy slope such as a grassy track (on the left in Figure 1). Another way is to climb up a rock face (shown in Figure 2). Either way, this could be a solo ascent or in guided party. But both are routes on one and the same mountain: you can see the rock face (in Figure 2) on the right slope in Figure 1. More important still is the fact that the 2,000 ft contour on this mountain (see Figure 3) sets the same height whichever route you climb and whether you do this alone (like Reinhold Messner in his solo ascent of Everest) or with others (like Hilary and Tensing in their siege-ascent of Everest).

In fact, on one and the same mountain there are countless routes – up, along the same contour, and down – over endlessly varied terrain – easy paths and steep rock faces – with massive variety in weather conditions – tropical-to-arctic – and countless variations on the company, if any, you might keep in mountain scrambles. A contour sets the successive levels on a mountain, where a contour is as objective as a grassy track or a rock face. This analogy serves to identify three aspects of intellectual development.

First, the analogy clarifies the common view that intellectual development occurs as a sequence of hierarchical levels or stages. It is common ground that this commitment is made explicitly by both Piaget and Vygotsky, for example:

> we do in fact find, in the analysis of forms of social equilibrium, these same three structures. . . . (just as the) cognitive mechanisms in children involve three distinct systems.

(Piaget, 1995a, pp. 56, 276)

Development consists in three intrinsic stages.

(Vygotsky, 1994, p. 216)

Figure 1 Mountain path

Figure 2 Mountain rock face

Figure 3 Mountain 2,000 contour

There is less agreement as to how such claims are to be understood since the available empirical evidence is taken to be incompatible with general stages of development (Case, 1991; Siegler, 1991). However, issues are not clear-cut and Flavell (1992) has reminded us that there is a major and outstanding problem precisely because there is so little agreement as to alternatives to 'general' stages of development. One way to avoid this stalemate is to draw a distinction between two senses of generality. In one sense, generality amounts to *transfer*, for example the transfer of knowledge across domains, contexts and cultures. In a quite different sense, generality amounts to *universalisation*, such as the development of knowledge of universal properties as opposed to merely observational properties. Universalisation does not mean universal consent across culture, nor that skills used in one context are used in any other, nor that knowledge of universal properties in one domain is thereby generalised to any other. Quite simply, the 'general' and the 'universal' do not mean the same thing (Piaget, 1995a, p. 178; for commentary, see Smith, 1995, 1996c). Thus even if the evidence runs counter to an account of general stages of development *qua* transfer of knowledge, this evidence has suspect relevance to an account of general stages of development *qua* universalisation of knowledge. It is the latter which is picked out by the mountain analogy. Just as each new contour is higher than its predecessor, so each new developmental level is more advanced than its predecessor. Gaining access to new levels – on mountains and during intellectual development – is an achievement in itself. Nothing detracts from the achievement if an individual in the sequel stays at one and the same contour level or backtracks down hill. Climbing to a higher contour level is not the only way to enjoy mountain scrambles. And so it is with intellectual development. Inhelder and Piaget (1964, p. 285) stated clearly that, in their account, developmental advance does not occur as mere ascent, and so not as 'simple emergence or creation *ex nihilo* but (rather) in terms of differentiation and coordination'. Mountain scrambles are endlessly varied – so too is intellectual development through hierarchically ordered stages. Universalisation occurs in indefinite ways through multiple means across invariant levels in the development of knowledge.

Second, a joint commitment to the social variability of intellectual development is also explicitly endorsed by both Piaget and Vygotsky:

> Human intelligence is subject to the action of social life at all levels of development from the first to the last day of life.
>
> (Piaget, 1995a, p. 278)

> The entire history of the child's psychological development shows us that, from the very first days of development, its adaptation to the environment is achieved by social means.
>
> (Vygotsky, 1994, p. 116)

It is evident that Vygotsky (1994, pp. 59, 63) has a tendency to move from a social to a cultural characterisation of development, a point that is exploited in commentary on his work (Cole and Wertsch, 1996). No doubt the basis of this shift is his commitment to a notion of society that is intrinsically cultural. This notion is not reducible to social interaction. It is equally evident that Piaget's (1995a, pp. 41–7) commitments are similar in this respect with due attention given to social relationships and the cultural availability of knowledge and values (Smith, 1996a, 1996b).

Third, a similarly joint commitment is made about a biological contribution to intellectual development by both Piaget and Vygotsky:

> The stages of development are far from being just the manifestation of internal organic maturation.
>
> (Piaget, 1995a, p. 296)

> We must, therefore, distinguish the main lines in the development of the child's behaviour. First, there is the line of natural development which is closely bound up with the processes of general organic growth and maturation.
>
> (Vygotsky, 1994, p. 57)

Although Piaget (1971) is widely credited with a biological epistemology, it is not always realised that Vygotsky's account includes a specifically biological element (Moll, 1994). One implication is that there are commonalities both within and between species with regard to intellectual development and that, at each and every level, there are primitive forms of intelligence and understanding which have a relational link with more advanced successors in the endless growth of new knowledge as universalisation over its hierarchically related levels.

The main conclusion to draw from this analogy is that there are similarities in the positions adopted by Piaget and Vygotsky. This does not, of course, mean that similarity is identity, since there are important differences to take into account as well. It does mean that there are common commitments which are central to their two accounts that can be used jointly, rather than unilaterally, in psychological and educational studies.

Even so, this mountain analogy is partial and breaks down for both accounts. Development is an open process with no assignable term, unlike a typical mountain which has only one summit. Piaget (1971, p. 155; 1986, p. 312) explicitly noted the open nature of the development of knowledge. Vygotsky's (1978, pp. 84–91) commitment to intellectual development through a zone of proximal development leaves open both the degree to which mediated assistance is successful and the extent to which successful mediation is generative of novel knowledge. Thus the mountain analogy with its fixed summit breaks down when applied to intellectual development. Even so, it stands as a clear alternative to monolithic analogies such as a staircase (Case, 1991) or ladder (Bidell and Fischer, 1992). There are fixed steps up or down a staircase or ladder which have unitary terms, unlike the indefinite number of routes up and down a mountain. However, an analogy is only an analogy. This leads to the second step.

The second step is an epistemological argument. This argument shows that there is an underlying similarity in the accounts of Piaget and Vygotsky. Intellectual development for Vygotsky is a transition from social unity to individual identity; for Piaget, it is the conquest of identity as the main element in social unity. Quite simply, their common mountain is the construction of objective knowledge.

To see this, consider first Vygotsky's position according to which knowledge available in a culture is socially mediated, resulting in the formation of psychological tools which are generative of sign-based forms of communication. Such communication can in its turn make a contribution to common culture with endless iterations of this cycle of 'voices of the mind' (Smagorinsky, 1995; Wertsch, 1991). This is an attractive idea, plausibly amounting to a developmental mechanism. Yet Vygotsky was acutely aware that there are specific problems to confront with regard to the human use of language. If intellectual development is made possible by socio-cultural interactions between individuals who share a common language, these interactions should be meaningful and indeed generative of novel meanings. Yet ambiguities can and do arise about meaning, as Vygotsky (1994, pp. 239, 243, 318) noticed in this example where

(1) the victor at Jena
and
(2) the vanquished at Waterloo

provide alternative descriptions which can be learned and used without the learner realising that their common reference is one and the same man, Napoleon. Quite simply, there can be a joint use of language by members of a social unit with underlying semantic differences and confusions. And this is a powerful argument. But it is not original to Vygotsky since the distinctive example in (1) and (2) has its origin in the work of Edmund Husserl (1970) who used this very example to make the point that descriptions whose *sense* is different can none the less have the same *reference*. Clearly, the sense of (1) is different from the sense of (2), even though each has the same reference. Husserl further noticed that there can be different references for an expression with a unitary sense. A horse is a horse and yet the same word *horse* refers to a quite different horse in

(3) Bucephalus is a horse
(4) That cart-horse is a horse.

Vygotsky used Husserl's example to pin-point difficulties which children may have over the ambiguities of meaning. Children may use the same words as adults both where the reference is the same and the sense is different and where the reference is different and the sense is the same (Vygotsky, 1994, p. 318). Thus Vygotsky's model of socio-cultural exchange is plausible because it shows that other people can act as the *source* of new knowledge on the basis of common culture and a shared use of language. But Vygotsky (1994, p. 241) was also aware that cultural mediation can break down in that 'children's words can coincide in their objective reference with adult words and fail to do so in their meanings'. Mistakes will arise if the use made by children of expressions diverges from that of adults. One outcome is the formation of pseudoconcepts, where a pseudoconcept is taken by Vygotsky to be one of the successive levels in the transition to true mastery of a concept. The common failing is the same, namely children's reliance on psychological rather than logical understanding. As Vygotsky (1994, p. 229) put it, in the formation of concepts during childhood there abounds 'factual connection rather than abstract or logical connection (in consequence of which) the contradiction between the late development of concepts and the early development of verbal understanding finds its real resolution in pseudoconcepts'. In short, social communication and cultural interaction is possible just because the words used by an adult (who has a true concept) and a child (who has a pseudoconcept) have the some meaning (reference) in common. But it does not follow that each has the same meaning (sense) in mind, since a pseudoconcept is not identical with a true concept. Vygotsky realised that objective knowledge can be constructed through socio-cultural exchange only when certain logical criteria are satisfied as well. It is the satisfaction of these criteria that is the hall-mark of internalisation. Vygotsky (1978, p. 57) noted that he had not supplied an adequate account of internalisation. His admission is important since such an account is required so as to show how in the developing mind of the child the identity conditions of commmonly available concepts are understood.

In short, Vygotsky (1994, p. 163 – his emphasis) was compelled 'to acknowledge the *unity, but not the identity, of higher and lower psychological functions*'. A social unity – peer interaction, family, group, culture – is one and the same social unit whether or not all of its members have access to, and put to the one and the same meaningful use, the cultural tools in the common pursuit of objective knowledge. What may be missing from the mind of a developing child is an understanding of conceptual identity through the indispensable but shifting uses of language in a myriad contexts *hic et nunc*.

It may be noticed that Husserl's argument arose out of Gottlob Frege's (1980) argument that the distinction between words and things is too simplistic in that any assertoric sentence has both a sense and a reference. His celebrated example draws on the difference between

(5) The morning star is the morning star
and
(6) The morning star is the evening star.

The reference of (5) and (6) is the same, namely the planet Venus. Yet the sense of (5) is different from the sense of (6). This difference is *not* due to the law of identity which states that anything is self-identical, and necessarily so (Marcus, 1993). Both (5) and (6) are true identities. Rather, grasping the sense of (6) rests upon the empirical discovery that Venus is one and the same planet which appears both as the morning star and as the evening star. By contrast, grasping the sense of (5) requires the realisation that this is an analytic truth. Frege's insightful proposal that any assertoric sentence has both a reference and a sense provides the means for retaining the necessity of identity, as in (5), whilst also showing how an identity can be understood empirically, as in (6). This insight secures Frege's notable contribution to philosophy.

It has been argued that Frege's contribution to epistemology is equally important and yet has been neglected (Carl, 1994; Sluga, 1980). Frege's epistemology was developed during the rise of empirical psychology in nineteenth-century Germany. Frege was the arch opponent of psychologism, denying that psychology could ever be explanatory of human rationality. Central to this denial was the distinction between thinking and thought. First, Frege (1977) argued that thinking is not always objective since it may be wrong. In the human mind, incorrect thinking is pervasive. If rationality implies objectivity, then the rationality of incorrect thinking is suspect. Further, a correct response may be based on muddled thinking. Such thinking is hardly rational. Yet it is the task of empirical psychology to explain the causal origins of thinking, whether correct, incorrect or flawed. Thus an explanation of the objectivity of thought cannot be solely psychological. By contrast, it is the task of epistemology to explain the rationality of thought, for example when a thought is judged as true or is based on true reasoning. Frege explicitly noted that the psychological investigation of causal laws of thinking is indispensable. But psychology alone is not enough since the distinction between truth and falsity is not a psychological distinction. Second, Frege (1977) argued that human thinking has a subjective element which is unique to its possessor. Yet objective thought is inter-subjective and accessible to us all. The Pythagorean theorem is an objective and inter-subjective thought which anyone can grasp. But access to any (objective and inter-subjective) thought is *in fact* mediated by human thinking as it occurs in the actual world on the basis of 'his idea' or 'her image'. It is in this sense that thinking is subjective since 'he' can no more have 'her image' than 'she' can have 'his idea'. It is a strict consequence of Frege's position that no thought can ever be grasped other than through thinking and in this respect language has an important contribution to make. The investigation of actual thinking is the task of psychology. But psychology is not enough since some further account is required which relates thinking through logic to objective and inter-subjectively accessible thought.

Providing such an account is the proper domain of epistemology, which is concerned to chart the laws of truth. Frege (1980, p. 57) went on to add that the sense of any linguistic sign – such as the words making up (5) and (6) – 'is grasped by everybody who is sufficiently familiar with the language'. Quite simply, Frege's (1980, p. 62) definition of inter-subjectivity as thought 'which is capable of being the common property of several thinkers' – that is, a thought accessible to anyone at all – is a sweeping claim. Something more needs to be said as to how access to rational thought is *in fact* secured on the basis of human thinking whose hallmarks include suspect objectivity and inter-subjectivity. In short, some form of empirical investigation is required. Frege apparently accepted the prevailing assumption that psychology is empirical and epistemology is non-empirical. Thus his rational epistemology showed no concern for empirical matters. In this respect Frege did not realise that there is a *tertium quid*, or third alternative, in empirical epistemology (Kornblith, 1985), cognitive science (Leiser and Gilliéron, 1990) or, indeed, what Isaacs (1951) has called the 'psycho-logic' in Piaget's work.

In Piaget's work, the questions which are central to rational epistemology such as 'How is knowledge accessible?' were replaced by the question 'How does knowledge in fact develop?' This latter question is empirical, leading to the study of children's minds or the formation of scientific thought in history. It is also epistemological since knowledge is constituted by truth-conditions which bear upon what reality is like. Questions about knowledge and reality are epistemological. In support of his *tertium quid*, Piaget had a twofold argument. One argument was an express denial of psychologism (Piaget, 1966). The other argument was a concern with 'normative facts' which had previously been ignored in rational epistemology, namely the extent to which some cognitive instrument specified in rational epistemology 'was actually at the subject's disposal. Here, whether we like it or not is a question of fact' (quoted in Smith, 1993, p. 7).

Two principles were central to Piaget's position. One is a constructivist epistemology, that objective and inter-subjective thought is developed in virtue of human thinking. The other is a developmental psychology, that human thinking can break down especially during childhood. A conspicuous example of such breakdowns was noticed by Piaget during his stay in Paris and the standardisation of Burt's psychometric tests such as the Edith task (see Smith, 1993, p. 116 for a typical protocol; see Harris, 1998 for a commentary). In the presence of such breakdowns, two types of investigation could arise. One is psychological directed upon their causal explanation. The other is epistemological, directed upon the development of rational thought from less than rational thinking. The joint concern with both investigations is Piaget's (1923, 1950) *tertium quid* between empirical psychology and rational epistemology. This is a progressive problem-shift, since it opens the door for psychological investigation as one essential element in epistemological inquiry (Smith, 1993, pp. 35–6). Note that this problem-shift requires *joint* concerns in both epistemology and developmental psychology. Yet Piaget (1963) himself noted that his own pre-occupation with epistemological rather than psychological issues had not been shared by all psychologists. Indeed, many psychologists are seemingly pre-occupied with the investigation of intellectual development to the complete exclusion of epistemological concerns.

Piaget's joint concerns are evident in his conservation studies. From an epistemological point of view, conservation is important for exactly the same reason that deductive validity is important. All *valid* deductions are truth-preserving, where truth is a constitutive element of rationality (Sainsbury, 1991). Similarly, 'all knowledge ... presupposes principles of conservation (in as much as) conservation is a necessary condition for all rational activity' (Piaget, 1952, p. 3; amended translation). From a psycho-logical point of view, non-conservation on a reasoning task excludes valid inference on that task. The realisation that an inference is valid requires some capacity to transform self-identical premises in one and the same train of thought *salva veritate* – with truth preserved. This capacity cannot be exercised, still less formed, in thinking based on non-conservation. In this sense, Piaget's notion of conservation matches Frege's (1977) objec-tivity criterion. Further, Frege's (1977) inter-subjectivity criterion is also secured. It is endorsed by Piaget (1995a, p. 154) in his claim that a good system of thought, such as the thinking made possible by a well-defined cognitive structure, 'is only a system of possible substitutions either within a single individual's thought (operations of intelligence) or within thought exchanges from one individual to another (cooperation)'. Egocentric thinking – of which non-conservation is a special case – excludes the inter-subjectivity of thought (cf. Piaget, 1995b, note 2). Egocentric thinking is particularly manifest where any one member of a social unit has 'the tendency to think that each of their thoughts is common to all the others' (Piaget, 1928, p. 207).

There are two further aspects of conservation which are epistemo-logically, and not merely psychologically, important. One concerns autonomy. Piaget (1995a) raised the question of whether 'reasoning is an act of obedience or is obedience an act of reason?' The former amounts to heteronomy, unlike the latter which is due to autonomy. The point behind this question is that external authority, such as that of a social group, is binding 'solely on condition of an individual's capacity to carry out the same operation on his own account'. Note well that this remark hinges on identity of operations, which Vygotsky (1994) pointed out is *not* guaranteed by social unity. Social mediation ensures the transmission of cultural tools, not their autonomous use. Second, Piaget (1995a) regarded intellectual development as the search for novelty, which in turn is such that 'each individual is called upon to think and to rethink – on his own account and by means of his own system of logic – the system of collective notions'. The point is not that new knowledge can arise in the absence of culturally available skills and knowledge – this is flatly impossible, as Piaget (1995a, pp. 37, 57, 291) stated explicitly. Rather, his claim is that transmission is not enough since transformation is required as well for new knowledge to count as an advance over commonly available knowledge (Smith, 1996b). The transformational aspects of intellectual development are also noted in Vygotskian commentary (Cole and Wertsch, 1996).

Piaget and Vygotsky were each concerned to provide a good map of the same mountain. They both realised that this mountain had been a major challenge in rational epistemology. They both realised that empirical investigation of this mountain is essential and can be illuminating, namely by ascertaining how children do develop novel knowledge. Each provided a map of this mountain with shared characteristics, including the delineation of distinct levels in developmental sequences which are in all cases shaped by socio-cultural experience as well as by individual internalisation. Finally, their accounts have an epistemological element, notably with regard to the objective, inter-subjective and accessible features of knowledge.

The argument has been that there is common ground between the positions of Piaget and Vygotsky. Even so, it may not be enough on two counts. One is that there are several 'maps' – not one 'map' – on offer in Piaget's work (Beilin, 1992; Halford, 1992; Smith, 1996a). And the same is true in the case of Vygotsky's work (Cole and Wertsch, 1996; Daniels, 1996; Moll, 1994). Are all of these available 'maps' self-consistent? Second, the available 'maps' may not be complete, neither severally nor jointly. Are there uncharted mountain ranges? Both questions are important and currently unresolved.

The works of Piaget and Vygotsky span many and various empirical and theoretical issues. It was our aim to identify issues which both reflected current concerns in child development and education and offered a forum for discussing evidence and ideas which would take the conceptualization of the issues forward in a constructive fashion. Five specific themes were identified which met our criteria and the practical limits of the conference together with one overview dealing generally with Piaget, Vygotsky and beyond.

The Postface was given as the Conference Address at the Piaget–Vygotsky 1996 Centenary Conference and is presented here without revision. In each of the five specific sections, a preliminary version of the first two papers was presented at the conference. Each was prepared independently and in advance. Specific commentary on the papers was then offered at the conference in an orally delivered discussant's commentary. The two lead papers and discussants' commentary were followed by discussion from conference delegates. The papers published in this book are the revised versions of these papers, variously drawing upon discussions at the conference, editorial feedback and subsequent reflections.

EDUCATIONAL INTERVENTION AND TEACHING

The link between psychology and education has long been a matter of debate. Yet major changes that have occurred in educational practice high-light the central role that could be played by strong accounts of learning and development. Both Piaget (1982) and Vygotsky (1994) made it clear that their psychological work was educationally important. Yet neither carried out, still less carried through, the educational application of their own ideas. Their followers have set out to remedy this oversight, but their work raises several questions (Brown *et al.*, 1996; Daniels, 1993). One is criterial: what exactly is distinctive about a Piagetian or a Vygotskian approach to education? A second is psychological: is there an opera-tionalised mechanism in their work which could lead to intellectual improvement? A third is educational: is there any evidence that education-ally significant changes can be brought about on the basis of either account? The argument in Michael Beveridge's paper is that anyone who sets out to study educational practice should have a good psychological theory, rather than a political ideology, at their disposal. Michael Shayer sets out his case to show that successful intervention in school settings is possible, notably when an intervention programme has its origin in Piaget's theory. Kathy Sylva provides a commentary.

SOCIAL COLLABORATION AND LEARNING

The role of peer collaboration in moulding successful learning has captured the interests of researchers and practitioners alike. In their accounts, both Piaget (1995a, 1995b) and Vygotsky (1978) identified a clear role for social exchange in intellectual development. In fact, research in this area has expanded to cover context and culture due to their instrinsic relation to human learning in society (Cole and Wertsch, 1996; Tryphon and Vonèche, 1996). A substantive problem to address is rationality and relativism (Gellner, 1992; Moshman, 1994). It is a plain fact that context and culture are variables, and potent ones at that. What needs to be shown is how an empirical account which is sensitive to such variability can avoid a com-mitment to relativism. The trouble here is that relativism is incompatible with the objectivity of knowledge. What also needs to be shown is how an account of rationality is compatible with social diversity without assigning privileged status to one socio-cultural group over all of the others. The paper by Anne-Nelly Perret-Clermont examines the early contextual effects on Piaget's own development, whilst in his paper Gerard Duveen focuses on social representation in accounts of intellectual development. Gerry Finn offers a commentary on their papers.

COGNITIVE SKILLS AND DOMAIN SPECIFICITY

The nature of learning mechanisms postulated by a theory is very largely dependent on its view of what develops. Underpinning much research in the development of cognition is the dichotomy between domain-specific and domain-general mechanisms. Each view has direct and profound implications for our view of what is developing. It is yet to be established how representational and procedural knowledge develop to create a cognitive domain. It is, for example, plausible that mechanisms that are general at an early point in development lead to domain-specific representations and procedures later. Piaget (1985) placed great store by domain-general mechanisms in his account of development as equilibration, though qualifications have been noted in subsequent work (cf. Case and Edelstein, 1993). The extent to which Vygotsky's (1978) account favours a domain-specific or a domain-general model is a matter of continuing discussion (Wozniak and Fischer, 1993). Many models of cognition which are currently dominant are more reliant – and in some cases exclusively so – on domain-specific mechanisms (cf. Carey and Gelman, 1991; Halford, 1993). Comparable positions are apparent in educational discussions (Brown *et al.*, 1989; Perkins and Salomon, 1989). Indeed, school children have ample experience of the differential demands arising from different subjects in the school curriculum. But human creativity is manifest as the detection and characterisation of similarities in and between bodies of knowledge, both within the arts and sciences as well as between them. In his paper, Peter Bryant reviews the research evidence on the development during childhood of knowledge and skills in arithmetic. Lauren Resnick and Sharon Nelson-Le Gall in their paper set out a case in which motivational, and not merely cognitive, factors are central to learning and development in real-world settings. Robin Campbell provides commentary on their papers.

MEASUREMENT OF DEVELOPMENT

The measurement of knowledge and abilities is a desirable element in a developmental theory and a standard feature of educational practice. Less clear is how such measurements are to be interpreted. Neither Piaget nor Vygotsky gave a lead in this respect. In fact, there is a stark dilemma here. On one side are batteries of psychometric tests, which are norm-referenced. Such tests have stood both the test of time and the methodological requirement of reliability (Anderson, 1992). But their validity is another matter and this ultimately rests on the assumption that all – and not merely some – abilities can be measured by tests which have been standardised through a bell-curve with an age-index. On the other side are batches of assessment tasks, which are criterion-referenced. Such tasks are typically subjected to meticulous experimental scrutiny, leading to results whose validity is attested through fine statistical analysis. The outstanding problem is that of showing which psychological interpretation best fits the statistically significant findings which arise from different assessment tasks. In fact, much current discussion about intellectual development centres on this issue with a consensus not yet in sight (Beilin, 1992; Flavell, 1992; Halford, 1992). Two approaches to the measurement of development are addressed in this section. Trevor Bond sets out a case for using Rasch analysis on the grounds that this technique is uniquely suited to the measurement of developmental differences just in case a good theory – such as Piaget's – is to hand. Margaret Chalmers and Brendan McGonigle base their position on the design and use of tasks which can be used with individuals from different species in the evolutionary spectrum. Jim Ridgway sets out his commentary on these issues.

DEVELOPMENT OF MODAL UNDERSTANDING

There are at least two demands which any account of intellectual development has to face. One is to identify distinct forms of knowledge. The other is to interpret them through a unifying account of human understanding. Modal understanding provides a good test-case. This is because modal knowledge has its own instrinsic features. Yet modal knowledge is also a prevalent and characteristic element in human understanding. In fact, there are several types of modal concepts (Haack, 1978; Piéraut-Le Bonniec, 1980). Each of these concerns the manner or mode in which something is known, for example with certainty (epistemic modality), as what should be the case (deontic modality), or as that which is necessarily so (alethic modality). Further, each is independent of the truth-value of what is known. Leslie Smith sets out a case for the investigation of necessary knowledge (alethic modality) in psychological and educational settings. Paul Harris and María Núñez elaborate their account of children's understanding of permission and obligation (deontic modality). The discussant in this section is Peter Tomlinson.

THE VIEW FROM GIANTS' SHOULDERS

Deanna Kuhn set out to look through the work of Piaget and Vygotsky in relation to current developments in psychology and education in the next steps ahead. This is both a liberating and daunting opportunity which is here carried through with special attention to current research on microgenesis, metacognition and social collaboration.

REFERENCES

Anderson, M. (1992). *Intelligence and Development*. Oxford: Blackwell.
Beilin, H. (1992). Piaget's enduring contribution to developmental psychology. *Developmental Psychology*, 28, 191–204.

Bidell, T. and Fischer, K. (1992). Cognitive development in educational contexts: implications of skill theory. In A. Demetriou, M. Shayer, A. Efklides (eds). *Neo-Piagetian Theories of Cognitive Development*. London: Routledge, p. 13.

Brown, A., Metz, K. and Campione, J. (1996). Social interaction and individual understanding in a community of learners: the influence of Piaget and Vygotsky. In A. Tryphon and J. Vonèche (eds). *Piaget–Vygotsky: The Social Genesis of Thought*. Hove: Psychology Press.

Brown, J., Collins, A. and Duguid, P. (1989). Situated cognition and the culture of learning. *Educational Researcher*, 18 (1), 32–42.

Carey, S. and Gelman, R. (1991). *The Epigenesis of Mind*. Hillsdale, NJ: Erlbaum.

Carl, W. (1994). *Frege's Theory of Sense and Reference*. Cambridge: Cambridge University Press.

Case, R. (1991). *The Mind's Stair-Case*. Hillsdale, NJ: Erlbaum.

Case, R. and Edelstein, W. (1993). *The New Structuralism in Cognitive Development Theory: Theory and Research on Individual Pathways*. Basel: Karger.

Chapman, M. (1988). *Constructive Evolution*. Cambridge: Cambridge University Press.

Cole, M. and Wertsch, J. (1996). Beyond the individual–social antinomy in discussions of Piaget and Vygotsky. *Human Development*, 39, 250–6.

Daniels, H. (1993). *Charting the Agenda*. London: Routledge.

Daniels, H. (1996). *An Introduction to Vygotsky*. London: Routledge.

Davydov, V. (1995). The influence of L. S. Vygotsky on education: theory, research, practice. *Educational Researcher*, 24 (3), 12–21.

Flavell, J. (1992). Cognitive development: past, present and future. *Developmental Psychology*, 28, 998–1005.

Frege, G. (1977). *Logical Investigations*. Oxford: Blackwell.

Frege, G. (1980). On sense and meaning. In P. Geach and M. Black (eds). *Translations from the Philosophical Writings of Gottlob Frege*. 3rd edition. Oxford: Blackwell, p. 56.

Gellner, E. (1992). *Postmodernism, Reason and Religion*. London: Routledge.

Haack, S. (1978). *Philosophy of Logics*. Cambridge: Cambridge University Press.

Halford, G. (1992). Analogical reasoning and conceptual complexity in cognitive development. *Human Development*, 35, 193–217.

Halford, G. (1993). *Children's Understanding: The Development of Mental Models*. Hillsdale, NJ: Erlbaum.

Harris, P. (1998). Piaget in Paris: 'autism' to logic. *Human Development*, in press.

Husserl, E. (1970). *Logical Investigations*. 2 vols. London: Routledge and Kegan Paul.

Inhelder, B. and Piaget, J. (1964). *Early Growth of Logic in the Child*. London: Routledge and Kegan Paul.

Isaacs, N. (1951). Critical notice: *Traité de logique*. *British Journal of Psychology*, 42, 155–8.

Jean Piaget Archives (1989). *Bibliography Jean Piaget*. Geneva: Jean Piaget Archives.

Kitchener, R. (1986). *Piaget's Theory of Knowledge*. New Haven: Yale University Press.

Kornblith, H. (1985). *Naturalizing Epistemology*. Cambridge, MA: MIT Press.

Leiser, D. and Gilliéron, C. (1990). *Cognitive Science and Genetic Epistemology*. New York: Plenum Press.

Light, P. and Butterworth, G. (1992). *Context and Cognition*. New York: Harvester Wheatsheaf.

Lloyd, P. and Fernyhough, C. (in press). *Lev Vygotsky: Critical Assessments*. London: Routledge.

Lourenco, O. and Machado, A. (1996). In defense of Piaget's theory: a reply to 10 common criticisms. *Psychological Review*, 103, 143–64.

Marcus, R. B. (1993). *Modalities: Philosophical Essays*. New York: Oxford University Press.

Moll, I. (1994). Reclaiming the natural line in Vygotsky's theory of cognitive development. *Human Development*, 37, 333–42.

Moshman, D. (1994). Reason, reasons and reasoning. *Theory and Psychology*, 4, 245–60.

Perkins, D. and Salomon, G. (1989). Are cognitive skills context-bound? *Educational Researcher*, 18 (1), 16–25.

Piaget, J. (1923). La psychologie et les valeurs religieuses. In Association Chrétienne d'Etudiants de la Suisse Romande (ed). *Sainte-Croix 1922*, pp. 38–82.

Piaget, J. (1928). *Judgment and Reasoning in the Child*. London: Routledge and Kegan Paul.

Piaget, J. (1929). *The Child's Conception of the World*. London: Routledge and Kegan Paul.

Piaget, J. (1950). *Introduction a l'épistémologie génétique*. Paris: Presses Universitaires de France.

Piaget, J. (1952). *Child's Conception of Number*. London: Routledge and Kegan Paul.

Piaget, J. (1963). Preface. In J. Flavell, *The Developmental Psychology of Jean Piaget*. New York: Van Nostrand.

Piaget, J. (1966). Part II. In E. Beth and J. Piaget, *Mathematical Epistemology and Psychology*. Dordrecht: Reidel.

Piaget, J. (1971). *Biology and Knowledge*. Edinburgh: Edinburgh University Press.

Piaget, J. (1982). Foreword. In G. Voyat, *Piaget Systematized*. Hillsdale, NJ: Erlbaum.

Piaget, J. (1985). *Equilibration of Cognitive Structures*. Chicago: University of Chicago Press.

Piaget, J. (1986). Essay on necessity. *Human Development*, 29, 301–14.

Piaget, J. (1995a). *Sociological Studies*. London: Routledge.

Piaget, J. (1995b). Commentary on Vygotsky's criticisms. *New Ideas in Psychology*, 13, 325–40.

Piéraut-Le Bonniec, G. (1980). *The Development of Modal Reasoning*. New York: Academic Press.

Russell, B. (1903). *Principles of Mathematics*. London: George Allen and Unwin.

Sainsbury, M. (1991). *Logical Forms*. Oxford: Blackwell.

Siegler, R. (1991). *Children's Thinking*. 2nd edition. Englewood Cliffs, NJ: Prentice Hall.

Sluga, H. (1980). *Gottlob Frege*. London: Routledge and Kegan Paul.

Smagorinsky, P. (1995). The social construction of data. *Review of Educational Research*, 65, 191–212.

Smith, L. (1992). *Jean Piaget: Critical Assessments*. 4 vols. London: Routledge.

Smith, L. (1993). *Necessary Knowledge*. Hove: Erlbaum Associates Ltd.

Smith, L. (1995). Introduction. In J. Piaget, *Sociological Studies*. London: Routledge.

Smith, L. (1996a). *Critical Readings on Piaget*. London: Routledge.

Smith, L. (1996b). With knowledge in mind: novel transformation in the learner or transformation of novel knowledge. *Human Development*, 39, 257–63.

Smith, L. (1996c). Universal knowledge. Paper presented at The Growing Mind conference at the University of Geneva, September.

Tryphon, A. and Vonèche, J. (1996). *Piaget–Vygotsky: The Social Genesis of Thought*. Hove: Psychology Press.

Van der Veer, R. and Valsiner, J. (1991). *Understanding Vygotsky: A Quest for Synthesis*. Oxford: Blackwell.

Vidal, F. (1994). *Piaget Before Piaget*. Cambridge, MA: Harvard University Press.

Vygotsky, L. (1978). *Mind in Society*. Cambridge, MA: Harvard University Press.

Vygotsky, L. (1994). *The Vygotsky Reader*. Oxford: Blackwell.

Wertsch, J. (1991). *Voices of the Mind*. Cambridge, MA: Harvard University Press.

Wertsch, J. and Tulviste, P. (1992). L. S. Vygotsky and contemporary developmental psychology. *Developmental Psychology*, 28, 548–57.

Wozniak, R. and Fischer, K. (1993). *Development in Context*. Hillsdale, NJ: Erlbaum.

Part 1

Educational intervention and teaching

1 Educational implementation and teaching
'School knowledge' and psychological theory

Michael Beveridge

THE OPTIMISTIC AGENDA

The development of psychology in the twentieth century can reasonably be seen as a success story. It has broadened and deepened its academic base as well as taking important steps as a profession. However, in the UK, psychology, which was once thought to make a significant contribution to the professional knowledge of teachers, is facing difficulties in influencing educational practices. In this paper I will examine some of the problems which we need to understand and overcome if future generations of learners are to benefit from the implementation of psychological research in educational contexts.

Many teachers, especially the newly qualified (Blandford, 1995), remain ignorant and deeply sceptical about the use of psychology in education. This is unfortunate because in the move away from grand theory, psychology has been making progress in the study of specific problems with practical applications in education. Psychology has put much effort into modelling processes. Of obvious relevance to education is the substantial body of work on cognitive processes in reading, writing and numeracy (e.g. Healy and Bourne, 1995). Other potentially useful areas of research include the roles of analogy, external representations, reasoning, implicit knowledge acquisition, social factors and the role of language in collaborative learning, the value of mixed modes of teaching, and cognitive apprenticeship (Pressley and McCormick, 1995).

Psychologists are also developing models of how learning develops over time, which take account of the structure of the tasks and the way they are taught. Work on small group teaching and peer tutoring shows that there may be many pathways to learning. Research is also continuing into how information technology can be used creatively to expand rather than narrow down children's learning environments. There is an urgent need for this research because designers of educational software are currently no better informed by research than textbook authors were fifty years ago.

This psychological research agenda looks promising for educational intervention with so many important new developments now being pursued.

New areas and methods of work will, of course, be required. For example, because teachers are concerned with student learning over an extended period of time and in different contexts psychologists should connect research on 'situated cognition' to studies of classrooms. In this connection there is a substantial body of research which has attempted to describe the 'meaning making' activities in classrooms which lead children to learn (Pollard and Filer, 1996). However this work is often highly interpretative, relies heavily on the subjectivity of the observer and fails to systematically test these interpretations. Nevertheless this research is attractive to practitioners because it presents data in narrative form from which they can recognise events similar to their own experiences. This work could usefully take account of psychological research into the long-term retention and use of both knowledge and skills. This would require studies of the individual learning histories of children, which investigate the scenes and situations they encounter in home and school.

Another fertile area of study which will benefit from this type of longitudinal research is that of teacher expertise. Developments in the study of expertise indicate that the intuitive knowledge of gifted teachers gained through experience can be formulated in ways which can be communicated to new recruits to the teaching profession (Borko and Livingston, 1989). Hopefully the pervasive idea that only teachers understand teaching will be less easy to sustain in future. Especially if, out of the usual complexities revealed by research, some useful simplifications emerge.

IMPLEMENTATION: PROCESS AND PROBLEMS

From the above, it might be concluded that the educational impact of psychological research is likely to increase with a consequent improvement in educational standards. Certainly the potential is there, but, as I will now suggest, the impact might well be minimal without careful consideration and resolution of the problems of research implementation in education. Simply doing the 'right' research will not be enough.

The relationship between research and practice in education has been a cause for concern for a considerable time. It has been the subject of several reviews and numerous formal and informal meetings. It is now clear that research-based educational intervention is not a straightforward process. Problems are well documented. These include (Havelock and Huberman, 1977) (see Table 1):

1 problems in managing the implementation process,
2 problems arising from the personalities and behaviour of those involved,
3 inadequate resources and organisational capacities, and
4 opposition from key groups in society to the proposed reforms.

Table 1 Problems in research utilisation

Problems in managing the innovation process	Personalities and personal motivation	Inadequate resources and capacities	Opposition from key groups in society
Not enough coordination of people in different roles	Personality conflicts on project team	Project materials not ready or delivered on time	Opposition to innovation by those in power
Insufficiently clear structure for decision-making	Some on project team lacked understanding and appreciation of feelings of others	Costs underestimated	Conflicting ideologies about change
Lack of common understanding of project objectives	Persons in key roles did not devote enough energy and enthusiasm to project	Difficulty locating and recruiting appropriate personnel	Slow implementation of the project
Lack of good communication with leaders	Some key persons too rigid and narrow-minded in understanding of project	High personnel turnover	Objections to project by special interest groups
Too much centralisation of decision-making	Faulty outside technical assistance	Inadequate financial support	
Too many rules and regulations that had to be followed	Persons in key roles not open to change in attitudes and behaviour	National economic priorities for education were low	
Formal authority to begin project was delayed	Insufficient rewards for implementors	Significant delays in delivery of funds	
Inadequate consideration of implementation problems		Inflation threw off original cost estimates	
Educators on project did not understand political realities			

Source: Adopted from Havelock and Huberman (1977)

These are factors which work against the application of new psychological ideas in education. However, even if psychological ideas are used there is, in addition to these other problems, the possibility that psychology can be distorted in the application process. For example, two decades ago Piaget was used as a theoretical justification for discovery learning. Piaget's ideas on the important role of certain child activities in the development of logical thought were seen as supporting a classroom environment in which children engaged with physical objects so as to inevitably discover relationships of e.g. quantity, size, volume and mass. Learning by discovery was seen as, in some sense, 'real' and meaningful for the child. This, in theory, was contrasted with didactic methods in which the meaning was seen to emanate from a teacher, but often failed to be clearly understood by children. Piaget's emphasis on the role of action in the genesis of thought was used to support the view that children could learn on their own. As we know, and as is demonstrated in this volume, Piaget paid great attention to the role of other persons in learning and development. But these aspects of his work were largely ignored by liberal educators with a particular agenda. The distortion of psychological theories by educators is difficult to avoid given their tendency to want simple, easily applied, solutions; especially if psychologists adopt weak techniques of dissemination to minimally satisfy funding conditions.

One particular problem to be addressed is the way that psychology has avoided the process of providing user communities with syntheses of current competing theories. Consider the following passage from Van der Veer and Valsinner's (1991, p. 392) *Understanding Vygotsky*:

> A present-day psychologist is most likely to adopt a non-dialectical, 'either–or' perspective when determining the 'class membership' of one or another approach in psychology. Hence the frequent non-dialectical contrasts between 'Piagetian' and 'Vygotskian' approaches, or the widespread separation of psychologists into 'social' versus 'cognitive' categories, which seem to occupy our minds in their meta-psychological activities. Even the existence of an overlap of the two ('social cognition') does not alter the non-dialectical classification of the psychological 'mindscape', since the focus of that taxonomy is mostly 'book-keeping', rather than synthesising ideas from opposing camps.

This quotation captures an important problem to be resolved if psychology is to be made useful to teachers. Many trainee teachers, when forced in their written assignments to decide which of two poorly understood theories was correct, promptly dismissed both as irrelevant. Without serious attempts at synthesis by the research community the case for relevance for the teaching context is not easily established.

The research implementation process in education is poorly understood. Attempts to characterise solutions to implementation problems have a tendency to end up with crude and relatively useless taxonomies and favour

---

SEVEN MODELS OF RESEARCH UTILISATION

The **classical linear model**: research → development → diffusion and dissemination → application.

The **problem-solving model** in which the researcher supplies evidence or conclusions needed to solve a policy problem or implement the policy: knowledge needed relevant to policy → search for relevant knowledge or commissioning of research → policy decision.

The **interactive model** which presumes some complex and disorderly to-and-fro dialogue between researchers and policy makers.

The **political model** in which research is used or interpreted selectively in a partisan way to support an already adopted position, or research is commissioned in the expectation that it will provide ammunition for the policy already adopted.

The **tactical model** or the burying of a research problem or of a problem in research to defend procrastination or the unwillingness to take action.

The **enlightenment model** (taken by Weiss to be the most common) by which research permeates the policy-making process not by specific findings or conclusions but by shaping conceptualisation and thinking relevant to the policy issue.

The **research-as-part-of-the-intellectual-enterprise-of-society model** in which research has no special impact but is just on influence among the huge number of factors that influence different policies in different ways at different times.

Figure 4 Weiss's seven models of research utilisation (Weiss, 1980)

diffuse connections between research and practice. For example, in Weiss's (1980) 'Seven models of research utilisation' (see Figure 4) the most popular was the enlightenment model. This is similar to the analyses presented by the Nisbet and Broadfoot (1980) review and of Murphy's (1995) BERA Presidential address.

In contrast, Beveridge (1995, and in press) and Hargreaves (1996) take a stronger line on developing explicit implementation processes. They cite evidence from medicine and engineering, which are more systems oriented, showing how a cultural shift in education towards a systems approach and away from the primacy of the individual teacher or lecturer is required. There are signs in, for example, new whole-school and inter-school policies which also involve parents, that this change may be occurring slowly (Beveridge, 1996).

Both Beveridge (in press) and Hargreaves (1996) argue that research implementation in education is hampered by the lack of an accepted technical language such as that of biological science in medicine or applied mathematics in engineering. Such an effective technical language must have the following general characteristics:

1 It must provide some useful specifications of the complexities of particular schools, classrooms, teachers and learners.
2 It must be able to enhance the process of creating expert teachers and learners.
3 It must be useable within educational organisations to enable them to learn from their own practices.

The development of such a language would require resolution of a number of different issues which can be broadly characterised as either (a) philosophical, (b) representational or (c) socio-cultural. This would be in addition to the practical problems listed above. Let me illustrate these in turn. An example based around the important psychological and educational question of motivation will serve to illustrate the epistemological issues. Motivation, as reflected in the time and effort given to study by learners of all abilities, is a concern of all teachers. And despite the general connection between educational success and economic prosperity, for both individuals and nations, many pupils do not, at least in the UK, just recognise this and work hard to succeed in their learning. It is an important research question as to why this is the case. And policy makers and practitioners are very interested in the answers.

But there is no clear agreement as to the appropriate account of motivation which might apply to education. There remain many questions that empirical research alone is unlikely to be able to answer. For example, can motivation be studied independently of the cultural meanings and values of the students? Is motivation, as many psychologists have assumed, a characteristic of individuals who can be said to belong to measurable motivational categories, e.g. having high achievement motivation? And is there an association between motivation and biological factors? Or, on the other hand, is motivation connected to Heidegger's 'basic modalities of the world', such as our separation from others, our anxieties about the future and our fear of death? None of these questions seem, at least at first sight, to be easily amenable to measurement using either questionnaires or biochemical techniques.

Many disagreements about psychological research and its value and its usefulness to education have similar elements of philosophical difficulty. Obvious examples include disputes about intelligence and ability. I have some concern, not that these issues arise, but whether they are being considered carefully enough by the educational community. There is a strong tendency for the serious philosophical debates that are necessary for the development of an accepted technical language for education to be reduced to quasi-political rhetoric. For example, it seems to be impossible to have an informed debate about genetics in relation to education.

The drive to empirical social science, which despite the short-termism associated with research assessment is a welcome move away from 'armchair' deliberation, has, in my view, left educational and psychological research short of synthesis as offered by the broadly based intellectual tradition of, for example, Piaget and Vygotsky. There are a growing number of technicians but relatively few thinkers and scholars. There is even in some academic institutions a prevailing anti-intellectualism which runs alongside views that all understanding and clarity of thought comes from the 'reality' of either the classroom or the experiment. This 'natural attitude', to use Husserl's term, is in itself an intellectual position but it is doubtful whether many of its protagonists understand its nature.

Moving on to the representational questions referred to above, in a recent review which consulted several hundred psychologists and educators the following conclusion was drawn: 'Research on knowledge representation, metaphors and analogies and explanations has much to contribute to the development of a technical language for education but at this point remains largely outside the purview of educational practitioners' (Beveridge, 1995, p. 26). (For a more extended discussion of these issues see Beveridge (in press).) These representational issues in developing a technical language are being studied by both psychologists and cognitive scientists, but these questions are also important for both teaching and the development of knowledge itself. Consider, for example, the problem of knowledge representation in visual mode through pictures and diagrams. Figure 5 shows the classical drawing of the way atoms behave, but, like all metaphors in science, it is considered by some to be inappropriate. As Quinn (1989, p. 29) wrote:

> One cannot draw a sensible picture of the atom. Apart from the problem of scales, there is the problem that the atom is a quantum mechanical system – the proper description of such a system is in terms of a probability distribution which, for example, gives the likelihood that an electron would be found at a certain distance from the center of the atom if one were able to make an instantaneous measurement.

Peter Cheng at the ESRC Centre for Research into Learning Development Instruction and Training is studying pictorial representation in scientific thought. His work shows how visual tools are powerful but not necessarily self-explanatory, as they are often taken to be by educators. There is considerable need to develop useful principles for visual knowledge representation based on an understanding of the way knowledge develops. If education is to benefit we need to extend psychological research in this area beyond studying simplistic 'laws' (e.g. the picture superiority effect) which have no practical uses and are probably experimental artefacts.

I will now turn to the socio-cultural difficulties in developing a research-based language for communicating about educational issues. Much has been written over the last fifteen years concerning socio-cultural issues in education and I will not attempt to summarise these discussions here. There is, however, one socio-cultural feature of the education system which does need to be emphasised in relation to the technical language

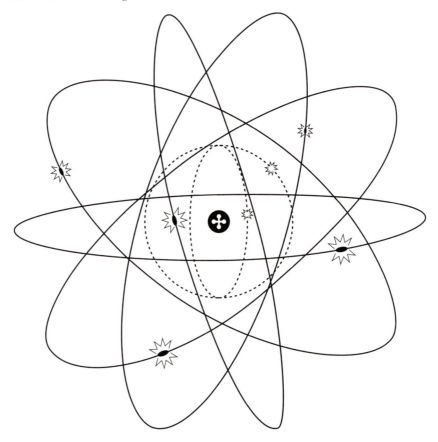

Figure 5 The atom model by Rutherford and Bohr

issue currently under discussion. This socio-cultural feature I will refer to as the 'commodification' of education. 'Commodification' is one of the conditions which economic sociology has regarded school knowledge as satisfying; which means that amongst its properties will be use and exchange value.

Doray (1988, p. 71) wrote: 'Assembly line work, or Fordism, has become a symbol of the modern way of working, and it is still that symbol that is branded on the body and consciousness of the worker.' In the educational context, in my view, the establishment of schools and universities along Fordist principles has led to an educational culture which extends an economic *raison d'être*, through the discourse of management and productivity, to the very subjectivity of teachers and students. This process has occurred with such force and pervasiveness that the results are seen by many practitioners, parents and children as inevitable characteristics of school culture. For psychological theories, including those of Piaget and Vygotsky, to have educational importance today, they must be able to connect with the aims and procedures of a school system which aims to develop, exchange and reproduce knowledge efficiently within the available resource constraints. The recent 'market' ideas of Thatcherism has only brought out the overt accounting which was latent in the organised culture of knowledge production.

Teachers and schools, often coerced by governments and education authorities, have, over many years, evolved a school curriculum based on the production of endless routine exemplar problems which facilitate short-term reproduction for assessment purposes. The resulting commodity, which I refer to here as 'school knowledge' has the following features. It:

1 assumes little knowledge beyond the curriculum,
2 is divided, often with no clear rationale, into subjects, topics and units,
3 is taught and assessed to produce graded performance,
4 leads to certification with little predictive power beyond the education system itself,
5 is premised on simplistic ideas of understanding and knowing,
6 often lacks 'active' input from pupils, and
7 distorts the real intellectual enquiry processes of, for example, science or history.

In the commodified culture of the school economy the goods, i.e. student learning, will be produced according to the interaction of many factors. Three of the most important are the cost to the student (Cs), the cost to the teacher (Ct) and the value (V) of the knowledge to the student. Let us further define (Cs) as the effort used by the student learner in acquiring the information, (Ct) as the effort required by the teacher in the presentation of the information, and (V) to include both formal accreditation which gives entry to other parts of the market (Vf) and knowledge (Vs) which will be useful to the student in reducing (Cs) in the future. The teacher's aim is to reduce costs (Cp) and (Ct) as well as to increase value (Vf and Vs). In schools, teaching and learning are managed within a culture with these economic forces at work.

Maximisation of value and minimisation of cost, in the sense outlined above, are key factors in the way ideas are evaluated in the culture of schools. The teachers' task is to construct a curriculum and a pedagogy, at reasonable cost, which maximises the cumulative value of what children learn. The production line of the school has led to particular ways of conceptualising and organising school knowledge; and the relationship between 'school knowledge' and 'knowledge' is not straightforward. School teaching has a ritualistic quality in which standard explanations are given, frozen metaphors in both verbal and diagrammatic form are pervasive, and standardised assessments built around these rituals are taken as measures of understanding.

Students engage with these social practices with different and variable degrees of motivation and success. And studies of teacher expertise show that organising these rituals is not a straightforward task. Nevertheless the product continues to be valued by most societies and the school system, despite much criticism, is maintained.

The value of this complex educational commodity called 'school knowledge' does not seem to lie, for most people, in its direct applicability in other arenas such as employment. For example school science, mathematics and humanities subject knowledge is not in itself used much beyond the school curriculum. Why then in most societies is schooling valued so highly?

One possible reason for the perceived value of schooling was illustrated by Vygotsky's student, Shif, in 1935. She investigated the use of everyday and scientific concepts. Following Piaget's format she gave children questions which ended in mid-sentence on 'because' or 'although'. A successful completion demonstrated correct use of the concept involved. Her somewhat surprising results showed that for younger children the causality questions were better understood when they were about scientific concepts. As always with this type of work there are methodological objections which can be raised to her studies but her explanation of the results hints at a more general phenomenon which connects school knowledge to thinking in the real world. She argued that explicit instruction in a subject at school leads to the use of certain ways of thinking within specific areas. Gradually these ways of thinking will spread and elevate the child's thinking to a higher level. Thus, the correct and explained use of 'because' conjunctions is first introduced in a 'school science' context and will only later generalise to everyday thinking. In Vygotsky's terms the explicit classroom instruction creates a zone of proximal development for the child. Education, therefore, prepares the road for the child's cognitive development through the pedagogic processes through which teachers construct commodified microworlds. These microworlds become the context in which many technical concepts have their prototypical meaning. The logical and scientific language is used to describe relationships within these microworlds, which are essentially descriptive and circular rather than explanatory and generative. An example is the teaching of Ohm's law using simple diagrams of circuits; within this microworld the concepts of resistance, current, etc. can be understood by pupils. Although these conceptions cannot easily be extended by them to the way electricity behaves in other contexts, some very limited and easily tested skill in using these terms has been acquired. And society presumably continues to regard its investment in this acquisition as worthwhile through its continued encouragement of this type of knowledge production.

However, the fact that in 1996 in the UK many children are reasonably competent at school subjects but are poor abstract reasoners, readers and communicators outside suggests that the school product needs reexamination. The ZPD (Zone of Proximal Development) may have been created but is not being crossed. The economic forces at work referred to earlier are creating a type of school knowledge which allows the costs to both learners and teachers to be manageable. The internal economy of the school creates its measures of value through assessments linked ever closer to the teaching process. But there must be doubts as to the generalisability of the skills engendered. The increased attention being given to work on thinking skills including Cognitive Acceleration and Philosophy for Children, suggests that this is a real problem.

One well-established view is that thinking is engendered by the teaching process. This view has had currency since Plato but has gained particular strength through the recent neo-Vygotskian arguments which interconnect 'dialogic processes (scaffolding)', tools for thought (writing, microscopes) and natural concepts (constructivism). Thinking is seen as developing through internalisation of the individual's engagement with these inter-connections.

Figure 6 (taken from Beveridge and Rimmershaw, 1991) gives an example of a teacher explicitly working to produce an educational commodity in a typical school context. In terms of its aims this whole lesson is an explanation of the concept of Brownian motion. During the lesson the teacher elicits ideas from the students. Sometimes he leaves their suggestions on one side and picks them up later. On other occasions he builds on them immediately. Sometimes pupils' ideas are ignored, usually by the teacher giving another idea himself. All the time he is leading the children to understanding that the movement of the smoke particles is caused by other invisible particles bumping into them. And that the movement is seen by the reflection of light off the smoke particles. The example in Figure 6 illustrates that engendering thinking through the school curriculum is not easy. Nor are the dialogic contributions to cognitive development clearly indicated.

Newman and Holzman (1993, p. 73) have provided a trenchant criticism of neo-Vygotskian attempts to understand thinking 'by focusing exclusively on the psychological aspects of adult child interaction' which they claim 'distorts the realities of human life'. They support the approach of Tharp and Gallimore (1988) who, while insisting on the importance of 'activity settings' (contexts in which collaborative interaction, intersubjectivity and assisted performance occur), argue that schools do not typically provide activity settings at all. There is, according to Newman and Holzman (1993, p. 73), 'rarely joint or collaborative productive activity either between administration and teachers or between teachers and students'. Indabawa (1992) connects these problems to the Marxist notion of 'fetishism' in which social relationships are 'disguised' and knowledge gives people 'alleged powers'.

Tharp and Gallimore (1988, p. 92) summarise their solution as follows: 'Every member of the school community should be engaged in the joint productive activity of activity setting whose purpose is an ever increasing competence to assist performance.' The outcome of which is 'a culture of

T: We've been thinking of materials as made up from particles. Now we're going to get as near as we can to seeing a single atom. You'll have realised from what you've done so far that atoms are very tiny, so they'll be difficult to see.

We're going to use what we can see through a microscope, and a model, and a computer simulation to try to get the idea.

Here's the apparatus (container, bulb, glass rod 'lens', plastic tube). I'm going to put smoke into the plastic tube. Is it empty at the moment?

P: No! Air's in it.

T: Here we go. (Puts smoke in.) What can you see?

P: Little white bits.

T: Are they doing anything?

P: Moving.

T: How?

P: Jumping.

P: Sharp.

T: Yes, fast movement.

P: Little bits, white circles.

P: Flashing on and off.

T: Do you mean they disappear sometimes?

P: Stardust, I think they're gold.

P: Dodging, bumping, shooting away from each other.

P: Like two magnets going for each other, but when they get near to each other they shoot away to the sides.

P: Is it?

T: Or is there a simpler explanation?

P: Are they just not attracted?

P: Is it cohesion being reversed, pushing each other away?

T: Let's piece together all these observations. First the colours – white, gold. What is it you're seeing?

P: Particles.

T: Of?

P: Smoke.

T: What is smoke?

P: Gas.

T: Alright, but it's tiny debris. This microscope isn't powerful enough for you to see the individual flakes. What is it you're seeing?

P: Heat – energy – oxygen burning.

T: What does energy do?

P: Makes things move.

T: So maybe it's involved in the movement. What about what you can see. When sunlight reflects off the car windscreen or a house window in the distance you don't know anything about the shape or size of the pane of glass. You're seeing particles of dust reflecting light in the same way.

T: Now what about the movement. You used the word 'dodgy'. Look at this computer simulation of just one speck, slowed down. The motion you're seeing is called Brownian motion. Could you predict which way that speck was going to move?

P: No.

T: So how is it moving?

P: Irregular.

P: Random.

T: Notice it's still there under the microscope as vigorous as ever. So it's also rapid and continuous. This is what the track of single particle could be like (computer demonstration). Some of you noticed the speck of light disappear. Remember, the microscope is focused on one level, but the movement is vertical as well as horizontal. So if the speck moves up or down it goes out of focus and you can no longer see it.

T: What causes the movement? What else is in the tube?

P: Air.

T: Air is also made of particles. Too tiny to reflect the light, but not to do something to the dust particles. A crowd in the corridor can't follow a straight path.

P: They zig zag, bumping and bouncing off each other.

T: So what might the air particles be doing to the smoke particles?

P: Deflection.

P: They're both moving, and bouncing off.

T: Yes, that's what we think is happening. A chap called Brown first discovered it by seeing floating pollen grains shimmering. Particles of water were moving at random and colliding with the pollen grains.

T: Here's a model to help you understand. Ball-bearings represent particles. I'll set the motor to give only a small amount of energy. The ball bearings are moving, but just vibrating up and down, closely packed together. That's how we think they might be in a solid. I'll give it more energy. What happens when it's heated?

P: Expands.

T: Becomes a liquid.

T: Look the particles are moving more freely. What about the spaces?

P: Further apart.

T: Right, so what about the forces between them?

P: They'll be weaker.

T: Yes and what's the next stage?

P: Gas.

T: Now here's a piece of paper representing a smoke particle. I'll put it in. Watch how it moves, what sort of path does it follow?

P: Zig zag.

T: Right, like the computer model showed. The ball bearings are bombarding it, pushing it sometimes one way sometimes another, giving a random motion.

So that's Brownian motion. It's close to seeing individual particles. It's evidence of the existence of particles, because how else would you explain what you're seeing under the microscope?

Figure 6 An illustration of the difficulties of engendering conceptual development through group dialogue in classrooms (from Beveridge and Rimmershaw, 1991)

learning'. Similarly, Newman and Holzman argue that the scenes and contexts of schools have been 'passivised' and as a result the real significance of the ZPD as a connection between learning and development is lost. I am suggesting here that we can begin to see how and why this passivisation has occurred through the concept of 'commodification'. More important, by examining how to understand this economic process we might become able better to connect psychological theory to educational practice in a way which contributes to the activation of a culture of learning both inside and outside school.

CONCLUSION

In this paper I have argued that despite the success story of twentieth-century psychology and its research agenda which is apparently increasingly relevant to education, we cannot assume a naturally occurring implementation programme. There are a range of questions which need to be addressed if students' education is to benefit from psychological research. The theories of Piaget and Vygotsky provide us with both warnings and examples. They both rightly took account of the intellectual riches of their time to set their theories in a culture of interesting ideas. This, I am arguing, is an approach needed today. However, the theories of Piaget and Vygotsky have been simplified and distorted to accommodate the simplistic ideas of learning and understanding that the educational system is inclined to accept. Both of these psychologists have told us much about the acquisition of knowledge beyond the assumptions of the school production line. We need to continue to extend their ideas in ways that will improve the quality of 'school knowledge'.

REFERENCES

Beveridge, M. (1995) *Strategic Review of Educational Research*. Report prepared for the Leverhulme Trust.

Beveridge, M. (1996) School integration for Down's Syndrome children: policies, problems and processes. In Rondal, J. A., Nadel, L. and Perera, J. *Down's Syndrome: Psychological, Psychobiological and Socio-educational Perspectives*. London: Whurr, pp. 205–16.

Beveridge, M. (in press) *The Context of Educational Research*. British Educational Research Association.

Beveridge, M. and Rimmershaw, R. (1991) Teaching and tutoring systems: explanatory dialogues in context. In Goodyear, P. (ed.) *Teaching Knowledge and Intelligent Tutoring*. New Jersey: Ablex, pp. 279–96.

Blandford, S. (1995) *The Relationship Between Educational Research, Theory and Practice*. Unpublished doctoral thesis, University of Bristol

Borko, H. and Livingston, C. (1989) Cognition and improvisation: differences in mathematical instruction by expert and novice teachers. *American Education Research Journal*, vol. 26, pp. 473–98.

Doray, B. (1988) *From Taylorism to Fordism*. London: Free Association Books.

Hargreaves, D. (1996) Annual Lecture to the Teacher Training Agency.

Havelock, R. G. and Huberman, A. M. (1977) *Solving Educational Problems: The Theory and Reality of Innovation in Developing Countries*. Paris: UNESCO.

Healy, A. F. and Bourne, L. E. (1995) *Learning and Memory of Knowledge and Skills*. London: Sage.

Indabawa, A. S. (1992) Issues in the ideology of educational knowledge. Unpublished doctoral thesis, University of Bristol.

Murphy, R. (1995) Presidential address to the British Educational Research Association, University of Bath, September.

Newman, F. and Holzman, L. (1993) *Lev Vygotsky: Revolutionary Scientist*. London: Routledge.

Nisbet, J. and Broadfoot, P. (1980) *The Impact of Research on Policy and Practice in Education*. Aberdeen: Aberdeen University Press.

Pollard, A. and Filer, A. (1996) *The Social World of Children's Learning: Case Studies from 4–7*. London: Cassell.

Pressley, M. and McCormick, C. (1995) *Cognition, Teaching and Assessment*. New York: Harper.

Quinn, H. (1989) *Learning Contemporary Physics*. Stanford: Stanford University Press.

Shif, Z. I. (1935) *Razvitie nauchnykh ponjatij u shkol'nika: issledovanie k voprosu umstvennogo razvitija shkol'nika pri obuchenii obshchestvovedeniju*. Moscow and Leningrad: Gosudarstvennoe Uchebno-Pedagogicheskoe Izdatel'stvo.

Tharp, R. G. and Gallimore, R. (1988) *Rousing Minds to Life: Teaching, Learning and Schooling in Social Context*. Cambridge: Cambridge University Press.

Van der Veer, R. and Valsiner, J. (1991) *Understanding Vygotsky: A Quest for Synthesis*. Oxford: Blackwell.

Weiss, C. (1980) *Using Social Research in Public Policy Making*. New York: Lexington Books.

2 Piaget and Vygotsky

A necessary marriage for effective educational intervention

Michael Shayer

INTRODUCTION: THE NOTION OF *INTERVENTION*

Intervention is a concept well understood in the medical literature; less well so in the context of education. It comes with an implicit reference to norms of development or health, and in the case of development it also implies a genetic programme which may not have been fully realised in the individual subject. Hence the need for some kind of medical intervention to assist the patient realise their genetic potential. The effect of an intervention is then assessed by measurements or clinical observations to see the extent to which the patient approaches the norms expected (Shayer, 1992). What then is the equivalent in the educational field of a suitable case for treatment?

In the early 1970s, when a Piagetian model of ages and stages of cognitive development was still in vogue, a large-scale survey was planned and implemented to examine the extent to which the model was true of the population as a whole. It was found, in fact, not to be true, as shown in Figure 7.

The Concepts in Secondary Mathematics and Science programme (CSMS) found that about 70% of the population do not achieve the formal operational stage at all (Shayer, Küchemann and Wylam, 1976; Shayer and Wylam, 1978). For interpretation these data need to be supplemented with data from three surveys on children from five to eleven years of age in Pakistan, Greece, England and Australia, and reported in Shayer, Demetriou and Pervez, 1988. The top 20% of the children in these surveys all developed exactly as Piaget and co-workers had described, reaching mature concrete operations by seven to eight years, having two years or so at the concrete generalisation level, and then beginning to develop formal operational thinking from about eleven or twelve. Children below average have not completed the concrete operations stage by the time they reach adolescence, and complete it only by the end of adolescence. This is part of the basis of the claim that Piaget had correctly described the genetic programme – realised in full only by 10% of the population, and in part by a further 20% – but not the general human condition. But one can only

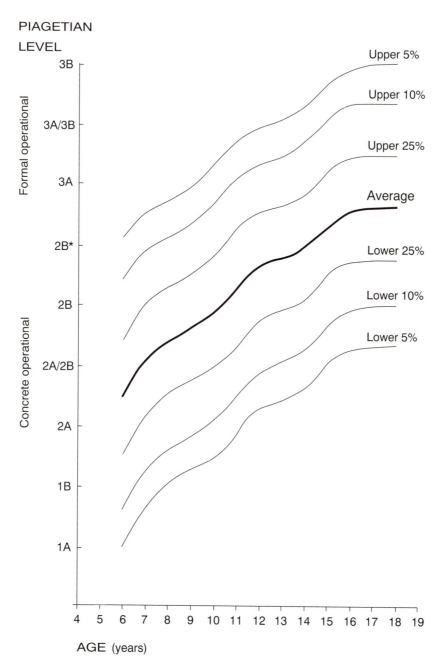

PIAGETIAN
LEVEL

Formal operational

Concrete operational

3B

3A/3B

3A

2B*

2B

2A/2B

2A

1B

1A

Upper 5%

Upper 10%

Upper 25%

Average

Lower 25%

Lower 10%

Lower 5%

4 5 6 7 8 9 10 11 12 13 14 15 16 17 18 19

AGE (years)

Figure 7 Cognitive development: boys (based on CSMS survey data, 1975–8)

claim that a genetic potential for cognitive development is there in all humans if it can be shown that by some educational intervention the proportion of children using formal operations can be increased, say, from some 20% at fourteen years at present to 50% or more.

That such an intervention would be desirable was shown by some associated research reported in Shayer and Adey (1981). This showed that unless pupils were using at least early formal operational thinking by the beginning of Year 9 their chances of success at O-level science (now GCSE C-grade or above) were slight. This is because the concepts of science themselves required formal operational thinking for their understanding.

Thus the educational application of the notion of intervention rests on the assumption that if children realise the last stage of the genetic programme and achieve formal operational capacity in early adolescence, they will then be qualitatively better learners, and will be able to benefit from good instructional teaching. Without it their learning will be frustrated. The evidence that this can be done will now be briefly examined. Evidence is required on both aspects: that *intervention produces measurable effects on psychological tests*, and that *this is accompanied by increased learning ability and hence achievement*.

EVIDENCE FOR THE EFFECTS OF COGNITIVE INTERVENTION

Initial CASE project

CASE II (Cognitive Acceleration through Science Education) (Chelsea College, 1984–7) was a small-scale research project designed to test the feasibility of the intervention model. One teacher in each of nine schools was involved, and they were trained in the conduct of intervention activities placed within the context of ordinary secondary school science learning. In each school an experimental class and a comparable control class were given Piagetian pre-tests, as used in the CSMS survey. The intervention took place over two years, and consisted initially of thirty activities, occupying about 25% of the science teaching time. In addition, teachers learnt how to 'bridge' between the CASE lessons and the content of their normal science lessons, through the Piagetian reasoning patterns involved in each, so that the overall amount of intervention was substantial.

The initial evidence on psychological tests was modest, but promising. In the 'laboratory' school where the lessons were taught by CASE staff, the experimental group moved from the 40th percentile at pre-test to the 65th percentile at post-test on Piagetian tests, compared with the control class who remained about the 50th percentile on both occasions. But of the four research school groups (11+ start boys, 11+ start girls; 12+ start boys, 12+ start girls) only the 12+ boys (N=56) showed substantial gains, compared with the controls, with an average gain of 23 percentile points on Piagetian tests over the two years. Even this evidence was equivocal, as the laboratory school involved an 11+ start (boys and girls). On end of year science achievement tests there was no difference between the experimental and control groups.

It was only as these cohorts moved on that the other aspect of intervention – that of increased learning ability – appeared. On science exams taken at the end of the year following the intervention there were now significant effects for two of the groups compared with their controls in the same schools, and positive effects for all. The 12+ boys showed an effect-size of 0.72σ, with the effect controlled for initial differences in cognitive levels at pre-test, and the 11+ girls had an effect-size of 0.60σ.

Finally, when all the groups took GCSE, the experimental and control groups were compared for long-term achievement differences in Grades in the three major school subjects, Science, Mathematics and English, and the effects are summarised in Table 2 (Adey and Shayer, 1994, pp. 100–2).

Table 2 Long-term achievement gains at GCSE from CASE intervention

		11+ boys	*11+ girls*	*12+boys*	*12+girls*
Science	Effect-size	-0.21σ	0.67σ	0.96σ	0.18σ
	Significance	n.s.	<.025	<.005	n.s.
	N	*35*	*29*	*48*	*45*
Mathematics	Effect-size	-0.19σ	0.72σ	0.55σ	0.13σ
	Significance	n.s.	<.005	<.005	n.s.
	N	*33*	*29*	*56*	*54*
English	Effect-size	0.22σ	0.69σ	0.32σ	0.44σ
	Significance	n.s.	<.025	<.05	<.01
	N	*36*	*27*	*56*	*57*

Although the intervention was set within the context of science, the intention was to affect the thinking of pupils generally, and for two of the four groups it appears that increased learning ability has resulted across the board. In the case of the third group of 12+ girls the effect appears to have shown up only in their English results, although one needs to bear in mind the possibility that the more able girls may have opted out of science before GCSE.

Post-CASE II INSET effects

Gains on psychological tests

The long-term effects of the CASE II project did seem to bear out the promise of the intervention model to deliver increased learning ability, and hence the possibility of raising standards in school (Adey and Shayer, 1994). By 1991 we had also gained more understanding of the underlying principles of intervention from the work of the CASE III project

(1989–91). It was now time to move from a primary effect and replication study to a generalisability study (Shayer, 1992, pp. 112–13), and at the same time to gather large-scale evidence on age and gender interactions which appeared to be present in the CASE II data. At this point the decision was made by King's staff to undertake the training of whole science departments in twelve schools. Again, Piagetian pre-tests were used in all schools in the term of pupil entry, and post-tests were given in the July of the second year of intervention (1993).

Data was collected from 8 schools, and 1,452 pupils, 568 of which received the CASE intervention in Years 7/8, and 884 in Years 8/9. The total number of school classes was 63. The effects are summarised in Table 3.

The concept of intervention itself is strongly supported by the data in the third column of Table 3. In the fifth column the national average is given of the proportion of 13- and 14-year-olds with early formal capacity or above. Those schools with intakes about the national average have doubled the proportion showing formal operational thinking, which is evidence that the potential was there in the pupils. In three cases there are also data from a previous year group who had not received the intervention, most of which did not realise their potential.

Overall, as related to the norms of the CSMS survey, there were mean gains of the order of 30 percentile points over the two years of intervention. Unlike the data from the original CASE II project, the age/gender interactions were much smaller. Further analysis of the data shows that there is little to choose between the average of the overall effect-sizes whether there is a Year 7 start or a Year 8 start to the intervention. For the boys, the average effect-size is much the same whether there is a Year 7 or a Year 8 start. The interaction is still there, though, in the case of the girls. Their mean effect-size was 0.27σ greater for a Year 7 start compared with a Year 8 start, so it appears desirable to start an intervention in Year 7 if it is at all possible. There is a major brain-growth spurt at about 10/11 years (Epstein, 1990) which would seem to be programmed to enable the development of formal operations. Neither Lovell and Shields (1967) nor Webb (1974), with samples of children four standard deviations above average (Wechsler), found any evidence of formal operations before the age of 10. Since this brain-growth spurt is twice as large in the case of girls, it may be that for them the next two years are particularly favourable for intervention, when the new inter-neuronal fibres are present in the cortex.

This evidence supports the overall intervention intention, but unless increased thinking ability, as assessed by psychological tests, is accompanied by subsequent increased learning and achievement, there would still be the suspicion that the CASE intervention was simply 'teaching-to-the-test'. The first large-scale evidence we have on this is from national data on Key Stage 3 tests, taken at 14 years of age at the end of Year 9, from those schools that began the CASE intervention in Year 7.

Table 3 General effects of CASE-INSET on teachers within schools, as tested over two years with pre- and post-tests (Piagetian reasoning tasks) on their pupils

School	Year	% early formal (3A) or above		Effect-size		Percentile points of school year pupil mean on the CSMS survey		
		July 1993	(previous year)	CSMS average[1]	(standard deviations)	1991 pre-test	1993 post-test	Change (%le points)
1	7/8	42.2	7.6	(17.9)	0.67σ	48	75	27
1	8/9	45.4		(21.9)	0.76σ	45	76	31
2	7/8	36.7		(17.9)	0.69σ	43	72	29
3	7/8	65.0	25	(17.9)	1.12σ	55	86	31
4	7/8	16.0		(17.9)	1.12σ	14	55	41
5	8/9	31.0		(21.9)	0.80σ	28	59	31
6	7/8	58.0		(17.9)	1.0σ	44	82	38
7	8/9	22.0		(21.9)	0.75σ	20	53	33
8	8/9	50.3	10	(21.9)	0.78σ	43	72	29

Note:
[1] These are the percentages of students showing 3A thinking or above in the CSMS survey for comparable year groups, and hence the proportion expected for schools with intakes near the 50th percentile.

Key Stage 3 results, Summer 1995

As part of the continuing programme of INSET based at King's College subsequent to 1991, there were pre-test Piagetian test data on school intakes where the year cohort who took Key Stage 3 tests in 1995 had not received the CASE intervention. These served as the control schools featured in Figures 8–10.

By plotting the statistic, percentage at level 6 or above at Key Stage 3, against the mean CSMS percentile of the school intake, it was possible to estimate the school to school variation, controlled for level of school intake. In each Figure the national average for the statistic, as published by the DfEE in February 1996, is added. The data for the schools that had used the CASE intervention were entered separately on the same graphs, and can be seen for the most part to lie above and outside the limits of sampling variation of the control schools. For Science and Mathematics the regression line lies above the national average, so the effects for the CASE schools may be slightly underestimated. In the case of the English results there was much more variability, both for control and CASE schools, and this is attributed to the poor reliability of the English test.

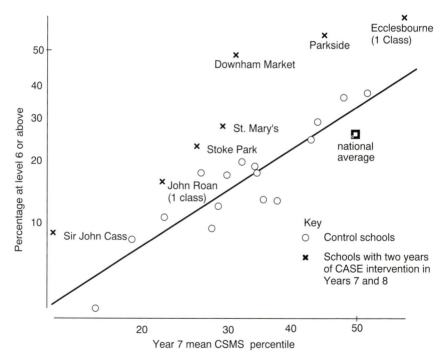

Figure 8 Key Stage 3 results, 1995: Science

Note: The regression line is derived from the control schools only, and thus the position of the CASE schools is a 'value-added' estimate of achievment given the level of the school intake. The number of percentile points above the regression line gives the magnitude of the effect. To obtain a linear plot, the percentiles have been transformed to logits: $\ln(\%/(100\%-\%))$.

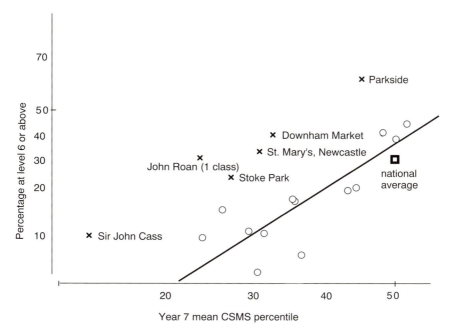

Figure 9 Key Stage 3 results, 1995: Mathematics
Note: For key and explanatory note see Figure 8.

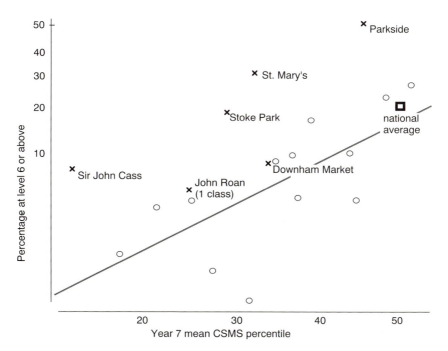

Figure 10 Key Stage 3 results, 1995: English
Note: For key and explanatory note see Figure 8.

Table 4 Key Stage 3 effects 1995: percentages at Level 6 and above

	School	Science			Mathematics			English		
		Predicted	Obtained	Difference (%)	Predicted	Obtained	Difference (%)	Predicted	Obtained	Difference (%)
Values in percentages	Ecclesbourne	39.6	64.3	24.7	—	—	—	—	—	—
	Downham Market	8.4	47.9	39.5	13.0	39.7	26.7	4.9	7.3	2.4
	John Roan	3.7	8.7	5.0	6.3	30.4	24.2	2.4	4.3	1.9
	Parkside	20.5	56.3	35.8	28.1	63.0	34.9	11.0	50.0	39.0
	Sir John Cass	1.1	3.6	2.6	2.0	10.2	8.3	0.8	6.6	5.8
	Stoke Park	5.5	15.4	9.9	8.9	24.0	15.1	3.4	16.5	13.1
	St. Mary's, N'castle	7.3	20.7	13.4	11.5	33.1	21.7	4.3	30.1	25.7
Values in logits	Ecclesbourne	-0.4236	0.588	1.0116	—	—	—	—	—	—
	Downham Market	-2.39	-0.084	2.306	-1.905	-0.42	1.485	-2.9635	-2.54	0.4235
	John Roan	-3.247	-2.351	0.896	-2.706	-0.827	1.879	-3.689	-3.093	0.596
$\ln(\%/(100-\%))$	Parkside	-1.357	0.253	1.61	-0.9387	0.5322	1.4709	-2.089	0	2.089
	Sir John Cass	-4.527	-3.28	1.247	-3.903	-2.171	1.732	-4.773	-2.646	2.127
	Stoke Park	-2.845	-1.704	1.141	-2.33	-1.154	1.176	-3.349	-1.624	1.725
	St, Mary's, N'castle	-2.54	-1.343	1.197	-2.045	-0.702	1.343	-3.0906	-0.8445	2.2461
	mean gain in logits			1.34			1.51			1.53
	Equivalent to gain for the national average	from 25% to		56.1	from 33% to		69.1	from 20% to		53.7

Note: Translation to logits is required to show that the relative increase for, e.g. Sir John Cass school, is of the same order as that for Ecclesbourne.

In Table 4 these data are reported quantitatively. Because percentages are not a linear variable, the analysis is done in terms of logits in order to compare effects (Tukey, 1977, pp. 501–9). This enables the data to be averaged, and then compared by computing the equivalent gain to be expected, over the national figures published by the DfEE. It can be seen that the magnitude of the effect (approximately a doubling of the proportion of Level 6 or above) is of the same order as that obtained from psychological post-tests reported above from 1993.

This is the evidence that early intervention in the secondary school can result in increased learning ability in pupils, not merely in the subject where the intervention was placed, but more generally. Inspection of the National Curriculum, in relation to what is examined at Key Stage 4, shows that attainment of Level 6 or above at the end of Year 9 would be expected to predict GCSE attainment at C-grade or above. In summer 1996 the final evidence on long-term achievement – that of GCSE results for schools that began the intervention in 1991 in Year 7 – will be available.

COGNITIVE DEVELOPMENT: PIAGET AND/OR VYGOTSKY?

Generally, the Thinking Skill literature tends to be long on inspiration and very short on quantitative evidence. This is the reason for the amount of space used above presenting evidence that intervention is a valid concept, and that it can be realised. Given that, it is then important to examine the detail of the causality of cognitive development, and hence to describe the professional teaching skills involved in changing it.

It is very strange that Piaget, as an ex-biologist, should not have made the small extra step from saying that he was studying the 'epistemic subject' to realising that this was equivalent to saying he was studying the genetic programme. It is strange also that given his early realisation that social factors were involved in cognitive development, he did not credit Vygotsky as having supplied the descriptions and concepts that might have complemented his own work. Piaget's own model of adaptation, being the result of the dialectic of assimilation and accommodation, does seem to contain implicitly the notion that it is only the child's own efforts which are the process of accommodation. A person accommodates to the environment when he/she realises that his own strategies have failed to solve a problem. The idea of 'cognitive conflict' – Piaget's contribution to the art – is certainly one cause of accommodation.

But – particularly for infants – various aspects of mediation are far more salient causes of cognitive development. The different aspects of retardation described in Clarke and Clarke (1976), together with evidence that various forms of intervention can remedy at least part of the deficit, can be interpreted more easily in Vygotskian concepts of mediation than they can in any concepts originating from Geneva.

In Feuerstein's (1980, chapter 2) interpretation of cognitive development, Piaget's stimulus-organism-response formula (S-O-R) needs to be extended to the formula S-H-O-R, in which a human mediator is interposed between the stimulus (James' 'blooming, buzzing world') and the organism. Various 'mediating agents' – parents, siblings, other care-givers – frame and organise the environment for the child, in such a way that the child not only learns more efficiently, but also comes to believe more in his own capacity to learn. The more mediating learning experience the child is given the more is he able to grapple on his own with stimuli. The less mediation he experiences, the less will be his belief in his own capacity, until the more extreme cases of institutionalised children described in Clarke and Clarke result.

This development of Vygotsky's original work by Feuerstein has been given, in the case of kindergarten children of five years of age, an experimental test. Tzuriel and Ernst (1990) set out to investigate what was the relation between distal factors such as socio-economic status (SES) and mother's intelligence, as estimated on Raven's Matrices (RPM), the proximal factor of mediated learning experience (MLE), and children's own cognitive modifiability, as estimated by pre-post-test gain scores on an analogical thinking test (CATM) given in dynamic assessment mode. The quality of MLE given by the mothers was assessed by videotaping two sessions of interaction between mother and child. In the first (fifteen minutes) mother and child were asked to play freely with toy and puzzle materials put in front of them. In the second the mother was asked to 'teach' their child two analogical thinking problems and two picture arrangement problems (fifteen minutes also). The analysis of the video recordings was by use of the MLE Observation scale, which involves structured descriptions of mediation of Intentionality and Reciprocity, Meaning, Transcendence, Feeling of Competence and Regulation of Behaviour.

It was found that although there were strong correlations between SES and mothers' Raven's score, and also between SES and the quality of mothers' mediation, there were no direct causal paths between either of these distal causes and the children's gains scores on dynamic assessment. Children's cognitive modifiability – as assessed by the gain scores between pre-test and post-dynamic assessment with the analogical reasoning test – was directly caused only by some of the mothers' mediation behaviours recorded using the MLE Observation scale. Subsequently, it was found that the mediation measures predicted children's achievement in the first two years of primary school (Klein and Aloni, 1993).

Important though mediation by adults and older and more competent siblings may be for the young child, other aspects of mediation as described by Vygotsky come to be more salient at the onset of adolescence. In this connection the interpretation of mediation by Bruner as 'scaffolding' is unfortunate. Such a description will probably be found useful when work seriously begins of developing intervention programmes for children in the first two years of primary education. But applied to adolescents it leads too easily to a 'short-circuit' between genuine notions of mediation and ordinary descriptions of teacher-dominated instruction, designed to make it easier for students to learn.

Two quotations from Vygotsky are needed here, introducing two essential concepts. First (Vygotsky, 1978, p. 86):

> there is a gap between any student's ... actual developmental level as determined by independent problem-solving and the level of potential development as determined through problem-solving under adult guidance or in collaboration with more capable peers.

Here he describes the concept of the Zone of Proximal Development (ZPD). One aspect of this was his original development of the practice of dynamic testing. By testing children first, quickly, with psychometric test items he tested their current unassisted level of functioning. Then through a structured programme of on-task mediation children are suggested broad strategies and allowed to talk them through and try them on comparable problems with the tester. When the children can take no more they are then brought back to the original items on which they had failed, and the extra items they can now succeed on is recorded. Vygotsky showed that these gain scores correlated more highly with the next two years of school learning of the students than the original unassisted test scores. Feuerstein and co-workers (1979) have developed this type of testing much further. Underlying the test model is the concept that children's assured competencies, as typically tested by performance on tests where – in one sense of the word – they have no time to *think*, is not all there is to know about the children's present minds. In addition there are many half, a quarter, three-quarters completed strategies already operative which are only waiting either the appropriate mediation or children's own mindful accommodation to the situation which requires them, for their completion. Dynamic assessment carefully done actually permits a description and measurement of these partial skills (Beasley and Shayer, 1990; Feuerstein *et al.*, 1979). The ZPD extends forwards, potentially in time, about two mental age years (Beasley and Shayer, 1990). Cognitive development, then, mostly consists in converting these potential, partially completed skills into present assured competencies. For how this may come about we need a second quotation (Vygtosky, 1981, p. 163):

> Any function in a child's cultural development appears twice, or on two planes. First it appears on the social plane, and then on the psychological plane. First it appears between people as an interpersonal category, and then within the child as an intrapsychological category.

Vygotsky goes on to explain that the meaning of this is that much of cognitive and also language development takes place through the child seeing a successful performance in another and instantly internalising it.

The nearer the 'successful performance' is to the child's present partially completed strategies the greater is the probability of the instant internalisation. But with adolescence the word 'nearer' takes on an extra connotation. Since at this point in their lives they are in the process of inserting into the present adult world newly created adult presences which are not just an imitation of present adult models, it is far more likely that it will be the style of successful performance from a peer who has just got there that will be internalised. Teachers' 'successful performances' – polished by time and familiarity – are often too far from where the adolescents presently are to be easily internalised and assimilated. One can frequently witness, in intervention lessons, the quality of attention which is commanded in a class by some student who has got there, and made it just in his or her own way, and can just express it.

PIAGET AND VYGOTSKY IN THE DESIGN OF INTERVENTION PROGRAMMES

FIE

The first successful programme – Feuerstein's Instrumental Enrichment (IE) – was a *context-independent* intervention (Adey and Shayer, 1994, pp. 51–4). Each of the IE lessons were designed to be delivered as a thinking skill activity placed outside the context of ordinary school subjects in which students may already have experienced failure. The initial set of ten instruments (containing each some twelve activities or more) meant to be used over a period of two years, were framed in terms both of mental abilities and Piagetian concrete operations so as to cover the whole spectrum of mental activity. In addition the first year's Instruments mostly began with tasks requiring only early to middle concrete operational schemata, but each taking students further towards the concrete generalisation level. The second year's Instruments began at the mature concrete level, and although the possibility of invoking formal operations was implicitly there, actual practice again mostly involves progress towards concrete generalisation. Thus the Piagetian contribution lies in the framing of the tasks themselves – as it were, the hardware – whereas the conduct of the lessons draws only on the Vygotskian aspect. Students spend some fifteen minutes in collaborative discussion of the implications of a worksheet provided, and are encouraged to generate several possible strategies to use on the task. After a period of around twenty minutes individual work on the task, they spend a further fifteen minutes in whole-class discussion comparing the success of the various strategies, and dealing with problems. Finally the students themselves summarise what has been important, and also try to imagine other contexts and situations where they can apply skills they have developed. Teachers are mainly unaware of the work which has gone into the framing of the tasks, and may not need to be aware of it.

CASE and CAME

In their replication of IE Shayer and Beasley (1987) found that there was a problem with context-independent intervention. Both students and teachers found it difficult to adapt their learning and teaching of their ordinary school subjects to utilise what had been achieved in IE lessons. Shayer therefore considered the possibility of creating a *context-delivered* intervention: that is, using the same thinking skill approach, but embedding it in the context of a major school subject. This led to an initial Primary effect study (CASE I), and the subsequent Replication study (CASE II). In the CASE project there was a strong Piagetian contribution to the framing of the *Thinking Science* (Adey, Shayer and Yates, 1995) lessons designed. On the assumption that IE was primarily targeted to the bottom 30% of 12- to 14-year-olds, CASE lessons were targeted to cover students from the 25th to 70th percentile approximately, and designed to promote formal operational thinking over a two-year period. Contexts were found requiring each one or more of the formal operational schemata (reasoning patterns) of control of variables, proportional thinking, etc. In the first year access to the task itself is possible from the middle to mature concrete level, whereas in the second year access requires at least mature concrete operations, and the last six activities require early formal thinking for access, and are aimed towards mature formal thinking. Over a period of some years of observation and analysis of teaching practice, some of the teaching skills were summarised, as is shown in Figure 11.

It can be seen that there is both a Piagetian and a Vygotskian contribution to these skills. The term 'Construction Zone Activity' (CZA) is borrowed from Newman, Griffin and Cole (1989). The Concrete Preparation phase is very similar to that used in IE: it is essentially a 'raising of consciousness' phase in relation to the subject matter of the activity, and its success depends on the extent to which the teacher engages as many pupils as possible in constructing ideas to be used in the task ahead. The possibility of cognitive conflict – the Piagetian aspect – is both implicit in the processing of the task itself, and can also be made explicit by tactical questioning from the teacher as she 'floats' from group to group. During this period of work on task there is the opportunity for some of the pupils to construct more powerful strategies. An essential phase of each CASE lesson is the period of whole-class discussion which follows group work on task, and it is not essential for this to work that all groups have completed all aspects of the experiment and questions on the worksheet. Managing this phase of the activity requires the teacher to be very aware of the working of the CZA described above. By questioning and chairing the discussion he has to ensure that every interesting insight, or difficulty encountered, in each of the working groups is now made available for all the pupils in the class, in their own language. Sometimes this is shown on the actual apparatus itself by the pupils, or notes scribbled on the board. This will maximise the

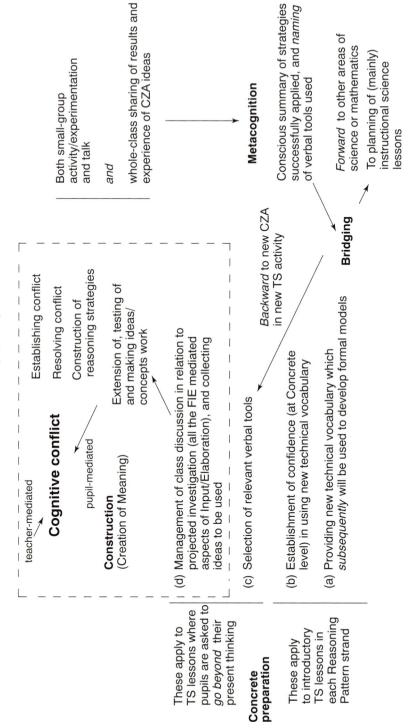

Construction Zone Activity (CZA)

teacher-mediated   Establishing conflict

Cognitive conflict   Resolving conflict

pupil-mediated   Construction of reasoning strategies

Construction
(Creation of Meaning)

Extension of, testing of and making ideas/concepts work

Both small-group activity/experimentation and talk

and

whole-class sharing of results and experience of CZA ideas

Metacognition

Conscious summary of strategies successfully applied, and *naming* of verbal tools used

Forward to other areas of science or mathematics

To planning of (mainly) instructional science lessons

Backward to new CZA in new TS activity

Bridging

(d) Management of class discussion in relation to projected investigation (all the FIE mediated aspects of Input/Elaboration), and collecting ideas to be used

(c) Selection of relevant verbal tools

(b) Establishment of confidence (at Concrete level) in using new technical vocabulary

(a) Providing new technical vocabulary which *subsequently* will be used to develop formal models

These apply to TS lessons where pupils are asked to *go beyond* their present thinking

Concrete preparation

These apply to introductory TS lessons in each Reasoning Pattern strand

Figure 11 Technical terms used to describe phases of CASE and CAME lessons

probability that each pupil will find in some other's 'successful performance' just what she needs to complete her CZA.

Thus in the practice of context-delivered intervention there is a richly-structured management of the whole class by the teacher. This move to whole-class teaching is even more noteworthy in the subsequent and present Cognitive Acceleration in Mathematics Education Project (CAME), for in Mathematics fashion has moved more strongly towards individualised learning than in Science.

The CAME project draws less explicitly from Piaget than the CASE project. This is because Inhelder and Piaget's (1958) work on adolescent thinking was taken almost exclusively from scientific contexts, and hence the reasoning patterns described embed nicely in a wide variety of biological and physical science concepts. Mathematical activity at the secondary school level is only sketchily addressed in the Genevan research, although clearly proportional and probabilistic thinking are widely used. The problem of hierarchy and progression was therefore addressed by starting with the National Curriculum (1991 version), analysing the Statements of Attainment (SoA) as to whether, broadly, they required mature concrete (2B), concrete generalisation (2B*), early formal (3A) or mature formal (3B) thinking. The result of this analysis is shown in Figure 12.

Hence nine broad strands were picked out, containing five more central strands. The thirty *Thinking Maths* activities were then designed in terms of a progression up the five central strands starting from Level 4, with contexts chosen in addition as far as possible from Ma4 (Space) and Ma5 (Data-handling). The essential 'shelf' to be attained, for success in secondary Mathematics as contrasted with primary, is that containing the various SoAs at the 3A Level, as this is where algebra proper begins, as contrasted with arithmetic.

Another important difference from Science is that mathematical activity in any one strand frequently involves mathematical language from several other strands, so there is a greater degree of reflexivity and recursion all the time for the learner, enriching his or her use of the language.

The Appendix shows a lesson transcript of the first *Thinking Maths* activity. This is 'work-in-progress' as we are only in the second term of the CAME II project, working intensively with twenty-two teachers in four schools. We have already been able to observe three different teaching styles which seem to be equivalent to the style described for FIE and CASE (although we have yet to gather the evidence that the effects *are* equivalent). The first style (not shown) is that adopted by some teachers who have top ability sets where there is streaming in Year 7. With the earlier activities, at least, such bright pupils, some of whom are already early formal thinkers, tolerate less easily the whole-class discussion featured in the description of Concrete Preparation given in Figure 11 for CASE. The teacher gets the pupils into the task as quickly as possible, and because the pupils are bright she can let them get on with it, 'floating' from

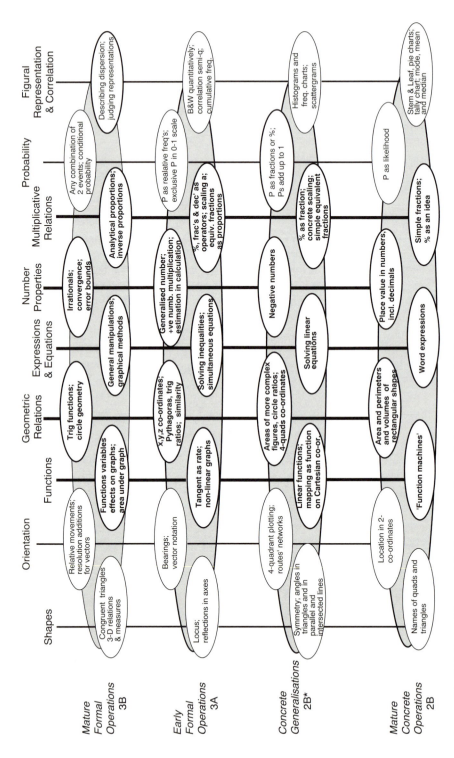

Figure 12 CAME working model of conceptual strands in secondary Mathematics

group to group and making sure that they handle all points that are problematic. Then, with the whole class having engaged on all aspects of the task, she just reserves that last five or six minutes for as many pupils as possible to sum up for the class as a whole what the problems were, and how they dealt with them. This puts all the metacognition and bridging into this last brief phase. It is to be expected that as the TM activities get more difficult, the teacher may tend towards one of the other two styles.

The second style, shown in the transcript of the Appendix, is by a teacher with a remedial class comparable in ability with those who might receive IE in a school using it. Here, with some success, she is using essentially the IE three-phase class management style, similar to that used in CASE as shown in Figure 11.

The third style, not shown, has been used successfully with both middle and bottom ability groups The style is one which, in CAME I, we have seen successfully used with a top ability group. The teacher spends the whole hour in whole-class teaching mode. By using the board and OHP well and recording and summarising each thing of interest he keeps the attention of the whole class on all aspects of the task. By asking questions all round the class that are genuine questions and not just 'guess-what-is-in-teacher's-mind' questions, and by giving each answer a welcoming attention, he gets the pupils to show their 'constructions' and successful performances as the lesson goes on so all can see and hear.

CONCLUSION

The objection is frequently met, from Vygotsky enthusiasts, that if one is pro-Vygotsky one must necessarily be anti-Piaget. In physics, who can doubt that Einstein gives a better understanding of action at a distance than does Newton? Yet 99% of current engineering calculations are done in Newtonian terms. It is hoped that in this paper it has been shown that by taking what Piaget and Vygotsky each offer in ways which are complementary an intervention practice has been achieved which delivers substantial results.

APPENDIX: THINKING MATHS, ACTIVITY 1: ROOFS

The (experienced) teacher realised from the outset that it wouldn't be possible to establish, in one lesson the class control which the collaborative learning style of the CAME lessons requires, and so her strategy was just to make the first steps with pupils recently in from primary school.

Teacher	Pupils	Description
11.35 Pupils in. T: 'You're going to be working in groups today.' *Groups are 3 or 4, left as they are sitting.*		
11.39 'Turn so you can see what's on the board.' 'You'll see some dotty paper, and I want you to use it in *landscape* shape, not *portrait*.' *Board has been prepared with a matrix of dots.* 'The *aim* of the lesson is to give someone else precise instructions (rules) how to draw something.'		
11.41 *Draws 1, 2, 1, 3 sequentially through board dots. Asks* 'What is the name of this shape?'	'Triangle shape'	
'Yes, but the top's cut off.' 'Good – correct: any other names?'	'trapezium' 'parallelogram' 'looks like a rooftop'	**Concrete Preparation (c): selection of relevant verbal tools** Teacher establishes the descriptive language needed for handling the task
'We'll call it ROOF – looks like the frame which the builders make when they are starting on a roof.'		

Teacher	Pupils	Description
Rehearses steps in drawing, and asks Ps to count and give numbers in the steps. 'Going up . . .' 'across . . . ?' 'down/along . . .' 'across and back'	'one' 'two' 'one' 'three' 'Are these centimetres?'	
11.45 'Good question! – no they can't be cms, they're the number of STEPS.' *Draws the roof:* 2, 1, 2, 3. *Draws the triangle* 3, 0, 3, 3 *and then asks* 'Is this a roof?' 'No (*then draws* 2, 1, 2, 3 *inside the triangle*) – but this one is, so triangles aren't allowed.' *Asks for code.* *Then checks idea by drawing* 1, 4, 1, 5. 'Is this a roof?'	Ps give code numbers Ps ? ? ? 'two' 'one' 'two' 'three' 'Yes' 'yes'	**Concrete Preparation (d): mediation of ideas to be used** The underlying intervention theme of the activity is the idea of generating counter-examples to check hypotheses Here the teacher prepares the pupils for this implicitly
11.48 'Draw some of your own, and then work out the code for each.' 'You can copy from the board to give you an idea.' *NB First worksheet not used: only dotty paper.*	Some Ps start with a code, and then draw the shape; most take the shape first and then derive the code. One P has great difficulty in connecting counting with numbers with the act of drawing the corresponding number of steps in drawing the roof elements. Same pupil not able to see point of making a not-roof. T goes round the groups and begins to ask their rules. Most groups have generated 3 or 4 examples.	**First Construction phase** Teacher assists with construction of reasoning strategies

Teacher	Pupils	Description
11.55 'Pencils down . . . look this way.' 'Lots of you have done lots of examples of roofs. Did anyone start with a code and then find it wasn't a roof?' *Draws, 2, 7, 2, 8 roof on board.* 'Yes – that's not a roof.' Draws it: '*Is a roof!*' 'Are you sure that is the code you used?' 'Yes.' 'In these sessions – one every few weeks – we will share our ideas, so share them sensibly. Any ideas about the rules?'	'2, 7, 2, 8,' '3, 2, 3, 5,' '1, 26, 1, 27!' 'always the same at the two sides' 'difference of 1 between top and bottom number'	**Concrete Preparation (a) (b): providing and establishing technical vocabulary** Teacher explicitly coaches pupils in the process of using disconfirming cases to test their rules Here the teacher is training the class in the behaviours which will enable pupils to use class discussion profitably
12.03 'Can you give an example?' 'Yes it's a roof, but does it fit your rule?' *Discipline problem here with two boys to do with willingness to listen to others without showing off disruptively. T breaks off to deal with it.* 'Now – rules?'	'3, 2, 3, 5,' '? ? ? no' 'top and bottom not always same' 'always four sets of numbers'	**Cognitive Conflict** Here the conflict is induced deliberately by the teacher Further training in class behaviour
'Certainly, that's always true.' 'You've shared good ideas. We have checked rules. Now I want you to make one rule of your own, and make shapes to check it.'	T goes to pupil who had produced rule of four numbers. Gives them 7, 7, 7, 7, and asks them to draw it. 'Does that make a roof?' P – 'No!' 'So four numbers has to be true, but it isn't *enough*.' T goes to all groups and does likewise.	**Second Construction phase** Cognitive Conflict induced implicitly by teacher
12.05 Gives out Worksheet 2.		

Teacher	Pupils	Description
12.21 *Many Ps more than a little confused about producing a second rule, and producing, or trying to produce, counter-examples.*		
12.23 'Pencils down – I want you now to share ideas again.' *Two boys again being silly because unused to this kind of expected class behaviour. Are dealt with.*		**Whole class discussion (Vygotskian aspect)** First step to promoting opportunity for pupils to learn from each other **Metacognition**
'What did I do when I came round and asked for your rule?'	'You gave me numbers that didn't make a roof!'	
'So what were yours?'	'If it goes 1, 2 . . . then the bottom is one bigger than the top'	
	'the two sides have to be the same'	
'Suppose I take 2, 3, 4 . . .'		**Further Construction**
'So what would the bottom be . . .?'	'5'	
'Carly has a rule she can depend on . . .' 'Suppose 3, 6, 3 . . .?'	(Carly) '9' 'Adds 1st and 2nd number – always gives bottom number'	**Construction** reported to class by pupil
'Another way of putting it?'	'Add the first and second – gives bottom line'	
'And what is the second rule that has to be there?'	'The two sides have to be the same'	
12.29 'Have you all these rules written down?' 'Put your names on your papers.'	*T gives one of the boys who have given trouble the job of collecting Ps' worksheets, and spends a minute or two with two of the other boys, giving counter-example, and also first three numbers of codes, and asks them to predict bottom. Then they co-operate intelligently.*	Further work towards training class in the behaviours teacher wants to promote with pupils newly arrived from primary school, and unused to whole class teaching

Teacher | *Pupils* | *Description*

'You've done good work on finding the *more* rules which were needed; and you've listened to each other well.'
*T here, I think, is reinforcing the behaviour that she **wants** the pupils to develop, and avoiding reference to any negative behaviour.*

12.35 Lesson ends.

Comment

Here the lesson strategy was to use a two-phase concrete preparation to lead to Worksheet 2 and a possible whole-class discussion on some of the problems about realising that one rule was necessary but not sufficient.

Initial phase (11.39–11.48). **9 min.** Preparing pupils for work on task with necessary ideas and technical terms.

Work on task (11.48–11.55), **7 min.** Assisting pupils who get into problems, using empty dotty paper only. Idea here was that counter-examples at this point would introduce diversionary confusion.

Further class discussion as preparation for Worksheet 2 (11.55–12.05), **10 min.** Here both examples and counter-examples were obtained from the pupils and shared on the board, so here was the first chance for pupils to begin to learn from each other.

Main work on task (12.05– 12.23), **18 min.** Pupils here were engaged as far as possible with counter-examples in the hope that they would see that, although their rules were true, they needed more than one.

Final whole-class discussion (12.23–12.29), **6 min.** Pupils somewhat tired by then, but (a) they were left with examples showing you need two rules, not just one, and (b) they were given a first idea of the collaborative learning style which they will later develop.

It might be a good idea to look for occasions in other Maths lessons where some reference back ('bridging') could be made to the idea of expressing rules and then testing them. It could help the pupils by realising they have met this kind of thing before.

Perhaps if time does not allow Worksheet 3 to be used (previous recorded lessons only show this when the overall time was 75 or 80 minutes) one should try to plan a few minutes on converting the code to letters at the end, in order to give the pupils a 'taster' for generalised number.

REFERENCES

Adey, P. and Shayer, M. (1994). *Really Raising Standards: Cognitive Intervention and Academic Achievement*. London: Routledge.

Adey, P., Shayer, M. and Yates, C. (1995). *Thinking Science: Student and Teachers' Materials for the CASE Intervention*. London: Nelson (2nd edition).

Beasley, F. and Shayer, M. (1990). Learning Potential Assessment through Feuerstein's LPAD: can quantitative results be achieved? *International Journal of Dynamic Assessment and Instruction*, 1 (2), 37–48.

Clarke, A. M. and Clarke, A. D. B. (1976). *Early Experience: Myth and Evidence*. London: Open Books.

Epstein, H. T. (1990). Stages in human mental growth. *Journal of Educational Psychology*, 82, 876–80.

Feuerstein, R., Rand, Y. and Hoffman, M. (1979). *The Dynamic Assessment of Retarded Performers: The Learning Potential Assessment Device, Theory, Instruments and Techniques*. Baltimore: University Park Press.

Feuerstein, R., Rand, Y., Hoffman, M. and Miller, M. (1980). *Instrumental Enrichment: An Intervention Programme for Cognitive Modifiability*. Baltimore: University Park Press.

Klein, P. S. and Aloni, S. (1993). Immediate and sustained effects of maternal mediating behaviours on young children. *Journal of Early Intervention*, 17, 1–17.

Lovell, K. and Shields, J. B. (1967). Some aspects of a study of the gifted child. *British Journal of Educational Psychology*, 37, 201–8.

Newman, D., Griffin, P. and Cole, M. (1989). *The Construction Zone: Working for Cognitive Change in School*. Cambridge: Cambridge University Press.

Shayer, M. (1992). Problems and issues in intervention studies. Chapter 6 in A. Demetriou, M. Shayer and A. Efklides (eds), *Neo-Piagetian Theories of Cognitive Development*. London: Routledge.

Shayer, M. and Adey, P. S. (1981). *Towards a Science of Science Teaching*. London: Heinemann Educational Books.

Shayer, M. and Beasley, F. (1987). Does Instrumental Enrichment work? *British Educational Research Journal*, 13 (2), 101–19.

Shayer, M. and Wylam, H. (1978). The distribution of Piagetian stages of thinking in British middle and secondary school children II: 14–16 year-olds and sex differentials. *British Journal of Educational Psychology*, 48, 62–70.

Shayer, M., Küchemann, D. E. and Wylam, H. (1976). The distribution of Piagetian stages of thinking in British middle and secondary school children. *British Journal of Educational Psychology*, 46, 164–73.

Shayer, M., Demetriou, A. and Pervez, M. (1988). The structure and scaling of concrete operational thought: three studies in four countries. *Genetic, Social and General Psychological Monographs*, 309–75.

Tukey, J. W. (1977). *Exploratory Data Analysis*. London: Addison-Wesley.

Tzuriel, D. and Ernst, H. (1990). Mediated learning experience and cognitive modifiability: testing the effects of distal and proximal factors by structural equation model. *International Journal of Cognitive Education and Mediated Learning*, 1 (2), 119–35.

Vygotsky, L. S. (1978). *Mind in Society*. London: Harvard University Press.

Vygotsky, L. S. (1981). The genesis of higher mental functions. In J. V. Wertsch (ed.), *The Concept of Activity in Soviet Psychology*. Armonk, NY: M. E. Sharpe.

Webb, R. A. (1974). Concrete and formal operations in very bright 6 to 11-year-olds. *Human Development*, 17, 292–300.

3 Psychological theory that 'works' in the classroom

Kathy Sylva

INTRODUCTION

When first invited to act as discussant for Michael Shayer and Mike Beveridge I wondered if they would produce 'head to head' papers, an intense academic debate which required me to find common ground and adjudicate fierce disagreements. I was pleased to find the papers complementary. Beveridge's masterly account of the socio-politics of educational reform creates a theoretical context, a political surround which neatly holds Shayer's carefully argued empirical demonstration of the power of Piaget and Vygotsky in the classroom. Thus Beveridge provides the macro-context for Shayer's micro-level paper.

THE RISE AND TRIUMPH OF CONTEXTUAL THEORY IN PSYCHOLOGY

Mike Beveridge's paper set the scene nicely with his description of psychology at the end of this century. Psychology is a 'success story'. He cited:

1 The move away from grand theory to context-specific behaviours, activities and processes. Psychology is potentially more useful to education than ever before. We now have a powerful theory which ought to be useful to practitioners. Useful concepts in education include situated cognition, analogy, external representations, reasoning in context, acquisition of implicit knowledge, and the role of language in collaboration.
2 Unfortunately, educators seek simple, easily applied solutions. However, when they try to put them to use, they quickly see their inadequacy. This is because simplicity is the enemy of application. Simple theories do not work and teachers soon realise this. Thus we have the dilemma of the 1990s. Educators want slogans and sound-bites but they will quickly decry and abandon them when they see their shallowness.

THE USE AND MIS-USE OF SCAFFOLDING AS AN EXAMPLE OF 'GIVING PSYCHOLOGY AWAY'

Educators wanted slogans and they found one in scaffolding. This was 'over-sold' (or perhaps, 'over-bought') in education. Recent research suggests that scaffolding either does not exist or does not work in classrooms. Bliss, Askew and McRae (1996) carried out research on thirteen teachers of Key Stage 2 (7–11 years) pupils. They asked the following questions:

- Did scaffolding of everyday knowledge (Rogoff and Wertsch, 1984) transfer to school knowledge?
- If scaffolding is found in the classroom, what is the best way to disseminate examples of good practice? Can good examples of practice help teachers to use scaffolding techniques in lessons on, e.g. sorting rocks, testing the strength of paper?

Much to the surprise of Bliss and colleagues, they found almost no scaffolding in science classes in London schools. What they found instead was 'pseudo scaffolding' as well as 'mis-fired scaffolding'. The researchers found few examples of 'activity settings' in science classrooms. They were surprised at this because so much has been written about the power of scaffolding theory to help us improve/understand practice in classrooms.

There are two recent studies where scaffolding took place successfully. These show that in certain educational contexts scaffolding is a useful conceptual structure for understanding practice. First, Wood and Wood (1996) showed how computer instruction can employ scaffolding in problem-solving contexts. Second, Hobsbaum, Peters and Sylva (1996) showed that Reading Recovery in a one-to-one tutorial intervention programme for children was successful in promoting literacy skills in poor readers. Although these two studies show that scaffolding *can* take place effectively in 1:1 setting (tutor or computer program), I am suggesting here that scaffolding is not a useful concept in normal classroom teaching.

In summary, it appears that classrooms are not the embodiment of Vygotskian principles. However, tutorial situations can embody Vygotskian principles. I believe that scaffolding is a good example of a Vygotskian concept which has been 'over-sold' or 'over-bought' by classroom teachers. It seems to work most effectively in 1:1 situations.

VYGOTSKIAN TEACHING IN THE CLASSROOM

Shayer's paper demonstrates that both Piaget and Vygotsky can contribute to improving practice in normal classrooms. I turn with great pleasure to the work of Shayer and colleagues who designed educational programmes based on *both* Piaget's and Vygotsky's work. Shayer's paper provides a convincing demonstration of the effectiveness of educational intervention based on cognitive developmental theory. He reports findings from many

London schools, including 'research schools'. His intervention was based on the following hypotheses:

1 If children reach the stage of formal operations, they will be better learners and better able to profit from instructional teaching.
2 If interventions assist pupils in formal operations, this 'development' will produce measurable effects on psychological tests and *also* on 'learning' outcomes. The latter happens because the psychological development can increase learning ability.

In Shayer's experiment, teachers were trained to deliver thirty activities, each fostering the move to operational thinking. Results showed that the intervention increased learning ability (gains on psychological tests) *but also* there were gains on Key Stage 3 assessment in Science, English and Maths. Most powerful of all Shayer's results is the generalisation to other school subjects such as English. The children have really 'learned how to learn'.

Shayer's view of why his intervention worked is fascinating. Cognitive and language development took place when a less able pupil witnessed a successful performance in another pupil and internalised it. The incomplete strategies of the less able child were 'improved' by his or her watching the successful performance of more able peers. Shayer claimed that the greater the match between the internalisations of the more and the less successful pupils, the greater was the learning.

How can this kind of learning be managed in class? Whole class discussion after small groups experimentation provided opportunity for pupils to construct more powerful strategies because each insight is shared in the class, and every difficulty encountered and eventually overcome is visible to other pupils who learn from it.

Shayer was asked the provocative question: 'Does Piaget or Vygotksy contribute most to the successful intervention?' He answered that what is to be acquired by the pupil ('framing of the tasks themselves, the intellectual hardware') is derived from Piaget. However, the pedagogy of the actual exercises/lesson draws on heavily on Vygotsky because various aspects of *mediation* were the cause of cognitive development, and because *mediating agents* (he draws on Feuerstein's work) frame and organise the learning environment.

The tasks themselves in Shayer's research are really contexts requiring formal operational schemata for solution. They include the control of variables and also the use of proportional thinking.

DEVELOPMENT VS. LEARNING IS AN OUTDATED DICHOTOMY

Should we encourage children's 'development' so it will form the basis for later school learning? Or should we encourage children's 'learning to use cultural tools' in subject contexts (Science, Maths) so they can be transferred within and across school subjects?

In Vygostky's view thinking develops from the teaching process. This view connects dialogic processes such as scaffolding with tools for thought such as writing and natural concepts like constructivism. Thinking develops through internalisation of the individual engagement with these interconnections. Shayer reminded us of the Piagetian description of different stages in cognition. He wished to encourage developmental progression and operational thinking, and his work shows optimal thinking will generalise to English. But the two approaches are very different.

Shayer's work assumes that:

Development → learning

whereas Vygotsky has claimed that:

Learning → development.

My suggestion here is to abandon these distinctions. Instead we might study 'learning in context'. In some cases this learning will take place in school (an educational context) and in others it will occur at home and in the neighbourhood. The specific context matters little; what matters is that the child has acquired new knowledge, skill or attitude and that this propels her towards maturity. The knowledge, skill or attitude will often be part of the 'cultural took kit'. Sometimes the learning will take place in a social context (in the Vygotskian tradition) and other times it will occur when the child is on her own (the Piagetian tradition). The child's being on her own matters little because the learner has an internal representation of 'others' even when she is learning (or developing) on her own. I make this radical suggestion because I believe that we have moved far enough from the old Behaviourist Learning Theory to reclaim the word 'learning'. The distinction between learning and development has created a schism between developmental psychology and education which I believe has excluded the former from practical debates.

THE RELATIONSHIP BETWEEN SHAYER'S RESEARCH AND BEVERIDGE'S SOCIO-POLITICAL STATEMENT

Beveridge described the 'commodified culture' of the school economy in which 'goods' called learning or knowledge are 'produced' by teachers and others in such a way as to maximise the 'value' to society (mostly industrialists) and to minimalise the cost to taxpayer. If Piaget or Vygotsky are to have educational salience today, we must be able to connect their theories with the aims and procedures of a school system which aims to exchange and reproduce knowledge efficiently within the available resource constraints. The product of this educational system is called 'school knowledge' and it is currently reified even though its direct applicability to other arenas of life such as employment is weak.

I return to Beveridge's optimistic beginning. Never before had psychologists so much 'useful knowledge' to sell to educationalists. If cultural tools enable more sophisticated learning, and if they are acquired in contexts of mediation, then we *will* convince 'economists' in education that they will 'pay off'.

But I'll not end here. I would like to see our research focus more squarely on Wertsch's (1994) concept of *mediated action* in that we should take the interaction between adults, pupils and tasks as the unit of analysis, not individuals.

Beveridge also suggested the need for effective technical language. However, it must be embedded in rich theories, not superficial ones. We might adopt a systems approach to explicit implementation processes. Beveridge decried the 'growing number of technicians but few thinkers and scholars'. Conferences such as this are one move against superficiality.

SUMMARY

1 I applauded the complementarity of the two papers.
2 I argued against the over-application of scaffolding to classroom learning.
3 I praised emphasis on mediated action, not forgetting the Piagetian operational slant of Michael Shayer.
4 I acknowledged the 'commodification' of education means we must show results. We need to make clear that 'development' leads to 'more educational attainment'.
5 I welcomed the rich theory on the process itself, not just outcomes.
6 However, I suggested that the new unit of analysis should be the activity in context (e.g. the school, classroom or small group) and not the individual learner.

REFERENCES

Bliss, J., Askew, M. and McRae, S. (1996). Effective teaching and learning: scaffolding revisited. *Oxford Review of Education*, 22 (1), 37–61.
Hobsbaum, A., Peters, S. and Sylva, K. (1996). Scaffolding in Reading Recovery. *Oxford Review of Education*, 22 (1), 17–35.
Rogoff, B. and Wertsch, J. V. (1984). Children's learning in the 'zone of proximal development'. In B. Rogoff and J. V. Wertsch (eds) *New Directions for Child Development*. San Francisco: Jossey-Bass.
Wertsch, J. V. (1994). The primacy of mediated action in sociocultural studies. *Mind, Culture and Activity*, 1, 202–8.
Wood, D. and Wood, H. (1996). Vygotsky, tutoring and learning. *Oxford Review of Education*, 22 (1), 5–15.

Part 2

Social collaboration and learning

4 Psychological development as a social process

Gerard Duveen

INTRODUCTION

The debate around the contributions of Piaget and Vygotsky for contemporary developmental psychology is usually constructed around an opposition between individual and social perspectives on the process of development, with Piaget construed as the individualist as against the social theorising of Vygotsky. There are good grounds, however, for resisting such a characterisation of these theorists. As I shall argue in this paper, Piaget has a stronger grasp of social processes than this view admits, while Vygotsky's grasp of social processes is limited in some important ways which this view does not recognise. While a review of some of the key themes in the classic contributions of these two authors will certainly entail a consideration of social aspects of development, I also want to argue that both of them ignore some central issues in considering psychological development as a social process. To make this argument it is also necessary to begin to reconnect developmental psychology with social psychology. There is something really very strange in the way these two endeavours have become so radically disconnected. Strange, because both of these traditions are fundamentally addressing similar concerns. As Moscovici has noted (1990, p. 169), they have a:

> common point of departure and are animated by such close underlying issues. Their different traditions and methods allow a deep similarity to show through and tie them together. It is as if social psychology and developmental psychology were concerned with the same thing, the former in space and the latter in time, the first by way of the exterior and the second by way of the interior.

If the problem for developmentalists is to understand how the child develops as a social actor, social psychologists forget at their peril that every social actor has a developmental history whose influence cannot be ignored.

In actual fact, although the designations 'social' and 'developmental' have come to signify distinct categories in the world of psychology, from the perspective of a constructivist epistemology the distinction necessarily collapses. Both Moscovici and Piaget share a common epistemological stance. The world that we know is the world as we have constructed it through our psychological operations. Piaget elaborated and defended his constructivist – or genetic – position against the claims of both *a priorism* and empiricism. Knowledge is neither the product of inherent character- istics of the mind, nor simply the reflection of environmental influences. Rather, for Piaget, knowledge develops in children through their inter- action with the environment, in the course of which they first come to co-ordinate their own actions and then to abstract more general operations from these co-ordinations. Similarly Moscovici (1972) elaborated and defended what he described as *systematic* social psychology against the claims of social psychological theories based on *a priori* or empiricist epistemologies. In a later work Moscovici (1976a) came to characterise his position as exemplifying a genetic social psychology, and the very use of this word *genetic*, so redolent with Piagetian overtones, ought to alert us to the harmony between these two authors. And it is in their common genetic approach that the harmony is heard most clearly.

A central assumption of genetic theories in psychology is that to understand something we have to understand the process through which it has been produced, that is we have to grasp its developmental construction. This assumption has been most clearly articulated in the classic texts of Piaget and Vygotsky, but it has also been evident in the theory of social representations. If we want to understand social representations we have to understand the processes through which they are produced and trans- formed. For Moscovici this means not only the processes of anchoring and objectification,[1] but also, as Doise (1993) has recently reminded us, the processes of propagation, propaganda and diffusion. In commenting on a collection of developmental studies of social representations, Moscovici (1990) suggests that there are two approaches to analysing the processes through which representations are constructed. The first, which he suggests is the more typical in social psychology, he describes as Bartlett's way, since it proposes to analyse the construction and reconstruction of representations as they pass from one social group to another. The second approach he characterises as Vygotsky's way (while noting that it is also Piaget's way, though, as we shall see, while they may share some character- istics Piaget's way is not always the same as Vygotsky's way), and it seeks to understand representations by analysing their successive transformations through the different phases of childhood and adolescence.

While Moscovici's comment suggests that these are two ways to achieve the same ends, there are nevertheless differences between Bartlett's way and Vygotsky's way. Bartlett's way has led to investigations of the processes through which representations are organised and the means through which they are communicated in society (Moscovici, 1976b), and, within this general approach, further reflections on the representations themselves has led to studies of the social psychological structures of the groups producing the representations (e.g. Jodelet, 1991). Some of the same concerns can also be observed in studies which have followed Vygotsky's way (though there is nothing here which compares to the richness of Jodelet's analysis of the underlying social psychology of her French villagers struggling to come to terms with the presence of the mad in their everyday lives), though the major focus for these studies has been the emergence of the child as a social actor. For the most part Vygotsky's way has been seen as an approach to a particular problem – if the child is born into a world which is already structured in terms of social representations, how does the child become a participating member of these communities? The emphasis, then, in studying social representations through Vygotsky's way has been rather different to that which has been evident from Bartlett's way. We could say that Vygotsky's way has been seen as an appropriate approach to questions of the *ontogenesis* of social representations, whereas Bartlett's way has been more generally adopted for the study of their *sociogenesis* (cf. Duveen and Lloyd, 1990).

Thus, a focus on ontogenetic issues has generated a concern with a different, if complementary, set of questions from those which are evident in sociogenetic studies. Primarily, of course, because ontogenetic studies have had to negotiate their way around the classical edifices of developmental psychology with their central assumption that the mental capabilities of children are themselves changing as the child develops. What contribution, if any, does the child's developing mental organisation exert on their acquisition of social representations? It is tempting to see the various responses to this question as illustrating two fundamental approaches, which either follow Piaget in emphasising the constitutive role of the child's own emerging mental structures, or share Vygotsky's emphasis on the internalisation of collective sign systems.

Before considering the contribution which the work of these authors can make to an understanding of the development of social representations, I want to outline the approach to this theme which has emerged from the work which Barbara Lloyd and I have undertaken over the past few years into the development of social representations of gender in young children (Duveen and Lloyd, 1986, 1990, 1993; Lloyd and Duveen, 1989, 1990, 1992). In this approach we have used Moscovici's theory of social representations as a starting point for considering psychological development as a social process. This approach provides a social psychological perspective of children as developing social actors, with a complementary emphasis on the symbolic aspect of their developing knowledge. It is this perspective which I use in the later sections of this chapter as a point of reference for discussing the contributions of Piaget and Vygotsky.

THE DEVELOPMENT OF SOCIAL REPRESENTATIONS

Children are born into a world which is already structured by the social representations of their communities, which ensure that they take their place within systematic sets of social practices and social relations. Contemporary approaches in developmental psychology demonstrate an increasing awareness of this situation, and nowhere is such a perspective more important than in relation to gender development, precisely because gender is such a powerful and ubiquitous dimension of the social world into which the child is born. Indeed, it seems inappropriate here to speak of 'the child' as though some shared set of characteristics could serve to identify the object of study. While Piaget could speak with some authority of 'the child' as an epistemic subject, and use this conceptualisation as a central strategic notion for pursuing an analysis of the development of intelligence, such a generalisation cannot be sustained in relation to gender, where it is difference which is more salient. The force of categorisation is so strong in the representations of gender which circulate around children, that they always appear as girls or boys developing particular social identities. From their earliest beginnings (which thanks to modern technology now frequently means while they are still in the womb) children are construed as gendered beings by those around them, who consequently act towards them in the light of this construction.

If children are born into a world which is structured by social representations of gender, and through which they are construed, this does not mean that they are born with the competence to be independent social actors in this world. Initially children figure as the objects of other people's representations of gender, and only gradually do they come to internalise these representations, and, as they do so, they also come to identify a position for themselves within the world structured by these representations. Representations of gender provide an important framework through which children acquire an identity which enables them to situate themselves in the social world. This relationship between representations and identities is not specific to the field of gender. Wherever representations are internalised they are linked to a process of identity formation, although the consequences of the identity are not always the same. For example, we do not usually think of children's internalisation of representations of mathematics as being linked to specific social identities, but this can indeed be the case. When the form of mathematics which children internalise is linked to their identity as the member of a marginalised social group this can lead to a disruptive relationship in their schooling, and it is only when we see the consequences of difficulties and failures in school that the sense in which representations of mathematics also express a social identity becomes apparent (de Abreu, 1993, 1995). If the relationship between representation and identity is usually opaque in the field of mathematics, it can nevertheless become clear in some contexts. The pervasiveness of variations and differences associated with gender ensures that the relationship between representations and identities is clear across a very wide range of contexts. That this should be so is due to the significance of gender as a dimension of power in the social world.

Representations are always constructive, they constitute the world as it is known, and the identities which they sustain secure a place for the individual within this world. As representations are internalised they come to express an individual's relationship to the world which they know and to situate them within this world. It is this dual operation of defining the world and locating a place within it which gives representations their symbolic value. Moscovici (1973, p. xiii) alludes to this when he speaks of social representations establishing 'an order which will enable individuals to orient themselves in their material and social world and to master it'. Once established in this way the order which is provided by representations takes on a fixed and objective character; it assumes a stability which can guarantee security for the individuals who find their place within this world. This aspect of cognitive activity has rarely been the explicit focus of discussion, although Shweder (1990) makes a similar point in outlining his idea of a cultural psychology when he speaks of cognition as functioning to reduce human existential uncertainty. Another example can be drawn from Mugny and Carugati's (1989) study of social representations of intelligence. They found that those groups of respondents such as students who were removed from the world of children had less clearly structured and organised representations of intelligence than groups such as parents and teachers who have to face an everyday reality in which differences between children require some explanatory framework. These authors talk about such social groups having a different 'social stake' in these representations, an idea which is close to what I have in mind when speaking of the symbolic aspects of representations. It is perhaps no accident that it is through reflecting on social representations of gender that I have come to emphasise their symbolic functions, for representations of gender, precisely because they refer to such a central dimension of social power and organisation, also carry central consequences for our definitions of self. We cannot think of ourselves as neutral in the field of gender, in some way or another we always think of ourselves as male or female, and these social identities arise in the course of internalising social representations of gender. Other representational fields may carry fewer existential consequences, in which case their symbolic value would also be reduced, as with Mugny and Carugati's students.

As a social psychological process, the construction of an identity is a way of organising meanings which enable a person to position him or herself as a social actor. An identity provides a means of organising experience which contributes towards the definition of self, but it does so by locating the self within the collective world. For the newborn child social gender identities are at first external; they are extended to the child through the practice of others. What we see in the development of social representations of gender is a grasp of consciousness, as children develop a reflexive awareness of the meaning of the social act of assignment to a gender group.

PIAGET'S WAY

There is not the space in this paper to offer a systematic appraisal of the relevance of Piaget's work for a developmental psychology of social representations. I have already alluded to the significance of his constructivist epistemology, and there are numerous other annotations which one could offer in this respect. Jovchelovitch (1995), for example, has emphasised the importance of Piaget's analysis of the development of representation and of decentering as contributions to a theory of social representations. One could also add the evident importance which Piaget's analysis of children's thinking held for the development of Moscovici's (1976b) analysis of the characteristics of social representations (and this reference to Piaget's work brings with it the influence of Lévy-Bruhl, who was also an important source for both Bartlett and Luria; indeed it may be in Lévy-Bruhl that one can see a clear common origin for the two ways which Moscovici describes).

No doubt a systematic analysis would bring forward many other points of confluence between Piaget and Moscovici. And yet for some authors Piaget has become a highly controversial figure from the perspective of social representations. Emler (1986; Emler, Ohana and Dickinson, 1990) in particular has attacked Piagetian work on two central grounds. First that it articulates the child as an autonomous individual engaged in the construction of knowledge through processes which are only marginally affected by social influences. Secondly that Piagetian theory presents a restricted image of the child as a solver of primarily logical problems. Emler can of course find evidence in Piaget's writings with which to condemn him for committing these sins, but this is based on too simplistic a reading of Piaget. Or perhaps we should say that in spite of the extraordinary theoretical integrity which sustained Piaget's work over the course of a very long productive life, there are nevertheless lacunae in this work which open up precisely around his articulation of the social character of knowledge. More than anywhere else it is in this arena that one finds not a single Piagetian theory but a multiplicity of Piagetian texts. There is on the one hand the Piaget who wrote *The Moral Judgement of the Child* (1932) and the *Sociological Studies* (1995) (and perhaps one should also add *Play, Dreams and Imitation*, 1951, to this list), where the social character of knowledge and the social processes of its constitution are of central concern. On the other hand there are numerous texts (particularly those of his later years devoted to an explication of developmental theory based on his conception of equilibration) where Piaget appears to elide any distinction between biological and social forces.[2] In short, the social is an unstable element in Piaget's analysis of the development of knowledge. Indeed one could go further and suggest that it is precisely this instability which has contributed to the construction of an image of Piaget's work as an 'asocial' theory, an image which is peculiarly deeply entrenched in the Anglo-Saxon world (one could conceive of a study of the social representations of Piaget's work, which would illustrate the way in which his theory is transformed as it becomes anchored in other psychological approaches). Emler's reading of Piaget is, I think, too closely linked to this image of Piaget, and fails to appreciate the more radical elements in his work which resist the interpretation which Emler seeks to sustain.

In the first place, Piaget's focus is not on the individual but on what he terms the knowing or *epistemic* subject, which he distinguishes from the *psychological* subject. 'There is', he writes (Piaget, 1966, p. 308),

> the 'psychological subject' centred in the conscious ego whose functional role is incontestable, but which is not the origin of any structure of general knowledge; but there is also the 'epistemic subject' or that which is common to all subjects at the same level of development, whose cognitive structures derive from the most general mechanisms of the co-ordination of actions.

One might legitimately accuse Piaget of a transcendentalism which obscures a view of cognitive structures as social and cultural formations (e.g. Buck-Morss, 1975), but there is no trace of a theoretical individualism in his work. The question of focus is paramount in appreciating Piaget's work. His central question was always 'How is knowledge possible?', and from this point of view sensorimotor co-ordinations and mental operations are not in themselves knowledge but the grounds for knowledge, the processes through which knowledge of the world is constructed. Thus from Piaget's point of view variations in the content of knowledge are less important than the uniformity of form which holds across social and cultural contexts. One can then see the point which a critical reading of Piaget needs to recognise, namely that what Piaget construes as universal forms of cognitive organisation are themselves particular social representations. In this sense to Piaget's question of 'How is knowledge possible?' we need to add the further question 'For whom is knowledge possible?', so that we can introduce a third term into Piaget's binary distinction. As well as the psychological and epistemic subjects, we need to consider the social psychological subject (cf. Duveen and Lloyd, 1986) for whom knowledge is not the product of an abstract universal but the expression of a social identity. To say this is not to deny the logical character of knowledge, but, rather, to assert that the use of a logic in constructing knowledge locates the subject in a social world where that logic is held to be legitimate.

Emler's second objection is that Piaget characterises the child primarily as a problem-solver. He cites his own studies on income inequality as evidence that such a view is in error. Far from solving problems, the children he interviewed responded as though they had access to ready made solutions which required little or no cognitive elaboration but which reflected primarily the child's social position. Thus he found little variation with age in children's judgements of relative income, but significant variations with social class (Emler and Dickinson, 1985).[3] Emler construes such results as providing evidence against a Piagetian view of the development of social knowledge, since there is little indication of any reconstructive activity on the part of children who seem merely to be repeating the common knowledge of their social class. But again this argument reflects only a very partial reading of Piaget, and a reading which ignores what is still one of the most important contributions which Piaget has to offer a developmental psychology of social representations.

In *The Moral Judgement of the Child* (1932) Piaget makes a fundamental distinction between two forms of acquiring social knowledge. On the one hand there is knowledge which he describes as the product of social transmission, where it is the authority of a dominant or privileged figure which is the source of knowledge. As against this Piaget also argues that there is knowledge which is acquired through cognitive elaboration in a process of reconstruction. The former, he argues, takes place in heteronomous relations where the asymmetry of power exercises a constraint on the less powerful. The latter, by contrast, can only occur in autonomous relations between equal partners, where each has the freedom to engage in argument and debate. Emler, it seems to me, has failed to take account of this distinction. The results he presents could be considered as a fine example of acquisition through social transmission. But there is also evidence from other sources which shows children engaged in a more productive cognitive elaboration of social knowledge. In this respect one could cite the Genevan research on social interaction and cognitive development (Doise and Mugny, 1984) as an exemplary instance, where collective engagement in a problem was found to lead to the construction of more complex solutions than either partner was able to find when working independently. Perhaps, though, such an example would be discounted by Emler as being too explicitly oriented towards logic and problem-solving. A different source of evidence for the reconstruction of social knowledge in symmetrical relations can be found in studies of pretend play among young children, in which the social world is literally reconstructed to the extent that children have understood it (cf. Duveen and Lloyd, 1988; Furth, 1992). Further evidence is offered by Corsaro's (1990) study of the constructive elaboration of social rules amongst peers in the world of the nursery.

To illustrate this point, consider these two excerpts from our video recordings of children at play during their first year at school (Lloyd and Duveen, 1992). The first extract contains a long domestic pretend episode which features Mummy, Daddy, their bed, their babies and marriage. Oscar asserts his role and responsibilities as Daddy in turns 1, 4 and 5. Sally initiates a scene shift from domesticity to courtship with princesses in turn

17. Adults are portrayed as actively searching for partners who presumably, upon marriage, become mummies and daddies. Physical contact between a boy and girl inevitably results in marriage, as Sally proclaims in turn 27. Betty's somewhat ambiguous comments in turn 28 leave little doubt that the Princess's marriage involves procreation. These episodes provide us with a glimpse of children's understanding of family life. It is based upon a view of adult sex group membership which offers little role choice or within-group variability. Sexuality is heterosexual and procreative.

Extract 1

Oscar is Daddy, Rachel the Mummy and Betty the Baby. There have been prior turns about eating and mending things.

1. *Oscar*: (*On mattress.*) I'm the Daddy.
2. *Sally*: (*To Rachel.*) Dinner's not ready, so just wait.
3. *Betty*: (*To Oscar.*) And you hear my crying a-ha-aah-aah.
4. *Oscar*: (*Goes to Betty who is still crying.*) Be quiet, baby, be quiet.
5. *Oscar*: I put that by your bed in case you wanted some dinner. (*He goes back to bed.*)
6. *Rachel*: (*Joins Oscar.*) No – aah!
7. *Oscar*: That's my bed. It's my bed. (*They both lie on it.*)
8. (*Break, followed by*)
9. *Sally*: This is Mummy's and Daddy's bed. (*Lying down on bed. Oscar goes over to her.*)
10. (*Character shift and Sally becomes Mummy.*)
11. *Rachel*: (*Rolling on bed.*) Hello Mum.
12. *Sally*: No! Get off Mummy's and Daddy's bed. You're being a very naughty girl today.
13. *Betty*: (*Crawling over to them.*) Googa googa.
14. *Sally*: Will you get that cover, Baby?
15. *Betty*: (*Hands cover to Sally.*)
16. (*Going to bed, Baby crying, tap dripping – relevant?*) . . .
17. *Sally*: I'm the Princess. (*Sits down on her bed.*)
18. *Betty*: Pretend, pretend, I want, pretend you was a bit beautiful and I was . . .
19. *Oscar*: I'm the Prince.
20. *Betty*: . . . beautiful. We were both beautiful. Decide who you want to marry.
21. *Oscar*: I'm the Prince.
22. *Betty*: You can searching for a beautiful woman.
23. (*Oscar pretends to dip between Sally and Betty. Meanwhile Rachel is pulling at his trouser leg.*)
24. *Rachel*: I caught him! I caught him! I caught him! I caught him! I caught him! I caught him!

25. (*Sally wins the dip and Oscar goes and puts his arms around her, sits beside her on the bed, puts his head on her shoulder.*)
26. *Betty*: [. . .]
27. *Sally*: He marries me.
28. *Betty*: [. . . ?] Yes, Yes, and I have to be the . . ? . . Princess, but with you little girl. Pretend you got married and you, you had a . . ? . . grown up. And I had to go to school.

The second extract illustrates once again children's belief that physical/ sexual contact between sex group members needs to be validated through marriage. Oscar is chased for some time by the girls but once he is kissed by Christine, perhaps somewhat to his surprise, he proclaims in turn 16 that he is going to marry her. Children create a simple world in which physical contact between sex group members is construed as sexual and involves marriage. In this world actions have direct and predictable consequences.

Extract 2

1. *Edith*: . . . and Lulu kiss, uhm, Oscar. Go on.
2. *Christine*: I'm not playing now.
3. *Edith*: Go away, then.
4. *Lulu*: No, you kiss Oscar and I kiss Darren.
5. *Edith*: I know. Look. You (*Joan*) kiss him Darren.
6. *Lulu*: And I'll kiss Oscar.
7. *Edith*: Joan kiss Oscar.
8. *Edith*: Joan kiss Darren, and Oscar kiss . . . you!
9. *Joan*: (*Starts for Darren, who runs.*) Hey!
10. *Edith*: Come here. (*Grabs Lulu and moves her towards Oscar, not unwillingly.*) No, kiss! Kiss her on the lips. Kiss her on the lips. Come on!
11. *Lulu*: No way!
12. *Edith*: Go on. Kiss her. Kiss her.
13. *Christine*: (*Makes a dash for Oscar.*) I kissed him.
14. *Oscar*: I kissed HER!
15. *Edith*: Oooh!
16. *Oscar*: (*Points at Christine.*) I'm going to marry her.
17. *Edith*: (*With Lulu, no longer struggling, very close.*) Kiss her.
18. *Oscar*: I'm going to marry her.
19. *Sally*: (*Also closing in on Oscar.*)
20. *Oscar*: All right. (*But which one should he kiss?*)
21. *Sally*: Kiss me. (*They kiss.*)
22. (*All laugh. Oscar throws himself back on sofa.*)

These examples illustrate the reconstructive processes at work in children's acquisition of social knowledge, which can be contrasted with aspects of social knowledge which appear to result from social transmission.

In arguing that from the perspective of social representations knowledge is only acquired through social transmission, Emler not only gives a partial view of Piaget's argument, but he also restricts the scope of social representations. If we consider for a moment other studies of economic knowledge, there is evidence of a constructive aspect in children's elaboration of such concepts as wages, prices and profit (e.g. Berti and Bombi, 1988). These notions are clearly not acquired simply by a process of social transmission, but does that mean that the idea of profit, for instance, is not a social representation? Clearly not.

From Piaget, then, we can draw an account of different processes at work in the acquisition of social knowledge. He himself associates social transmission with children's acquisition of the collective representations of their society (and in using that term he makes explicit reference to Durkheim), while reconstruction is for him a function of engagement in cognitive activity. But if we read Piaget's argument in the light of the critical perspective outlined above, what he construes as cognitive activity also needs to be understood as social representation. And from this point of view it is interesting to return to Moscovici's contrast of social representations with Durkheim's analysis of collective representations. For Moscovici Durkheim's conception is too static, and his major reason for preferring the adjective 'social' is to emphasise the dynamic aspects of representations. He wishes to focus on social knowledge in the process of formation and transformation, rather than social knowledge as received wisdom (or what Sartre referred to as the *practico-inert*). There must, of course, be a relationship between social representations and collective representations, for even collective representations must at one time have emerged from a more dynamic elaboration (just as the practico-inert is no more than the accumulated products of past human praxis). In childhood much of what appears to be the static common sense of the adult world is subject to a more dynamic form of elaboration. And where children are engaged in such elaboration we can learn from Piaget to expect that they will articulate representations which reflect their cognitive development rather than being the immediate reflection of adult thought. Piaget also offers us a further lesson, that cognitive elaborations occur in the context of symmetrical relations where thought is not constrained by hegemonic power. In the life of children it is in their relations with other children that this condition is most frequently found, so that the constructive cognitive elaborations in the development of social representations will be most clearly seen in analyses of children's interactions with their peers in situations where they have the freedom to invent.

If we take Emler's arguments to their most extreme conclusion they imply not only that we should abandon Piaget, but that we should also abandon a commitment to any idea of cognitive development as an autonomous process. I have tried to argue that these positions do not hold, and that there is much to be gained from continuing a constructive dialogue with Piagetian theory. The constructive moment of cognitive elaboration is one of the most important elements in Piaget's genetic psychology, and adopting the perspective of social representations does not mean abandoning a notion of cognitive development, but rather seeing that the structures which emerge are themselves social and cultural products. This may make us see cognitive development as a moment of relative autonomy (to adopt a phrase of Althusser's), but it also serves to remind us that between the 'thinking society' of adults and the emergence of the child as a social actor there is a process of construction which needs to be addressed.

VYGOTSKY'S WAY

Within the corpus of Vygotsky's work the concept of internalisation appears to be at once both the most enigmatic and provocative of his contributions. Enigmatic because although internalisation is identified as a law of psychology, the 'general genetic law of cultural development', the process is described only through the briefest sketch of its contours which rarely provide a sense of detail in the way in which the process operates. What is provocative in Vygotsky's formulation is that it suggests a simple solution to what is a complex problem, the relations between social and cognitive processes, so that it seems to dissolve the mysteries of the socialisation of cognitive functions and thereby to offer a resolution of some of the deepest problems of developmental psychology.

Since the emergence of Vygotsky's work in the Western world, his account of the process of internalisation has exerted an ever-growing influence in developmental psychology. It is not, perhaps, too difficult to identify at least some of the reasons why this should be so. Certainly, a primary reason lies in Vygotsky's insistence that internalisation is a social process, both in the sense that it takes place in the interactions between people and in the sense that what is internalised is a semiotic system which is itself a collective or social product. This emphasis on social processes was seen as an alternative to what was considered to be the irremediably individualist perspective offered by Piagetian theory (although, as I have argued above, this is a particularly myopic view of Piaget's contribution). In particular, cross-cultural evidence appeared to expose serious difficulties in the Piagetian assumption of universal forms in development, while a Vygotskian perspective seemed to offer a means for understanding cultures within the terms of their own semiotic productions (although again, this view of Vygotsky fails to grasp his own evolutionary perspective on culture and society). In short, Vygotsky's work seemed to offer a perspective from which social relations and cognitive processes could be brought into a single productive framework. And yet doubts remain about the extent to which the Vygotskian framework is able to achieve this resolution. Serge Moscovici, for one, has commented (1990, p. 179) that the Vygotskian formula is 'too good to be true', since it assumes a direct relationship between social practices and individual functioning. The suspicion here is that the lack of attention to any mediating structures between these two levels limits the usefulness of Vygotsky's work for social psychology. It is this suspicion which I want to explore in this paper.

Vygotsky's idea of internalisation finds its most succinct expression in what he termed the 'general genetic law of cultural development' (1981, p. 163):

> Any function in the child's cultural development appears twice, or on two planes. First it appears on the social plane, and then on the psychological plane. First it appears between people as an interpsychological category, and then within the child as an intrapsychological category. ... Social relations or relations among people genetically underlie all higher functions and their relationships.

Internalisation is the process through which functions which are first established in the child's external relations with others are re-constructed internally. The connecting thread in this process is given by Vygotsky's analysis of sign functions. In his characteristic metaphor he speaks of these functions 'turning inward', so that what once could be sustained only in interaction with others, takes on the character of an internal function which the child can achieve independently. This transformation may be the 'result of a long series of developmental events' (1978, p. 57), but it creates a profound and radical restructuring of the child's activity.

A prototypical example which Vygotsky (1978) gives of internalisation is the development of pointing in the young child. When the young child tries to grasp an object which is out of reach, this gesture is initially directed at the object itself. It is through the actions of others that the child's gesture is made meaningful. It is the intervention of another (an adult or older sibling) who interprets the gesture and gives the child the object which changes the situation. Gradually, the action of grasping is replaced by the action of pointing, which, as Vygotsky notes, is directed not at the object but at a person. The form of the action itself changes; from the outstretched fingers of the whole hand to the use of a single finger to indicate the desired object. The emergence of pointing not only serves to establish relations with others, but also transforms the child's own sphere of activity by bringing within its horizons objects which cannot be directly grasped.

The constitutive role of others in internalisation led Vygotsky to formulate another key notion, the idea of a zone of proximal development, which he defined (1978, p. 86) as: 'the distance between the child's actual developmental level as determined by independent problem solving and the level of potential development as determined through problem solving under adult guidance or in collaboration with more capable peers'. This image of the child developing through their interaction with adults or peers with greater expertise has had a powerful impact in psychological and educational thinking, being elaborated in terms of 'scaffolding' (Wood,

Bruner and Ross, 1976), 'guided participation' (e.g. Rogoff, 1990) or as the 'construction zone' (Newman, Griffin and Cole, 1989). In all of these guises Vygotsky's notion is the principal idea. It is through their participation in culturally patterned activities that children internalise the semiotic systems of their culture, and thus emerge as competent cultural subjects.

The power of Vygotsky's idea, as Moscovici recognised, is its simplicity. The child is born into a world which is already culturally structured, and this culture is mediated for the child through the activities of those around them. In this way the child comes to take their place within this culture, and eventually, through their own activities to become a mediator of the culture to successive generations. The process through which the child develops is social, and the products of this development are internalised sign systems, which, like all sign systems, are collective in character. Internalisation, then, stands at the centre of Vygotsky's argument that psychological activities are social processes.

However, as powerful as Vygotsky's idea may be, there are nevertheless limits to its usefulness. Wertsch (1991, p. 46), for instance, points to weaknesses in Vygotsky's approach to the way 'historical, cultural and institutional settings are tied to various forms of mediated action'. In responding to these issues, Wertsch has sought to extend Vygotsky's semiotics by including Bakhtin's notion of 'voice'. Other writers have emphasised the significance of social identities as mediators between the interpersonal and the intrapersonal (e.g. Goodnow, 1990; Litowitz, 1993; Duveen, 1994). Although both of these responses to Vygotsky are derived from a consideration of limitations in his grasp of the structural influences at work in the process of internalisation, they draw on different traditions to articulate this concern.

One way in which to examine the limits of Vygotsky's theory is to consider the body of work constructed around the notion of an apprenticeship model of cultural learning. This has become a major form in which Vygotskian ideas have been elaborated in contemporary developmental psychology (e.g. Rogoff and Lave, 1984; Lave, 1990; Rogoff, 1990). The metaphor of apprenticeship is employed to give concrete expression to Vygotsky's idea of a zone of proximal development. A novice acquires cultural knowledge through participation in social practices under the guidance of an expert. Guided participation serves to structure and organise the task for the novice, so that eventually they are able to take independent responsibility for the task. Litowitz (1993, p. 185) identifies the principal characteristics of this model as:

> (1) cultural knowledge is transferred not from one person (adult) to another (child) but from two persons (the dyad) to one (the child); (2) the transmission is accomplished through semiotic means; and (3) the nonknower demonstrates equality in the dyad by becoming equally responsible for solving problems and accomplishing tasks.

As Litowitz makes clear, an important element in this model is a notion of equality between the partners based on mutual respect for the initial differences in expertise. The model emphasises a sense of intersubjectivity based on mutual engagement in a joint activity which subordinates differences between the partners.

This model has been employed with considerable success in the analysis of some specific processes of cultural learning, for example in Greenfield's (1984) study of young women learning to weave in Zinacantan, Mexico, and Lave's (1990) study of apprentice tailors among the Vai and Gola in Liberia. In these analyses one can trace the relations between the cultural patterning of a particular practice, the mediating activities of the expert and the gradual acquisition of independent skill by the novice. It is the engagement of expert and novice in a joint activity which provides the arena for transmission of a particular skill which is embedded in a cultural tradition of practice. And yet the very power of the apprenticeship model to render this situation theoretically accessible points to the limits of the applicability of the model. Reflecting on these analyses one can in fact identify a series of conditions which limit the model, or set boundaries to the range of its applicability.

1 The apprenticeship model applies only to well-structured social practices. The model has been most successfully employed in situations where what is being acquired is a practical skill which depends on mastery of particular coordinations of actions, and it is the regulation of this co-ordination which is the focus of the expert's guidance of the novice's participation. Yet not all cultural knowledge has this concrete quality.
2 The social practices which are being transmitted need to be highly valued by the community so that they are seen as a legitimate expression of the culture. In the examples of the Mexican weavers or the Liberian tailors, it is clear that these practices have an economic value for the community as well as practical and symbolic value.
3 The model assumes a community of interest between novice and expert, so that no conflict arises between them as to the value of what is being learned. For an apprenticeship to be established both expert and novice need to see themselves as being engaged in a joint activity which, whatever their different roles may be, is meaningful to both parties. The novice must be willing to learn and the expert ready to guide their participation. In circumstances where such a community of interest does not exist, where there is instead dissent or resistance, it is difficult to see how an effective apprenticeship could be established. Some of the most persistent problems in secondary education, for example, seem to arise precisely because the students do not recognise any community of interest with their teachers. In championing the 'practice of understanding' as against the 'culture of acquisition' Lave (1990) herself discusses this problem.

4   The model does not account for individual variability in the acquisition of cultural knowledge. Some young Zinacantan women will become better weavers than others, and some young Liberian men better tailors than others. But all will have passed through the same process of apprenticeship. The model itself offers no means for discussing such diversity, which, at the extreme, means that it provides no explanation for failure in the transmission of cultural knowledge.

5   The model offers an account of how specific social practices are transmitted from experts to novices, and in this sense is focussed exclusively on the reproduction of existing social relations. One can legitimately ask how social change can be brought about through a process of apprenticeship.

If we consider these five conditions as a whole, it is possible to recognise a common theme running through them. This is that the model treats social life as though it were in some important way undifferentiated. It is as though children progressively internalise the collective practices of their community through interaction with competent adults or more knowledgeable peers in the absence of any complications arising from the effects of any differential valorisation. Indeed, a certain homogeneity is the most striking characteristic of culture and of the child as they figure within the Vygotskian perspective. Culture as it appears in the Vygotskian formula is an ensemble of signs embedded in social practices, but, importantly, there is no significant diversity of values within this image of culture. It is as though social life were constructed without the differences of value and perspective, of power and conflict which structure social phenomena and which have been at the centre of social psychological concerns. And as a corollary to this one-dimensional culture, the child who develops within it is a subject unmarked by the vicissitudes of social life, a subject who is constituted only as a reproduction of the culture within which they live.

The Vygotskian model establishes a dynamic which moves from the practices established as interpersonal relations through internalisation to the intrapersonal achievement of this practice. But what exactly should be understood by the term 'practice' here? In the examples I quoted earlier, as in most research bearing on the theme of apprenticeship, the practices which are being internalised are established first as dyadic structures. While this may be appropriate for the learning of weaving or tailoring, it is not the case that social practices are limited to dyadic situations. There is, of course, no clear reason why Vygotsky's model should be limited to dyadic interactions. Both the examples he gives and his formulation of the zone of proximal development focus on dyads, but these instances illustrate his thinking rather than define his terms. In principle, internalisation should apply to the acquisition of any social representations where these are articulated through interpersonal relations. If, for example, we consider representations of gender as a set of social practices, it is of course the case that at times the child is a participant in dyadic interactions with adults who structure the child's activity in terms of these representations. Yet gender is also a more diffuse phenomenon which surrounds the child through a variety of semiotic media: the toys which children play with carry gender markings; the social roles articulated in comics, picture books and in television programmes are also marked for gender; and in the collective institutions, such as the nurseries and schools which children attend, representations of gender structure complex patterns of interaction. In all of these media the categories of gender are articulated as a collective semiotic system which effect a fundamental division in the social world. Becoming a part of this world means both internalising the social representation of gender and establishing an identity with one category or the other.

Further evidence for the significance of social identities as mediating structures comes from our recent study of the development of gender identities through the first year of schooling (Lloyd and Duveen, 1992). An initial ethnography undertaken in the reception classes of two infant schools,[4] enabled us to investigate the way in which gender figures as a structural element in the organisation of the classroom (cf. Duveen and Lloyd, 1993). This structure is not limited to dyadic interactions, but is rather characteristic of the pattern of interactions throughout the classroom, which will include dyads, but also extend to larger scale interactions. Children bring with them into school the gender identities which they have acquired in their pre-school years. As they enter the reception class, however, they encounter representations of gender which are embedded in a set of social practices which are at first unfamiliar, but which are linked to the process of education itself. In short, as they enter school children encounter a set of representations of gender embedded in a novel institutional context, representations which exert a powerful influence on their subsequent educational careers. Sometimes these representations are indeed presented to children through dyadic interactions with their teacher or with a peer, but more frequently they are presented to them through larger scale social interactions. In our study we used our ethnographic account of gender as a dimension of classroom organisation to construct systematic observation schedules and a series of interview based tasks which explored children's knowledge of gender marking in the classroom.

The extent to which their activity was organised around a dimension of gender was clear from a number of indices related to patterns of peer associations. At the beginning of the school year boys were observed more frequently in single sex groups and in groups with more boys than girls, while girls were observed more frequently in groups with more girls than boys and in groups with even numbers of girls and boys. Further, single sex groups of boys were larger than single sex groups of girls. These patterns were observed in settings where children's activity was not immediately directed by the teacher. When the teacher did organise children's activity the differences between girls and boys in the gender composition of groups was less apparent, particularly for single sex groups. By the end of the first year these patterns had changed somewhat. Girls' participation in single sex groups in peer organised contexts had increased (though still not to a level which matched that of boys), while in teacher organised contexts there were fewer observations of girls in single sex groups. As well as influencing patterns of peer association, children's sex group membership also influenced their choice of materials for play, with boys being observed in active and constructive play more frequently, and girls more frequently in creative and role play.

So far I have described differences between girls and boys in the gender composition of groups which form in the classroom in terms only of a contrast between sex groups. In these contrasts the data have been aggregated for boys and for girls. Yet anyone who spends time in a reception class will also notice that there are variations within sex groups: not all boys are alike and neither are all girls. Different types of masculine and feminine identities can be observed developing within sex groups. For example, when we looked at individual patterns of association in single sex groups it was apparent that some children tended to associate particularly with some specific friends, while other children interacted with a much wider circle of peers. This variation was more noticeable among girls than among boys, to the extent that we observed some small groups of girls, who practically interacted only with each other, forming small isolated groupings in which they had little contact with other children in the classroom, girls or boys. These observations suggested to us that it was important to investigate varieties of gender identity which emerged within sex groups,[5] and to do so we constructed an index of gender identity based on the proportion of time individual children were observed in single sex groups.[6]

Using this measure of gender identity we found a series of differences within sex groups in the ways that children made use of elements of the material culture of the classroom. For example, girls with low gender identity (that is girls who were observed less frequently in single sex groups) made as much use of activity play materials as did the boys, while girls with high gender identity (who were observed more frequently in single sex groups) made much less use of these materials. Some differences emerged when we compared children's activity at the beginning and end of their first year at school, as was the case for the use of directed play materials in peer organised contexts (these are materials usually associated with teacher organised activities such as books, reading schemes, writing materials, etc.). In the autumn term all children made much the same use of these materials, but in the summer term high gender identity girls made twice as much use of these materials, while low gender identity girls and all the boys continued to use these materials at the same rate as they had in the autumn term. Finally, some differences were also specific to particular schools. In the autumn term all girls made much the same use of constructive play materials, although not as much as did the boys who used them between two and three times as much. By the summer term, however, not only had differences emerged among girls, but these differences varied also between schools. In both of the classrooms we observed, low gender identity girls continued to use these materials at the same rate. It was among the high gender identity girls that differences emerged. In one classroom their use of these materials declined dramatically in the summer term, while in the other classroom it increased to the level at which boys were using these materials. These data are complicated because in the latter school the teacher set aside time when these materials were only available to girls, so that the greater use of them by girls in single sex groups can be seen as the consequence of the teacher's intervention. But the decline in the use of activity play materials by high gender identity girls observed in the other classroom was not related to any action by the teacher.

Overall these results indicate that variations of gender identity emerge within sex groups through the course of the first year of schooling, particularly among girls, and in relation to the local culture of gender within a school. Further indications of the significance of these emerging gender identities came from the results for some of our interview based measures. For example, in one task children were asked to identify the odd-one-out from a set of three figure drawings. Each figure showed a child playing with a toy, and each triad was composed of one figure of a boy playing with a masculine marked toy, one figure of a girl playing with a feminine marked toy and one figure of a child playing with a toy marked for the opposite gender. Children were asked to pick the odd-one-out for six triads, in three of which the third figure showed a girl playing with a masculine marked toy, and in three it showed a boy playing with a feminine marked toy. Children's judgements for each triad could therefore focus on either the actor in the figure (e.g. picking out a boy in a triad with two girls), or the gender marking of toys (a feminine marked toy in a triad where the other two figures showed children playing with a masculine marked toy), or the figure in which there was a mismatch between the gender of the actor and the gender marking of the toy they were shown as playing with. The mismatch choices are more cognitively complex because they demand a coordination between the two dimensions of actor and toy, and overall it is perhaps not surprising that children did not make a great many such choices. In general, too, there was little change in children's performance from the autumn term to the summer term. However, in one class the high gender identity girls showed a notable increase in the number of mismatch choices from the autumn term to the summer term. These were the same girls whose use of activity play materials (generally a masculine marked activity) declined quite sharply across the school year, suggesting that something in the local gender culture of this classroom is making the gender marking of persons and objects particularly salient.

One might look at the results from these studies in reception classes and suggest that in general they follow a Vygotskian line from social practice to intraindividual accomplishment, even if it means displacing the Vygotskian formula from dyadic interaction to social practice on a broader scale. However, this generality obscures an important point, namely that variations of gender identity within sex groups emerges through the course of the year. If we accept that there is a representation of gender structuring the social practices in a classroom, why should these practices lead to differentiation within sex groups? Why should one group of girls acquire a different set of practices from another? The Vygotskian formula does not explain how interindividual practices can lead to different intraindividual formations. To do so we need to consider the role of developing social (in this case gender) identities in mediating the transition from interindividual to intraindividual practices.

CONCLUSIONS

These reflections on the contributions of Piaget and Vygotsky to a developmental psychology of social representations lead to an interesting comparison between them. From Piaget there is an important lesson to be drawn from his distinction between two modes in the acquisition of social knowledge. There is acquisition through social transmission, characterised by an asymmetry of power so that knowledge is reproduced because of the influence and prestige of its source. But there is also acquisition through reconstruction in symmetrical social relations between peers. As always in Piaget it is conflict which is at the heart of this process, but for conflict to be productive it has to be situated in a context where thought is unconstrained by hegemonic influences, so that thinkers have the freedom to invent and construct. Vygotsky's work really only addresses the first of these modes. It describes the acquisition of social knowledge through social transmission in asymmetrical social relations. Here knowledge truly is power, for it is the possession of expertise and the prestige that it brings which distinguishes the expert from the novice.

This conclusion may seem somewhat paradoxical, since the images of Piaget and Vygotsky which circulate in the contemporary world of psychology have more generally associated Vygotsky as a theorist of cognition as a social process and Piaget as a theorist of individual cognition. But, as I have tried to demonstrate, this paradox is more apparent than real. If my comments on Vygotsky have been sharper than those on Piaget it is because I have sought to emphasise this contrast. And yet neither of these authors really provides a ready made model in which to pursue an analysis of the child as a developing social actor. Piaget's analysis always returns to a focus on the 'epistemic subject', and gives only a limited acknowledgement of the significance of the social representations which structure the collective world within which children develop. If Vygotsky's theory can be said to focus on the child as a 'cultural subject' it does so by reducing culture to a set of signs which function as cognitive tools and excluding the sense in which signs also express the values of particular social groups.

In their different ways, both Piaget and Vygotsky present a view of the developing child centered on an idea of the child as a single, unified subject, 'epistemic' for Piaget, 'cultural' for Vygotsky. In each case the child appears to live in a world which is marked by a homogeneity of meanings, so that in neither case is there a clear recognition that the social world is a world of differences and contrasts. To consider the developing child as an emerging social actor means to construe the child as a social psychological subject. From this point of view the social is neither simply an influence which can accelerate or retard the child's development, nor is it simply a body of knowledge about the social world (in terms of rules, norms, etc.). What children know and believe also serves a symbolic function, since it provides a primary means through which children are able to locate themselves in the social world. It is in this sense that we can consider children's developing representations as expressions of their social identities. In many instances social identities act to promote children's development, since they provide the source for the community of interests which facilitates learning in the zone of proximal development. But there are also instances where children's social identities can be a source of conflict for them. This was the case for the Brazilian children studied by de Abreu, and also in our studies of the development of social representations of gender in primary classrooms. It is in these instances where defending a social identity leads children to resist the influences of others that a sense of psychological development as a social process emerges most clearly.

NOTES

1 For Moscovici the process of social representation is always concerned with the way in which the unfamiliar is made familiar, and he distinguishes analytically between two complementary aspects of this process of construction–anchoring refers to the way in which the unfamiliar is located within the context of existing representations, while through objectification representations are projected into the world as concrete objects (cf. Moscovici, 1981; Duveen and Lloyd, 1990).

2 Equilibration is a complex concept in Piaget's account. While he suggests that it is as much a social as a biological process (e.g. Piaget, 1970; and Furth, 1980, uses the example of developing social knowledge to explicate the idea of equilibration) this generates problems for a social psychological perspective. The equilibration of cognitive structures results in the construction of necessary knowledge, and it is by no means clear that we can characterise all social knowledge in this way. Divisions within society result in different representations, and it is these differences which are the focus of social psychological concerns. However, as I make clear in the following pages, Piaget himself makes an important distinction between two forms of social knowledge.

3 These results have been challenged by Burgard, Cheyne and Jahoda (1989) on the basis of their attempt to replicate this study. However, my purpose here is not to attempt to resolve this dispute, but rather to concentrate on the way in which Emler's use of his evidence reflects his reading of Piaget.

4 In England, where the research I shall describe was undertaken, children enter school at the beginning of the year in which they will be five. Thus the reception class (which is the term used for the first year of school) contains children between four and five years of age.
5 This is a theme which has received very little attention in developmental research, to the extent that some authors have suggested the terms *sex* and *gender* should be used interchangeably. Maccoby and Jacklin (1987), for example, have argued that since research designs usually employ a contrast between girls and boys there are no grounds for distinguishing sex and gender. While they may be right to point to a weakness in the logic of such research designs, their argument loses its force when research designs encompass contrasts within sex groups as well as between sex groups.
6 This is far from ideal as a measure of gender identity, since it uses a single dimension to index a much more complex reality. However, even this rather rough measure served to demonstrate that it is possible to distinguish important variations within sex groups among young children.

REFERENCES

Berti, A. E. and Bombi, A. S. (1988). *The Child's Construction of Economics*. Cambridge: Cambridge University Press.

Buck-Morss, S. (1975). Socio-economic bias in Piaget's theory and its implication for cross-culture studies. *Human Development*, 18, 35–49.

Burgard, P., Cheyne, W. and Jahoda, G. (1989). Children's representations of economic inequality: a replication. *British Journal of Developmental Psychology*, 7, 275–87.

Corsaro, W. (1990) The underlife of the nursery school: young children's social representations of adult rules. In G. Duveen and B. Lloyd (eds) *Social Representations and the Development of Knowledge*. Cambridge: Cambridge University Press.

de Abreu, G. (1993). *The Relationship Between Home and School Mathematics in a Farming Community in Rural Brazil*. PhD thesis, University of Cambridge.

de Abreu, G. (1995). Understanding how children experience the relationship between home and school mathematics. *Mind, Culture and Activity*, 2, 119–42.

Doise, W. (1993). Debating social representations. In G. Breakwell and D. Canter (eds) *Empirical Approaches to Social Representations*. Oxford: Oxford University Press.

Doise, W. and Mugny, G. (1984). *The Social Development of the Intellect*. Oxford: Pergamon.

Duveen, G. (1994). Crianças enquanto atores sociais. In S. Jovchelovitch and P. Guareschi (eds) *Textos em representações sociais*. Petropolis, Brazil: Vozes.

Duveen, G. and Lloyd, B. (1986). The significance of social identities. *British Journal of Social Psychology*, 25, 219–30.

Duveen, G. and Lloyd, B. (1988). Gender as an influence in the development of scripted pretend play. *British Journal of Developmental Psychology*, 6, 89–95.

Duveen, G. and Lloyd, B. (1990). Introduction. In G. Duveen and B. Lloyd (eds) *Social Representations and the Development of Knowledge*. Cambridge: Cambridge University Press.

Duveen, G. and Lloyd, B. (1993). An ethnographic approach to social representations. In G. Breakwell and D. Canter (eds) *Empirical Approaches to Social Representations*. Oxford: Oxford University Press.

Emler, N. (1986). The relative significance of social identities: a comment on Duveen and Lloyd. *British Journal of Social Psychology*, 25, 231–2.

Emler, N. and Dickinson, J. (1985). Children's representations of economic inequalities: the effects of social class. *British Journal of Developmental Psychology*, 3, 191–8.

Emler, N., Ohana, J. and Dickinson, J. (1990). Children's representations of social relations. In G. Duveen and B. Lloyd (eds) *Social Representations and the Development of Knowledge*. Cambridge: Cambridge University Press.

Furth, H. G. (1980). *The World of Grown Ups*. New York: Elsevier.

Furth, H. G. (1992). The developmental origin of human societies. In H. Beilin and P. Pufall (eds) *Piaget's Theory: Prospects and Possibilities*. Hillsdale, NJ: Lawrence Erlbaum Associates.

Goodnow, J. (1990). The socialization of cognition: what's involved? In J. Stigler, R. Shweder and G. Herdt (eds) *Cultural Psychology*. Cambridge: Cambridge University Press.

Greenfield, P. (1984). A theory of the teacher in the learning activities of everyday life. In B. Rogoff and J. Lave (eds) *Everyday Cognition*. Cambridge, MA: Harvard University Press.

Jodelet, D. (1991). *Madness and Social Representations*. London: Harvester Wheatsheaf.

Jovchelovitch, S. (1995). Social representations in and of the public sphere: towards a theoretical articulation. *Journal for the Theory of Social Behaviour*, 25, 81–102.

Lave, J. (1990). The culture of acquisition and the practice of understanding. In J. W. Stigler, R. A. Shweder and G. Herdt (eds) *Cultural Psychology*. Cambridge: Cambridge University Press.

Litowitz, B. (1993). Deconstruction in the zone of proximal development. In E. Forman, N. Minnick and C. Stone (eds) *Contexts for Learning*. Oxford: Oxford University Press.

Lloyd, B. and Duveen, G. (1989). The reconstruction of social knowledge in the transition from sensorimotor to conceptual activity: the gender system. In A. Gellatly, D. Rogers and J. Sloboda (eds) *Cognition and Social Worlds*. Oxford: Oxford University Press.

Lloyd, B. and Duveen, G. (1990). A semiotic analysis of the development of social representations of gender. In G. Duveen and B. Lloyd (eds) *Social Representations and the Development of Knowledge*. Cambridge: Cambridge University Press.

Lloyd, B. and Duveen, G. (1992). *Gender Identities and Education: The Impact of Starting School*. London: Harvester Wheatsheaf.

Maccoby, E. and Jacklin, C. N. (1987). Gender segregation in childhood. In H. Reese (ed.) *Advances in Child Development and Behaviour*, vol. 20, London: Academic Press, 239–87.

Moscovici, S. (1972). Society and theory in social psychology. In J. Israel and H. Tajfel (eds) *The Context of Social Psychology*. London: Academic Press.

Moscovici, S. (1973). Foreword to C. Herzlich, *Health and Illness*. London: Academic Press.

Moscovici, S. (1976a). *Social Influence and Social Control*. London: Academic Press.

Moscovici, S. (1976b). *La psychanalyse, son image et son public*. Paris: Presses Universitaires de France.

Moscovici, S. (1981). On social representation. In J. Forgas (ed.) *Social Cognition*. London: Academic Press.

Moscovici, S. (1990). Social psychology and developmental psychology: extending the conversation. In G. Duveen and B. Lloyd (eds) *Social Representations and the Development of Knowledge*. Cambridge: Cambridge University Press.

Mugny, G. and Carugati, F. (1989). *Social Representations of Intelligence*. Cambridge: Cambridge University Press.

Newman, D., Griffin, P. and Cole, M. (1989). *The Construction Zone*. Cambridge: Cambridge University Press.

Piaget, J. (1932). *The Moral Judgement of the Child*. London: Routledge and Kegan Paul.

Piaget, J. (1951). *Play, Dreams and Imitation in Childhood*. London: Routledge and Kegan Paul.

Piaget, J. (1966). Part Two of E. W. Beth and J. Piaget, *Mathematical Epistemology and Psychology*. Dordrecht: D. Reidel.

Piaget, J. (1970). Piaget's theory. In P. Mussen (ed.) *Manual of Child Psychology*, vol. 1. New York: J. Wiley and Sons.

Piaget, J. (1995). *Sociological Studies*. London: Routledge.

Rogoff, B. (1990). *Apprenticeship in Thinking*. Oxford: Oxford University Press.

Rogoff, B. and Lave, J. (eds) (1984). *Everyday Cognition*. Cambridge, MA: Harvard University Press.

Shweder, R. (1990). Cultural psychology: what is it? In J. W. Stigler, R. A. Shweder and G. Herdt (eds) *Cultural Psychology*. Cambridge: Cambridge University Press.

Vygotsky, L. S. (1978). Mind in society. Cambridge, MA: Harvard University Press.

Vygotsky, L. S. (1981). The genesis of higher mental functions. In J. Wertsch (ed.) *The Concept of Activity in Soviet Psychology*. Armonk, N.Y.: M. E. Sharpe.

Wertsch, J. (1991). *Voices of the Mind*. London: Harvester Wheatsheaf.

Wood, D., Bruner, J. and Ross, G. (1976). The role of tutoring in problem solving. *Journal of Child Psychology and Psychiatry*, 17, 89–100.

5 Revisiting young Jean Piaget in Neuchâtel among his partners in learning[1]

Anne-Nelly Perret-Clermont

Science cannot impose its premises to value judgments. The premises of value judgments arise from a direct awareness and cannot be demonstrated. If I start from the following assumption: 'I want to live and what helps me living is good for me,' this value judgment is immediate and cannot be countered by any man or science.

(Piaget, 1923, p. 65)

Science states, whereas faith values, and in the end, this evaluation always depends on a personal decision.

(ibid., p. 80)

with Renouvier ... are we going to keep hoping for an alliance between the religious search and the cult of classical logic, both rational and experimental?

(Piaget, 1921a, p. 410)

Piaget, right from the beginning of his long career, makes a clear distinction between what pertains to reasoning and logic and what results from another order of phenomena, which he names (together with his interlocutors[2]) 'value judgments'. These are considered to be the immediate and direct results of an *ethical* attitude towards life and reality. In this acceptation, 'value judgments' do not concern so much aesthetics (these had no central part in Piaget's interests) but primarily basic philosophical, moral, social, political and religious stands. They reflect the dignity of life and of the person and, as such, are important guide marks for the meaning of individual and collective action.

What *were* the premises of young Piaget's value judgments? This contribution will try to examine the implications of this question and to show that by taking into account some aspects of the socio-cultural and historical context, it is possible to illuminate the meaning Piaget gave to his system by theorising the first stands he took. Hopefully this approach will spotlight dimensions of his psychology that often remain implicit in contemporary debates, and thus create a critical distance encouraging the same boldness that was shown by this elder researcher in facing the great issues of his time.

In the first part of this paper, the approach will be explained: an account of the socio-historical context during Piaget's years in Neuchâtel through conceptual tools mainly borrowed from the contemporary psychological study of socio-cognitive processes. After this epistemic introduction, there will be an attempt to identify *who* were young Piaget's partners in learning. The second part will deal with the *stands taken* by him as an adolescent and later as a young researcher, in his quest for meaning, as well as their *significations in their context*. His premisses are not necessarily shared by the coming generations. But the reader might be incited to re-open the debate and to add to it the acquisitions made by contemporary psychology in other cultural areas.

FOREWORD: THE NATURE OF THE PRESENT APPROACH

What were, then, the premisses of young Piaget's value judgements? This question could be asked and examined according to the programme designed by Piaget himself, in his attempt to found a psychology of moral values. In order to submit him to his own method, one should therefore start from his premisses as if they were given data, and then proceed to 'check them against the experience from which [these value judgements] arose, [by first verifying] that the individual has indeed remained consistent' (Piaget 1923, pp. 55 and 64).

But this is not the purpose of the present contribution: firstly, Piaget prized so much thought consistency, elevating it indeed to the status of a *value* – and a capital one! – that he can most probably be trusted in that respect. According to young Piaget's conception of cognitive psychology, the greater part of the thinking subject's processes aim at explaining the conservation of his/her premisses and the consistency of his/her thought. In other words, there is little ground to believe that Piaget might have changed his mind about the premisses of his own value judgments. Therefore the aim here is not to submit him to a genetic approach in order to see whether his premisses have evolved during his life time. The working hypothesis (not demonstrated here, because this would need separate research) will be that Piaget was 'conserving' in this field.

So, what is the purpose in looking for the origin of Piaget's premisses? It is precisely to emphasise that from the beginning, before caring for consistency, young Piaget did actually take stands (which shall later become *premisses*) on a certain number of issues, affectively and socially involved in a milieu that encouraged debate, but that he was also marked by practices and tensions, and structured by institutions (family, school and university, churches, political parties, youth clubs, scientific societies, etc.) providing a framework for ideological discourses and for modalities of interpersonal relations, and by psychological and concrete conditions that made some projects feasible and stood in the way of others.

Thus, the focus of interest here is not so much the study of social influence *per se* on Piaget (a theme dealt with by others, in particular by Ducret, 1984, and Vidal, 1994), nor this young man's theorisation of his relations to his milieu (which remained very rudimentary, as will be evident below), as the observation (unfortunately *post hoc*!) of the social inter-actions in which he was actively involved. In this light, Jean appears to be concerned about the meaning of life, in a social setting that is also aware of the meaning of youth education for society (Reymond, 1931).[3]

This paper does not take an individualistic psychological approach, trying to explore the sole interior dynamics of the subject through a nice case study, nor a socially deterministic approach, according to which Piaget would be the 'product' of social factors influencing a predisposition for scientific creativity. It tries to contextualise the development of young Piaget's cognitive activity.

Thus, Piaget's youth will be considered from a contemporary vantage point, marked by the re-reading of Vygotsky and influenced by the con-textual approach of speech acts and thought (Bruner, 1990; Rogoff, 1990) and by the observation of social interactions (Perret-Clermont, 1980; Perret-Clermont and Nicolet, 1988; Pontecorvo, 1993). At a time when psychologists speak of 'situated cognition' (Resnick, Levine and Teasley, 1991) and insist upon the importance of 'communities of practices' (Lave and Wenger 1991), the endeavour will be to observe Piaget's thought at its origin, in its historical context and in a 'multi-voiced' world.

And of course, during the Neuchâtel years (1896–1929) considered here, Jean Piaget, as a child, pupil, adolescent, student, young researcher and young professor, will not appear as solitary or abandoned to himself among inanimate objects in his epistemic quest! On the contrary, as he says himself in his autobiographical writings, he was in continuous interaction with his peers (Juvet, for instance) and his elders (Godet, Reymond, Bovet, his own father of course, and still others). These persons 'scaffold' him in trials to take an active role in 'real' scientific activities of that period and within very lively debates. He was given this opportunity at an early age that might provoke the envy of young people who, at the end of the twentieth century, are confined for many years in the role of 'peripheral participants'.

It is important to rediscover the circumstances, the people and institutions that formed the social and cultural landscape in which Piaget constructed his model. This should contribute to an understanding of the value priorities underlying Piaget's theory and the meaning given by him to his scientific commitment, and by way of consequence, to define its reach. Piaget's intellectual activity is no abstract, timeless reality, but it is historically situated. By putting Piaget's theory of psychological devel-opment in perspective, this awareness should allow us to examine critically its present relevance.

Obviously, in some manner, this purpose is too ambitious for current means. Many pieces of information, needed to really grasp the context in which Piaget grew up, are still lacking. Nevertheless, the hope underlying this paper is that its boldness (after all, Piaget himself taught us to tackle

big topics boldly!) might incite other researchers to follow interesting paths
leading to a reflection on the psychological activity, not only of the child,
but also of those who would describe it (Gilliéron, 1985). The reader
will have understood that the intent here is not to produce a biographical
study of Piaget, or a historical reconstruction of his interests. It is rather to
attempt to re-discover some of his programmatic declarations and theses,
considering them *as a practical, contextualised activity of someone trying
to assert himself among the questions and requirements of his social and
cultural setting.* In this perspective, Jean Piaget's reflections can be seen in
part as *answers*[4] to his milieu, i.e. to his masters and to the people he met,
including the child who called him a 'rigolo' (a joker, a comic – cf. Piaget,
1972).

Many years later, when he re-examined his life-course, Piaget (1965,
p. 22) declared:

> I was strongly struck, after the First World War . . . by the repercussions
> that the social and political instability, which dominated Europe at that
> time, had on the movement of ideas, and this led me naturally to doubt
> the objective and universal validity of philosophical declarations made
> in those circumstances. In my small country, so quiet and relatively
> sheltered from outside events, many symptoms showed this dependence
> of ideas on social unrest.

Obviously, one of Piaget's aims was to stress the importance of what he
often called the autonomy of thought, i.e. its *freedom*. The purpose is not to
deny here the liberties taken by Piaget, but to show on the contrary that
they represent significant answers amidst the expectancies and constrictions
of the milieu he came from.

YOUNG PIAGET'S PARTNERS IN LEARNING

> On the day in which Piaget was born, the town and canton of Neuchâtel
> were getting ready to commemorate feverishly the 50th anniversary of
> the proclamation of the republican regime, a recent consequence, like
> so many other such regimes in Europe, of the great revolutionary 1848
> upheavals . . . Thus, it was in this naturally peaceful environment, still
> agitated however by the aftermath of a rich and recently perturbed
> history, in this little city forced by events to exchange overnight its
> status as a capital of a principality for the less glorious one of the mere
> main town of a confederate canton, in this place enriched by an intense
> past and passionately interested in scientific research, in this canton
> where the quest for technical progress always rivalled with the ability in
> traditional crafts, in short, in this city of Neuchâtel, both humane and
> humanitarian, that Jean Piaget was born.

(Jelmini, 1996, pp. 27, 37)

Who were Jean Piaget's partners in learning? This section will present first those of his restricted family circle, then the ones he met at his primary and secondary schools, at the University, but also in his extra-curricular activities and in the Church.

Jean Piaget was born in 1896 in Neuchâtel, the main town of a very small territory on the border between the Swiss Confederation and France. This region had become the twenty-first Swiss canton in 1815 although it remained a property of the Prussian king, then a democratic republic and fully fledged canton in 1848. But the Neuchâtelois had to wait until the Paris Treaty in 1857 to be free from all feudal bonds and foreign allegiances. This event sharpened the internal division that had appeared in 1848, and incited many local families to expatriate, as did Piaget's grand-parents, who settled in Yverdon (Jelmini, 1996).

The town of Yverdon is in canton Vaud, roughly 40 km away from Neuchâtel. There, Frédéric Piaget 'directed a watch-making factory exporting its products as far as America, under the trademark "Piaget et Allison"' (de Tribolet, 1996, p. 39). Their son Arthur, born in 1865, grew up in Yverdon until he went to Lausanne and then to Paris for his studies. He came back in order to submit his PhD thesis at the Faculté des Lettres (Faculty of Arts) of the University of Geneva. Already in 1895, he began to teach at the Académie of Neuchâtel (of which he became *recteur*, i.e. vice-chancellor, when it became a university).

Thus Piaget was born in an area forming a small political entity which was very aware of its past, or at least of its myths, and combined the virtues of the watch-making craft, of foreign trade and of local cultural and economic development (Liengme, 1994). At least in that respect, Piaget seems to have truly assimilated the spirit of his birthplace. Many years later, in his acceptance address for the Erasmus Prize, he declared (1972, p. 27):

> I am happy to see that the distinction offered me is placed under the sign of Europe and comes from a country of modest size, like mine, because I strongly believe in the essential part played by small European countries in contemporary culture. There, as far as I can see, researchers in all fields enjoy a freedom of spirit and an informality more difficult to achieve in bigger countries where national traditions, and above all, fashions and 'schools', sometimes weigh rather more heavily'.[5]

Who were Jean Piaget's partners in learning in this local context? His family, of course, but also his school-fellows, his teachers and the members of many associations and societies, which were extremely lively in Neuchâtel at that time, and where Piaget played an active part. He certainly remembered this when he theorised the function of peers in the structuring and sociability of thought. But in spite of the Piagetian model's insistence on the function of peers, the figures of some important elders who have marked the path of his entrance in the scientific, philosophical and political debates of his time are worth exploring.

Family

Jean Piaget does not say much about his parents. Yet the important part played by his father, Arthur Piaget, in the Neuchâtel intelligentsia has been evidenced (de Tribolet, 1996). He was a professor of literature and, as a historian, he refused all compromises in his quest for objective facts. He took many initiatives, for instance by reorganising the cantonal archives and editing the local historical journal. He had come to the limelight by brilliantly demonstrating the spuriousness of the *Chronique des chanoines* (Chronicle of the Canons), a document to which the local historians of that period attributed a great importance in the construction of a Neuchâtelois identity strengthening Swiss patriotic feelings in the citizens of the canton. 'The polemic provoked by the exposure of the Chronicle, which gave a direct blow to the intellectual conformism of some Neuchâtelois' profoundly hurt Arthur Piaget, 'who considered the idea of leaving the city for other places that might prove more hospitable and more congenial to his independent mind' (ibid., p. 44). This exile project was abandoned by Arthur Piaget, but his son Jean, living near him for at least twenty years, was able to witness the *psychological pressure exercised by social institutions* when a free mind demonstrates something that goes against the grain of received ideas.

Thus Jean Piaget's father was active, committed, rigorous in his thinking, and he took on important public responsibilities. He was a figure of authority. His son praised his qualities in later years (cf. Ducret, 1984; Vidal, 1994) and tried to emulate him (Piaget, 1976, p. 2). But there are *no traces of co-operation* between father and son, in the sense of joint activities aimed at the realisation of a concrete project. It can be surmised that their exchanges were mainly intellectual, which is indeed the meaning that Piaget was to give later to the word 'co-operation' in his theory.

Jean Piaget's mother, too, was a striking personality. She unfortunately left him painful memories, because of her nervous fragility (Piaget, 1976, p. 2):

> My mother was very intelligent, energetic and, at bottom, really good-hearted; but her somewhat neurotic temperament made our family life rather difficult. As a direct consequence of this situation, I gave up childish games at an early age in favour of serious work, partly because I wanted to imitate my father, but also because this work provided me with a kind of sanctuary.

She was an ardent believer and belonged to the Independent Church, one of the fractions created by the schism that split Protestantism in Neuchâtel towards the end of the nineteenth century, gathering those who were 'convinced that from then on, their Church could not remain true to its Master and to its mission, and who wished to remain independent from the state' (Thomann, 1996, p. 112).

Jean Piaget had two younger sisters, Madeleine and Marthe, and a step-sister, Henriette. He rarely mentions this feminine familial setting whose members do not belong, apparently, to the peers who significantly influenced the intellectual life of this budding scientist, who identified with his father.

Piaget mentions several times his godfather, Samuel Cornut, a well-known man of letters in French-speaking Switzerland, but he only seems to have appeared, at a crucial moment of Piaget's adolescence, in the context of philosophical queries.

Studies

Among his school-fellows, Piaget remembered his friend Gustave Juvet, who was already at the same school when they were ten (Schaller-Jeanneret, 1966) and remained his companion through secondary and university studies. They also shared many extra-curricular activities. Their relation continued in particular within the Société philosophique (Reymond, 1931). As Schaller-Jeanneret demonstrates, many former school-fellows of Piaget's had impressive scientific careers, inside or outside university. But there are few traces of significant social interaction *at school* between these pupils. Apparently, this socialisation happened outside school.

His relation with the professors is a different matter: Piaget often mentions the influence of some teachers who knew how to encourage him, such as Arnold Reymond 'who followed my juvenile attempts with admirable patience and sympathy' (Piaget, 1965, p. 14).

Extra-curricular activities

Outside school, some elders strongly influenced the intellectual activity of Piaget during his pre-adolescence: 'I started with biology, because I had the good fortune, when I was very young, to be initiated by an old naturalist to a rather special branch of zoology, malacology, or in plain words, the science of snails and similar animals' (Piaget, 1972, p. 27). The old naturalist was Paul Godet, curator of the Museum of Natural History, who gave Jean (between the age of eleven and fifteen) the opportunity to participate fully and regularly in zoological research. Thanks to this training, he soon started publishing in this field. In this instance, Jean Piaget participated in 'joint actions' situated in a well-defined scientific field. The affective relationship with this 'old' specialist was such that it soon enabled this young neophyte to abandon the status of an apprentice (of 'legitimate peripheral participant', to quote Lave's coinage) and to become a full fledged researcher.

Another elder contributed to create socio-cognitive conditions that were particularly stimulating for Jean as an adolescent: I am thinking of Pierre

Bovet, who was professor of philosophy, psychology and pedagogy at the University of Neuchâtel, but at a time when Piaget was too young to attend his lectures. Therefore it was not as a professor that Pierre Bovet influenced our future thinker, but more directly still – if I may say so – through the concrete conditions of a co-operation (in the full meaning of the word) between peers and of intellectual confrontation made available to Jean Piaget and to his friend Gustave Juvet (among dozens of other boys) at the Club 'Amici Naturae' (Friends of Nature), founded by Bovet and, among others, his friend Carl-Albert Loosli in 1893, when they were themselves adolescents. In the years when Piaget was a very active member of the club, Bovet still regularly encouraged its projects through his presence and advice. Other elders involved in the intellectual and, above all, in the scientific life of the country, also attended some of the meetings and gave acknowledgement and encouragement to these adolescents by supporting their activities and answering their questions with their extraordinary competences. What is striking is that these activities were largely based on *autonomous initiatives taken by the young people themselves* (in this, the club was close to the scouts and to other youth movements created at the turn of the century). Surely, the adults played an important part, but their commitment was rarely direct. They approved, encouraged, offered contributions (mainly intellectual, at times material), but they never directly organised the young members' activity, limiting themselves to monitor its 'setting', as it were (Guinand and Lüscher, 1993).

Church

During Piaget's adolescence, he also met his peers in other venues, for instance at the official church 'where he attended classes of religious instruction and was confirmed in 1912' (Thomann, 1996, p. 112). Piaget reflected on the content of these classes, but they probably reminded him more of the teacher-directed atmosphere of school than of his beloved Club of the Friends of Nature. The vehemence of his essay 'La mission de l'idée' (1916; see Vidal 1994 for a partial translation) suggests that, on that occasion, he was confronted with figures of authority who tried to impose beliefs and dogmas, rather than with real interlocutors in his quasi mystical search for the sense of life.

In this field, one may wonder why neither Piaget nor Zundel, who were both to achieve international fame – the former as an epistemologist, the latter as a theologian – ever mention each other when discussing topics connected with *faith*, although they attended the same school and belonged to the club of the Friends of Nature as young adolescents. Yet Piaget wrote many pages on the relationship between science, philosophy and faith; and Maurice Zundel focused several of his writings on issues he was probably already reflecting on as a young Friend of Nature: 'What drives a scientist towards research? Is the possibility of mastering the world offered by applied research? Is it the liberation from imposed reality? Is it the thought of an always imperfect truth? Is it the aspiration towards Truth? How should we interpret this perpetual struggle of Jacob fought by the scientist against reality? Is it a delusion, a possession, a contemplation?' (quoted in Donzé, 1980, p. 62). Of course, they were still young. It may also have been a difficult time for religious debates. Jean Piaget was a Protestant, whereas Maurice Zundel was a Catholic.

Years later, Zundel (1976a, p. 3) wrote:[6]

> As a child, I lived in a Protestant country, I heard the polemics and the demonstrations of the *anti* who kept disparaging the Catholics. My grandmother, who was a Protestant, never missed an opportunity to attack the Catholic world. On the other hand, local Catholicism was very ritualistic and it offered a facile world where there was no need for personal involvement: to find fulfilment, you just had to know the liturgical formulas by rote. A lot of opposition, a lot of words, very little Gospel: all this did not amount to a religion. We listened to the readings from the Gospel, delivered in the usual monotone, and the meaning escaped me completely. All this could be summarised as a religious practice without the slightest experiencing of God: the ritual formulas were right and true, hence acceptable, but dull. Salvation was reduced to well-chosen set phrases . . . a family religion imposed without meeting the slightest resistance.[7]

Later on, as a priest, Maurice Zundel encouraged the Catholic youth movement Jeunesse Ouvrière Chrétienne, he became deeply involved in the quest for a live and cultivated faith, and his preachings were important references and support for a large number of people. But he also often met incomprehension and exclusion on behalf of the clerical institution until 1972, when Paul VI invited him to preach during a retreat at the Vatican (published after his death – Zundel, 1976b), drawing him very late away from this formal marginalisation and giving official recognition to his international fame.

Jean Piaget wrote later (1965, p. 12):

> Brought up as a Protestant by a faithful mother, and as the son of an agnostic father, I already felt the conflict between science and religion rather strongly . . . Reading Bergson was a revelation . . . in a moment of enthusiasm close to ecstasy, I was overwhelmed by the certitude that God was life, in the shape of this *élan vital* or vital force of which my interests in biology allowed me to study a small section. I thus found inner unity by following a kind of immanentism which fulfilled me for many years, though in more and more rational forms . . . I had taken a decision: I would dedicate my life to philosophy, and my main purpose would be to reconcile science and religious values.

Piaget is almost militant in this quest for an immanent faith against the idea of a transcendence beyond the human mind. Piaget's discourses on that topic reflect his polemical attitude against churches, and in particular against Catholicism. He stated clearly his stance towards Church tradition and authority, which he apparently perceived as the social constriction *par excellence*: 'No other social institution demonstrates better the fundamental kinship between the idea of transcendence and the reality of authority, than the Catholic Church' (Piaget 1930a, p. 35; quoted by Barbey, 1982, p. 309).[8]

For Maurice Zundel, God was not an 'idea', and the encounter with Him was an encounter with alterity and not a constriction. In these years of his attending the Friends of Nature, Maurice Zundel was having mystical experiences that were decisive for him (Donzé, 1980, p. 21). But could these young people discuss such themes in a secure socio-affective setting, considering the polemical atmosphere of the time and the formal aspect of their religious instruction? It might have been possible at the Friends of Nature's. But it is not certain that, even in that venue, their exchanges went beyond merry adolescent bantering. The Cahiers des Présences (attendance register) of this club[9] contain some allusions to these ironic jokes: for instance, the nickname Thiécelin, borrowed from the *Roman de Renart*, was given to Maurice Zundel at the suggestion of Jean Piaget: 'Thiécelin, because the raven has an ecclesiastic appearance that fits Zundel perfectly' (15 September 1911). It is worth noticing that Piaget's own nickname was Tardieu (a slug in the same *Roman de Renart*), and that it was sometimes spelt 'Tar-dieu' (slow God or late God). Apparently, Piaget and Zundel were good comrades, perhaps even friendly accomplices, as apparent from in the notes they jotted down in these Cahiers. Tardieu was chairman and Thiécelin secretary.

A few years later, Piaget, as a young man, became committed to the liberal fringe of Protestantism, who believed in the social vocation of Christianity. He met in particular an enthusiastic clergyman, Paul Pettavel (1861–1934), described by Thomann as 'sparkling with activity, loquacious, impish, and above all, a happy Christian . . . [advocating] the improvement of the workers' social status through a forceful political action conducted without infringing democratic rules' (Thomann, 1996, p. 116). Paul Pettavel had aroused the interest of several young Neuchâtelois. In 1915, Piaget wrote to him, submitting an article he wished to publish in *L'Essor*, a small Protestant review published in Geneva but covering the entire French-speaking part of Switzerland, edited by Pettavel. The latter accepted the article, because he wished to dedicate a space in his paper to the opinions of young people. Soon after that, Piaget joined the editorial board (Thomann, 1996, p. 118). In 1914, he became a member of the Association chrétienne suisse d'étudiants (Swiss Christian association of students), a venue for strong debates to which Piaget contributed personally, in particular during the well-known Sainte-Croix conferences (Piaget 1923). After that, Jean Piaget grew gradually more distant, not only from theology, but also probably from faith. In this field as well, it was an older person, Paul Pettavel, an 'expert' (as he would be described in contemporary psychological parlance) who encouraged his younger friend to speak out, by initiating him to the social life of his circle and by integrating him in it.

Jean Piaget's relation with his socio-cultural matrix

So far, a few elements connected with Jean's social life have been mentioned, and attempts have been made to emphasise some character-istics of his socio-cognitive interactions in the French-speaking and Protestant area of Europe where he lived at the beginning of the century (Barrelet and Perret-Clermont, 1996). In this personal, intellectual and social context, Jean learned how to take a stand, how to give expression to his ideas and defend them (he also learned how to find a venue, bargain for its rent, stimulate his comrades and recruit collaborators ... these competences proved very useful later on!). This is the starting point of what he very soon called 'his system', which will now be examined from four viewpoints: affective relations; relations with authority and opportunities offered by his elders; respective roles of peers and experts; border-crossing.

The expressions of affective feelings are very scarce and understated in Piaget's writings. He mentions clearly his great friendship for his childhood comrade Gustave Juvet; one can feel a certain complicity between him and his master Godet; he expresses his gratitude for the help he received from his professor Arnold Reymond, as well as his profound admiration and respect for his father. He apparently hid away from his mother. His memories of her are often painful and may have fostered both his interest in psychopathology (Piaget, 1976, p. 2) and his desire to stop his didactic analysis when, through the transference, it revealed elements connecting him with this eccentric mother (Appignanesi and Forrester, 1992, quoted by Soyland, 1993).[10] 'I never felt any inclination to proceed further in that particular direction, because I have always preferred to study normal cases and the workings of the intellect, rather than the tricks played by the unconscious,' as he says in his autobiography (Piaget, 1976, p. 2). Thomann (1996) mentions that in 1927, Piaget asked Paul Pettavel to convince his mother that she should be admitted to a psychiatric hospital.

Beyond this troublesome maternal presence, few female figures are mentioned. Virtually nothing is known of Cécile-Marie Berthoud (1848–1931), his teacher at the private school he attended when he was eight years old (Schaller-Jeanneret, 1996). After her, only male teachers are recollected by Piaget. It is true that at that time, boy and girls did not attend the same secondary schools. The Friends of Nature did not have female members until 1987. Nevertheless, there were women students at the university when Piaget attended it but it is very striking to see that most of them were foreigners: from 1911 to 1918 the university registers record at least 110 women students coming from the vast Russian empire.[11] Thus Piaget seems to have lived in an essentially male environment, except for the rather marginal presence of these women.

Pierre Bovet, in his book about the development of religious feeling in the child (1925), gave a good description of these feelings of love and fear, based on the experience of respect for the elders, feelings which, according to him, dominate the growth of the psyche and of faith in the child. Jean Piaget, eighteen years younger than Bovet, reflected in other terms (and in other years) on the problem of the relation to authority. Was it because of the way he related to his father and to the hierarchical society of his home town? Or (perhaps 'and') was it a reaction to the troubled atmosphere of his first years, when the echo of pre-revolutionary activities in Russia was heard in the Neuchâtelois town of La Chaux-de-Fonds, together with the forebodings of the First World War? Clearly, Piaget resented the limitations imposed by his milieu and doubted that what he was to call later 'social constrictions' were of any value to him. He often judged negatively the inheritance of his forefathers on various levels: in religion (see his passionate attacks in 'La mission de l'idée', 1916), philosophy (he feared the notion of a transcendence situated outside understanding – *op. cit.* and 1929), and even in science, as can be seen in the foreword to his doctoral thesis in malacology, where he mainly expressed his dissatisfaction with existing research methods (Piaget 1921b, pp. 1–3). In his psychological works, Piaget came back several times to the idea that transmission from one generation to another cannot be the source of understanding, because this transmission is organised by an authority principle that precludes the autonomy of thought (see for instance Piaget, 1960).

Yet the elders who had the status of experts in the milieu of the adolescent Piaget were not all – by far – pompous professors or dogmatic thinkers! On the contrary, they often seemed keen to let younger people have their say. So did Arthur Piaget in the journal he edited, *Le Musée Neuchâtelois* (de Tribolet, 1996), Paul Pettavel in his own publication, Arnold Reymond in the dialogue with his students, and Pierre Bovet, mainly through the Friends of Nature, but also in the activities organised by his family in Grandchamp,[12] as well as Paul Godel in his laboratory at the Museum of Natural History.

In fact, Jean Piaget frequented two kind of circles: venues where peer-relations were privileged (first and foremost the Amici Naturae), and others where he had to learn how to find his place among experts: the Club Jurassien, and later, from 1912 to 1914, the Société Neuchâteloise de Sciences Naturelles, the Société Zoologique Suisse and the Société Helvétique des Sciences Naturelles (Vidal, 1996), in addition to those already mentioned before.

Surely Piaget drew profit from interactions with his peers: but were they really 'peers'? Piaget seems soon to have accepted – with the approval of his friends, who found him amusing and interesting – the status of official deviant. This is the image given of him in some of the minutes for the meetings of the Friends of Nature, of whom he had soon become chairman.

Piaget rarely describes experiences of debates between equals and apparently never mentioned at that time the results of exchanges with people who were less expert than him. Did his status as an erudite, already during his adolescence, deprive him of such exchanges? This would be worth checking. Actually, his first experience of a cognitive advantage drawn from an asymmetric relation happened apparently during his exchanges with children in Th. Simon's research laboratory in Paris (Piaget, 1972). One may wonder whether the pleasure Piaget drew from these interviews was not due in part to a projection allowing him to reconstruct a situation he had often experienced successfully: that of the brilliant child who knows how to take part in the grown-up's discourse.

During his childhood and youth in Neuchâtel, Piaget evolved in a social space left relatively open by his parents: in between two churches, with parents who held different religious convictions; living in Neuchâtel but in touch with La Chaux-de-Fonds, the other important town of the canton, which tended towards socialism; joining students' societies where theological, philosophical and scientific issues were debated; a student at the Science Faculty but often attending lectures at the Faculty of Arts (Liengme Bessire and Béguelin, 1996) in a university that was small, but international in its recruitment, before he left Neuchâtel to pursue his studies in Zurich (in another language) and then in Paris, from where he was to return to Geneva, where Claparède and Bovet had invited him.

THE SEARCH FOR A CONSTRUCTION OF MEANING: THE STANDS TAKEN BY JEAN PIAGET AND THEIR CONTEXTUAL RELEVANCE

This paper has dealt so far with the attempt to describe the socio-cultural world in which Jean Piaget grew up. This new section will focus on the stands he took and his early participation in his elders' debates. In his quest for meaning, this young man, strongly influenced by his philosophical readings, attempted to elaborate a system based on a certain number of premises in which he strongly believed, as if they were the foundation, not merely of his thought, but of his very identity. The relation between reason, society, transcendence (or rather, immanence) and action played a crucial part in his reflections. Starting from his interest in natural science, Jean Piaget discovered philosophy and theology and tackled the big issues of his time (God, war, justice, freedom, truth, social order, evolutionary theories, etc.), trying to find an answer in a personal vision of Man.

Piaget's leading ideal: reason and personal thought

Even in the texts Piaget wrote as an adolescent, it appears clearly that he did not conceive the individual as a born disciple. As a young natural scientist specialising in snails, when Piaget became interested in philosophy and discovered this other living species, *homo sapiens*, he was evidently enthralled by the problem of the access to *knowledge*. So much so that he considered it as the main characteristic of Man, his 'essence', as it were (even though he does not actually use this word). At that time, there were lively discussions at the university, but also in the churches, about the evolutionary theories propounded by Darwin, Lamarck and others. His standpoint as a biologist and his focusing on thought as the source of knowledge led him to take a very idiosyncratic approach in the philosophical and theological issues debated then.

His inaugural lecture in 1925, when he became professor of philosophy, history of science and psychology at the University of Neuchâtel, makes his standpoint explicit. In it, he first considers a return to Kant and his notion of *a priori*; then the idea, which according to him is its opposite, 'of a radically contingent spiritual development, such as the one Léon Brunschvicg believes he can perceive in the history of human thought'. Yet Piaget does not seem very convinced by this alternative and he opts for a third possibility: his own method (which he sees as impartial) of genetic analysis in psychology, because he believes he can intuit that 'it is possible, moreover, that such a method imposes the notion of a kind of *ideal that directs reason*,[13] an ideal both active and unfulfilled' (Piaget, 1925, p. 210).

Earlier on, for instance in an unpublished essay he submitted for a competition, 'Réalisme et nominalisme d'après les sciences de la vie' (1917)[14] Piaget had already treated this *ideal*. His philosophy professor, Arnold Reymond (1917, quoted by Liengme Bessire and Béguelin, 1996, p. 85), who wrote an ample discussion of this essay, regrets

> the ambiguous aspect of the definition [Piaget gives] of God, at times presented as a 'mere ideal', at times as a 'reality existing independently from our judgments'. The author hovers all the time between those two value judgments, and we think that this indecision is due to the fact that he has not made a clear enough distinction between the fields of metaphysics and psychology.

Many years later, in his book *Biology and knowledge*, under the heading 'Life and truth', Piaget defined his standpoint with greater precision (1967, pp. 414–15):

> If truth is not a copy, then it is an organisation of reality. But who is the organiser? . . . The philosophers who wish to promote the notion of absolute have all devolved this function to a transcendental subject, beyond man and, above all, beyond 'nature' so as to situate truth outside

the spatial and temporal contingencies of the physical world, and to make this nature understandable in an atemporal or eternal perspective. ... Before deciding to place the absolute in the clouds, it might be useful to look within things. In that case, if truth is an organisation of reality, we should first try to understand how an organisation is organised, and this is a biological issue. ... Before settling for a transcendental organisation, we should first exhaust the possibilities of immanent organisation ... [and look for] the secret of rational organisation in the vital organisation, *including what goes beyond it.* The method should therefore be an attempt to understand knowledge through its own construction, and this is not absurd at all, as knowledge is *essentially a construction.*[15]

On this level, it is no more a question of an essential and abstract 'reason', but of a kind of 'biological reason' which Piaget attempts to account for in his publications on the self-regulation processes.

Therefore, this evolution towards a more and more 'biologising' explanation of life and thought has not modified his initial fundamental standpoint, or his refusal of a reduction of intellectual processes to phenomena of cultural transmission. For him, thought is first and foremost an *individual* issue which only gradually becomes socialised: 'children aged 4–5 ... are not yet subjected to social and objective thinking habits' (Piaget, 1925, p. 207). But this socialisation will only permit the birth of personal thought if, as Piaget wrote later (1931a, p. 115), the child is 'brought up in a spirit of co-operation between minds, and not forced to respect the word'. Society can transmit opinions and beliefs, but it cannot endow the subject with comprehension *per se*. The latter requires a kind of personal enlightenment, an interior conviction infusing a sense of balance. Its only 'constriction' is intellectual consistency, which can be established with the help of a particular type of social co-operation: a verification by peers outside all hierarchic imposition.

The social element as a constriction

Piaget always rejected intellectual constrictions of any kind. His refusal of an impersonal thought might at times be surprising in its vehemence, for example in the texts he wrote as an adolescent (1916) or as a young professor, when he not only dismissed static dogmas and visions about knowledge, but even the implicit constriction exercised on the child by the language he is being taught (1925, pp. 204–5):

from his first smiles, and above all from his first words, the baby is subjected to a social influence, which is at first very slight, but becomes more and more constricting. At the beginning, it only orients his mind, but in the end, it shapes it, and may even modify it profoundly. In fact, the language he is taught is not only a system of signs. It is mainly a system of implicit judgments and notions. It is a kind of crystallised and impersonal thought inherited from former generations. An infinitely tyrannical thought which shall heavily influence every state of individual conscience, even the most intimate.

What provoked this refusal of a certain kind of inheritance in Piaget? His elder, professor Arnold Reymond, in his comment on Piaget's competition essay mentioned above, suggests the following interpretation: 'this essay is directly inspired by a contemporary circumstance . . . the war . . . raises again the ancient problem of the individual's relations to the social organism he belongs to'[16] (Reymond, 1917, passage quoted in Liengme Bessire and Béguelin, 1966, p. 84). In fact, Piaget belongs to the generation of people who were eighteen when the war broke out in 1914. These young people were the inheritors of, and potential soldiers in, an unbearable situation. Other elements from the socio-historical context contributed to Piaget's mental frame: the Russian Empire, with which the people of Neuchâtel were in touch, in particular through the Russian students at the University and the watch trade, was undergoing at that time the violent repressive actions of the tsarist regime. And locally, the ideological atmosphere of the canton was still marked by the recent refusal of feudal inheritances which Neuchâtel had only got rid of a few decades before. What meaning was to be attributed, in these circumstances, to the *relation between individual and society*?

In his quest for the meaning of life, young Piaget's answer was to assign a mission of salvation to the individual's free thought. In this, he paid allegiance to Protestant ethics, which distrusted social mediations and devolved a great responsibility to the individual who, in the end, must judge according to his sole conscience. Was it in the wake of this religious attitude that Piaget perceived the explanation of his reflections as the fulfilment of a *mission* based on the highest values? He apparently looked for the meaning of life in an enhanced freedom of the mind, in the protection of essential values and in the struggle against ideological enrolment and against war. For him, this commitment is the same as the quest for more social justice.

From his youthful experience, Piaget evidently remembered the importance of peer interactions. According to him, knowledge (including religious knowledge) comes from an intellectual exchange ruled by an ethic of debating (see for instance Piaget, 1923, p. 82). Piaget neglected the inter-generation dimension of the access to knowledge. In this field, he was in contradiction with his Russian contemporary Vygotsky, who based his research paradigm on an actual concomitance between the higher social position of the elder and his expertise (Perret-Clermont, 1995).

In consequence, Piaget's vision of knowing cannot be static. Knowledge is neither preformed in the objects nor in the subject; it undergoes a living development concerning both the historical evolution and the ontogenetic development. The categories of thought are not immutable. They evolve according to the subject's *experience*, because the latter brings concrete facts and is therefore needed by thought, which does not find its nobility in pure speculation. Piaget, as a biologist, focused on the dynamics of living beings, and tried to observe the processes through which the creative spirit – he had read Bergson – makes the construction of intelligence possible.

Following Piaget's reasoning, one becomes aware that through this focusing on the dynamics of individual intelligence, he also tried to state the autonomy of each person and to speak of his or her possible blossoming within a freedom of thought unhampered by the social context, and above all, by the pressures exercised by elders. But he rarely used the word 'person' to describe the subjects he submitted to his epistemic research interviews.

He took courageous stands, in various fields, against what he perceived as illegitimate social encroachments, in particular by institutions. This *social element*, which Piaget so strongly distrusts, seems to sum up several different things: collective opinion (is this perhaps a reminiscence of Durkheim's 'collective representations'?) based on unchecked utterances; states and churches; and all sources of constricting ideological thought. The social element is also everything not embattled in favour of a social justice that would make room for women (in a country which took a very long time to acknowledge women's right to vote and constitutional equality between men and women, Piaget, like his parents [de Tribolet, 1996] almost anticipated his century!) and for the deprived. Piaget denied the virtue of education when it is an intellectual constriction, instead of awakening the spirit of research and questioning. He condemned former generations who, through the use of their authority, prevented the growth of personal judgement. On the other hand, he pleaded in favour of exchanges between peers, which alone could respect the autonomy of thought and enrich it with the experience of reciprocity and free interpersonal co-ordination.

Considering that Piaget was a young man, barely out of an adolescence he himself describes as a period of 'liberation, through the primacy of exchanges between peers over the obedience owed to adults, and at the same time through this kind of intellectual rebellion of each new generation against the former', as a stage which enables 'the adolescent to eschew, at least within himself, the authority of adults in order to look for the living source of his future activity in relationships with people of his age group' (Piaget, 1931a, pp. 96 and 99) – how come that this former adolescent was the object of magnificent praise from his elder, Arnold Reymond, who saw in him 'the exceptionally brilliant continuator of his elders' (Reymond, 1931, p. 13)? The fair play of his professors who were apparently able to recognise and support the abilities of this younger man, without holding his kicking against him, is worth underlining.[17]

Piaget and the debates among his elders

Did Piaget, in the structuration of his own theoretical thought, progress mainly by taking stands that expressed his breaking away from his milieu, as in a game made of cognitive conflicts with his elders; or on the contrary, as Reymond says, did this young thinker shine out in the debates of his elders, and by using their own methods? Did Piaget start by imitating his elders, before he overtook them? The working hypothesis in this section will be that, at first, Piaget gradually appropriated the concepts and the processes of the scientists around him, in Neuchâtel and in French-speaking Switzerland, before he transformed them in his own way.

Through his family relations, history was the first academic topic Jean Piaget became acquainted with. His father, professor of medieval French language and literature, had studied under Gaston Paris at the Collège de France. The time spent in the circles of the new French historical science impressed upon Arthur Piaget 'the constant need to go back to the very sources' and gave him a 'critical mind that never accepted unverified opinions' (de Tribolet 1996, p. 41). In 1929, Arthur Piaget created a seminar of History of Reformation in collaboration with the Faculty of Divinity (ibid.). This historical-critical approach was not universally accepted; people wondered in particular whether it was wise to display all the doubts raised by the historical criticism of documents. Châtelain (1994, p. 138) quotes Alexandre Daguet's remarks in the paedagogic journal *L'Educateur* (1872, pp. 211–12):

> We must not play lightly with this sacred feeling [patriotism]; extreme care must be taken when contemplating the rectification of facts belonging to the historical literature written for the young and for a general readership, because once you destroy the belief of youth and of people at large in some of the traditions they hold most dear, which are for them symbols of freedom, independence, and republican virtues, you also destroy every kind of historical and patriotic faith.

Châtelain observes that in Switzerland 'historians [were] caught in the following dilemma: on the one hand, the objectivity to which methodical historical research aspires, on the other hand the need to convince most citizens of the importance of republican values' (ibid., p. 139). Did Piaget follow the path of critical history traced by his father? According to him, he didn't, and in fact, he never published any purely historical work. Yet one can see that he was deeply interested from the start by the lectures in history of science given by his philosophy professor Arnold Reymond, of whom he was to remember the 'historical-genetic stance' (Piaget, 1931b, p. 20). Moreover, like his father, he developed a critical, scientific mind, looking for facts even if (or particularly if) these facts went against received ideas.

It was probably Arnold Reymond who taught Jean Piaget how to read critically, underlining how much Kant's opinions seemed to him dependent on a state of science which had undergone great changes in the meantime. Thus Reymond raised the issue of the historical relativity of ideas, and in particular of the debate on the nature of scientific knowledge. Piaget pursued his training in that direction during his stay in Paris. A few years later, when he succeeded Reymond at the University of Neuchâtel, he declared: 'History has shown that mental categories are not fixed or immutable, and contemporary thinkers are so penetrated by this idea that, in a strange reversal of values, mobility appears as . . . the defining characteristic of any work conforming with intelligence' (Piaget, 1925, p. 196).

Did Piaget borrow from his elder Pierre Bovet his methods of 'observation and tests through interrogation'[18] (cf. Reymond, 1931, p. 13)? Usually Piaget's method of clinical interviews is considered as his own adaptation of an approach he took from psychiatry (Vinh Bang, 1988, p. 39).

Piaget studied psychological growth in several fields, as did Bovet (1922 and 1925) for the development of religious feeling, and Claparède (1915) in his studies on the evolution of interests and on the role of games for the child. But Piaget made this kind of observation more systematic and he went further than his elders in theorising the very processes of the psychological genesis of knowledge, both on a historical and on an individual level. It is interesting that his historical and genetic relativism provoked, up to a point, the same opposition as his father's historical critical relativism. Piaget remembers how his colleague P. Godet, Professor of Philosophy at the University of Neuchâtel, often told him straight 'that his psycho-genetic viewpoint in epistemology would suit him well if he were to abandon himself to the seduction of intellectual considerations alone, but that these views were dangerous for society, because man needs stable realities and absolute values' (Piaget, 1965, pp. 23–4). Even his close childhood friend and companion of his scientific and philosophical studies, Gustave Juvet, told Piaget that: 'I believe in ontogeny because a permanent Order is needed in intelligence as well as in Society.' Piaget comments: 'In French-speaking Switzerland, a Maurassian [right-wing patriotic] influence spoiled the metaphysics of elite individuals, although they were educated as Protestant democrats' (ibid., p. 24). So, in spite of his peers' reactions, Piaget remained true to his father's uncompromising attitude, which was Protestant, democratic and critical. The genetic approach took a central part in his work, where, for decades, he tried to establish parallels between the history of ideas and of individual intellectual development. Phylogeny and ontogeny: in these two perspectives, the biologist in Piaget reappears.

In fact, from his biological studies, Piaget remembered in particular the important post-Darwinian debate on evolution. The question of the respective role of nature and nurture in the individuals' adaptation to their environment was always present in his mind. Piaget studied malacology for many years. He went on to experiment about the adaptation of molluscs when transferred into another lake,[19] wondering if acquired factors could be inherited. He studied this same question again, extending its implication, in his examination of adaptation processes on a psychological level.

Pierre Bovet had studied 'the social instinct', endeavouring to understand under which circumstances it could be educated' (Bovet, 1922, for instance). Piaget was not particularly interested in the social instinct (as seen above, he distrusted the 'social element' and he saw reason as its counterpoise), but he did present a model where instincts acted as biological premises for the development of adaptation processes, which, according to him, later expanded on the level of thought into a process of self-regulation and equilibration. In his perspective, reason does not 'educate' instinct, but supplants it. The social element can only contribute to this development because it is the locus of the learning of how to regulate exchanges between peers.

As one can see, Piaget entered his elders' debates and remembered the issues discussed, but he distanced himself from them, by adapting them according to his own perspective. The stands he was to take on the sources of knowledge and faith were for him an opportunity to theorise his difference.

Finding his own autonomy from his elders and from the concept of transcendence

In the debates on the sources of knowledge and faith, Piaget took a clear position in favour of immanentism which, for him, 'in differentiated societies, gradually supersedes the notion of transcendence. . . . [because] when reciprocity and mutual respect develop, unilateral respect, as well as the source of belief in transcendental gods, become proportionally less important' (Piaget, 1929, p. 149). For Piaget, knowledge is neither a revelation progressively conceded by the Creator to the mind of His creature, nor an adapatation of the creature to the Creation that would enable it to understand the latter. Knowledge finds its source in the evolution and in the very dynamics of thought: 'Thought explains being, but in so far as we thus learn to know it, being explains thought' (ibid., p. 150). Piaget apparently considers 'meaning' and 'understanding' as synonymous. Like his predecessors and contemporaries, Piaget looked for the 'meaning of life' (this was actually the title of Bridel's paper at the already mentioned Sainte-Croix encounter in 1922)[20] and, like them, he gave a prominent place to ethics and to individual thought (Reymond, 1931, pp. 14–15):

> It is no mystery for anyone that most philosophers from French-speaking Switzerland have started by studying theology and, all in all, these studies are an excellent initiation, *provided one gets away from them*, and provided they are conducted, as is the case in our country, *in a spirit of free research and of respectful independence*.[21]

But in these debates, Piaget's location of God was apparently idio-syncratic, even though he tried to demonstrate that it was not fully opposed to the one upheld by his interlocutors (1929, pp. 151–2):

> The two great ideas of a Creator God and of a God underwriting truth remain important when they are translated into immanentistic speech ... No perception, no notion, no judgment is possible within each of us, without implying in these acts a supreme Ideal, a norm both intellectual and moral that illuminates our thought as well as our conscience! If God is not present as the source of intellectual light and love, where is He? ... Being limited by given reality on one side, by the laws of thought on the other, we thus dive into Being and Spirit, in the hope of grasping Unity one day. Where does human thought stop, and where does God begin? It is mainly a moral problem: God steps in when we give up our Self, when we renounce intellectual egocentrism as well as practical egoism. .... Immanentism is also entitled to the spiritual food of the One who said: 'the Kingdom of God is within you.

A way of thinking departing from action

To summarise, next to elders whose authoritarian influence he feared, and in a social world he perceived as conservative and repressive, young Piaget made a bold quest for meaning. He wanted to see the individual as the source of meaning, which he should reach through a reflexive activity endowed with a kind of divine underwriting for rationality. From this con-cept, he elaborated a system which, surprisingly, started from the problem of meaning and ended in a *logical and abstract model* of consistency.

Why? Probably Piaget, while taking an active part in these debates, gave such a priority to *thought* that he may not have realised how much this thought fuelled – at least for some of his teachers and for Bovet in particular – concrete and committed *actions*. Piaget's description might lead us to think that these questions were only occasions for debates. Yet the political and educational issues that were at stake for his elders were pregnant with meaning. Their epistemic models had immediate social and pedagogical implications. Thus, for instance, the stands taken by the clergyman Pettavel identified him very precisely on a political and ecclesiastic level, in the middle of vivid tensions. Pierre Bovet certainly did put forward very interesting ideas in the field of psychology and pedagogy, but they only find their full meaning when considered in the long tradition of Grandchamp, not far from Neuchâtel, where his family was actively involved in social institutions[22] (Bovet, 1965; Mouchet, 1967; de Rougemont and Bovet, 1992). One should bear in mind here that this same Pierre Bovet did not only reflect on the education of young people, but created and supported the club of the Amici Naturae, where Piaget spent so many important hours. It is true that Piaget, in his system, granted a fundamental role to *action*, and presented it as the very base of thought. But from a developmental point of view, he left action at such a primitive stage that he did not even study its adult forms. Therefore, in his psychological research, Piaget actually abandoned the field of action in order to concentrate mainly on the study of *judgement* and of *rational thought*, in an evolution where thought eventually becomes totally detached from action. Piaget explicitly praised this move towards abstraction, without apparently considering the practical consequences of this position. This led him to prefer logic to an understanding of the problem of meaning such as it is psychologically experienced, i.e. in direct touch with individual and collective daily life.

Piaget and his cultural inheritance

At a time when it is fashionable to collate and compare the works of Piaget and Vygotsky, who were both born a hundred years ago, it might be fruitful to recall the specificities of their socio-cultural inheritances and of the historical contexts in which they shaped their positions and thoughts.

As can be seen from the previous pages, Piaget grew up among social influences that were very different from the ones known by his Russian contemporary. He belonged to a political entity within what might be termed a 'confederation of minorities' (and not an empire), which offered few opportunities of identification with the leaders of a nation or of a dominant culture. The Neuchâtelois citizen did not feel the need to 'civilise the world' through his culture – but perhaps through his religious ethic. The transactions he was familiar with were often business transactions.[23] He was not the citizen of a colonialising country but of a nation of agriculturists, watch-makers, mercenaries, merchants and bankers. Neuchâtel was not a Catholic region which might consider instruction as a commodity to be shared out by a central authority in order to insure the consistency of the social body, but a state of Protestant tradition where the religious atmosphere would underline the dignity of the individual (and not of the Church), who was meant to communicate directly ('democratically', as it were) with God. Personal experience – and in particular, its highest part, religious experience – was seen as unique and personal, as a kind of incommunicable premiss.

Piaget also came from a political, cultural, religious and familial tradition encouraging a critical distance from authority. His lack of interest in social factors influencing development, beyond its roots in his biography and his personal inclinations, was perhaps also caused by the ideological climate in which he lived, where authority was generally perceived as something extraneous, repressive – at best as a protection – and where local institutions had long been forced to negotiate a relative autonomy with foreign powers.

But Piaget went further by expressing an almost egocentric individualism:[24] for him the development of personal thought was a fundamental and universal duty. In his system, this led him to ignore the importance of concrete social and educational solidarities and of relational interdependencies which make psychological growth possible and offer an access to knowledge that is already prepared by the efforts of former generations. This 'egocentrism' of Piaget led him to undervalue the role of elders and of peers.

REOPENING THE DEBATE FROM THE MODEL'S PREMISSES

Starting from this (unfortunately partial) 'case study' of the future scientist's thought, many questions can be opened or re-opened. Today's researchers do not necessarily share Piaget's premisses, which do not have to remain implicit. The same holds true, of course, for the implicit premisses of other 'grandfathers' (Vygotsky, for instance) of contemporary psychology.

It is important to examine the present historical and social situations and to ask if the great theories, in particular those propounded by these two elders, may not present useful instruments of thought, but also *distorting lenses*, because of their historically situated choices, whose implications (and at times, inopportunity in today's circumstances) tend to be now neglected out of ignorance. To re-examine these premisses (which often remained implicit *a priori*) instead of dismissing them beforehand as incompatibly different might also be an opportunity to work on the elaboration of new ways of understanding the psychological and social world, as well as the nature of cognition.

More precisely, it might be important to reconsider, taking seriously the prevailing circumstances in the last years of the twentieth century, the transmission of knowledge and its elaboration. Attention should be paid to the new terms in which political and technological mutations set the questions of freedom, identity and inter-generational relationships. Young people faced with great social and ideological upheavals cannot be contented with entering the matrix of former generations. A denial of cultural inheritance would deprive them of landmarks and instruments; they would be left without capitalisation of experience, without memory.

The psychology of the relations between experts and novices would gain from being revisited, taking explicitly into account the relations between elder and younger people, between persons involved in action with different responsibilities and experience. Cultural contexts structure in part the ways in which people act and think. The search for abstraction – outside social relations and outside time – is not necessarily the most adequate norm in all circumstances. The universality of thought might not be where it is usually looked for. In this matter, present researches have stressed other dimensions than the ones tackled by Piaget. The 'case' study of the adolescent Jean Piaget, whose thought was so lively, may be used to illustrate several characteristics of the cognitive activity such as it can be understood with the theoretical instruments currently available, briefly listed hereafter.

Cognitive activity appears in relational spaces that make it possible, and at the same time, it contributes to their structuration (Hinde, Perret-Clermont and Stevenson-Hinde, 1985; Grossen and Perret-Clermont, 1992). The epistemic quest is not its sole motivation. The learning subject summons and constructs various strategies according to the stakes he perceives in the situations he meets with. Thought does not unfold in a vacuum, without social relations and actions.

Recent researches on learning have also stressed the importance of considering the specificities of the different domains and of distinguishing conceptual learning from procedural learning (Hoyles and Forman, 1995). What were the subjects in which Piaget was educated and to what kind of learning was he confronted as a child? How have these marked his intellectual path? The learner is not only faced with a feeling of logical necessity and with the feed-backs from physical reality, but also with the actions and interpretations of other social agents, in institutional settings that do or do not legitimate some approaches and some memories. Memory and action are organised according to goals that are sometimes contradictory, and to patterns that are more or less consciously taught. The individual's 'micro-history' influences the ways in which he interprets new situations on the basis of the elaborations he has already made of those previously encountered.

This transfer of former psychological experiences does not only concern the cognitive aspects but also, obviously, the emotional and affective dimensions, which are connected for instance to the meaning given by the learner to his adventures, in social fields marked by institutional and ideological traditions, and by familial affective stakes.

The *mediation* between the object of knowledge and learner, since the invention of printing and with the growth of modern means for the communication of information, seems (rightly or wrongly) to have lost its *directness*. It does not present itself anymore through speech, through the face and hands of the elder, of the teacher or of the expert. On the contrary, this mediation more often appears to be *indirect*, coming from a teacher 'transmitting' (and not 'creating') knowledge, or from semiotic instruments reifying speech: books, recordings of images or sounds, computerised data, etc. What are the psychological impacts of these symbolic mediations on the subject's relationship to knowledge? Can they replace the contacts between expert and beginner? This question leads to another one, which concerns Piaget's experience. To what extent did the possibility he had to hear directly the descriptions of the struggles fought by the historian Arthur Piaget, to work at the museum with his old naturalist friend, to meet the ebullient Paul Pettavel, to train in philosophical interrogations with his teacher Reymond or with his godfather Samuel Cornut, and in scientific research with the experts who supported the club of the Friends of Nature

– to what extent did these personal, face-to-face meetings act as levers in Piaget's development? Are they available to secondary and high-school pupils nowadays?

And to come back to the philosophical and theological debate in which Piagetian psychology was born, it is possible to ascertain nowadays – at least among many adolescents in Neuchâtel – that the question of meaning is no longer formulated in the same terms as in the years of Piaget's youth: they are no longer those of *history* (which the adults tend perhaps to omit to mention), nor of the *meaning of the person's relations to his/her Creator*, nor of the intellectual and moral adequacy of the ways in which these relations are conceived.

Perhaps contemporary thought has taken seriously God's image in the human being: man is also a creator, and in his search for understanding, he finds himself urgently faced, not only with the Creation but also with the effects of his own material, relational, ecological, social and intellectual activity. Do elders know how to discuss these issues with young people? Do they care to enable them to do so among themselves? Or are they so profoundly marked by the Second World War, which was even more violent than the First, by the deep splitting of Europe, by the revolutions in their former colonies and by other collective ordeals, that their conflictual relation to the inheritance of the past prevents them, as in Piaget's case, from accepting and transmitting memory?

Will the destruction of ideological iron curtains offer to a less hemiplegic Europe other spaces for action and thought, where it will be possible to discuss these issues? And with other aims than theological, ideological or scientific domination?

NOTES

1 Thanks are due to Claude Béguin for the translation of this contribution into English.

2 Among which French-speaking Swiss liberal Protestants engaged in vivid debates in the face of the revival of neo-orthodox movements (for further information on this Protestant scene, see Vidal, 1987).

3 For instance, the report on the activities of the Société de Philosophie en Suisse Romande (Reymond, 1931, p. 7) asks some questions rising from the research about *Le droit d'éduquer*, elicited by Edouard Claparède: 'What and whom do we have in mind when we educate a child? Do we want to create a given type of society (nation)? But what right has this society to do this? In the name of an ideal? But what are the bases of this ideal, and how can it be justified?'

4 Piaget did indeed *practise* thought as an *answer*: he often said to his students in Geneva: 'In order to develop an idea, always choose a couple of scapegoats and act as if you were answering them.' Following this advice, this paper will endeavour to keep track of its 'scapegoats': the first one is Vygotsky, because he pays too little attention to the creative and involved activity of the individual as a person in his model of thought development where the cultural expert appears as the ultimate point of reference, and because he overestimates the necessity of dissymmetry between expert and apprentice in the construction of

understandings. The second one is Piaget himself, for the scarce attention paid in his model to the affective, relational and cultural processes connected with the development of thought products, including his own.

5 This interpretation of social reality by Piaget is rather ironic and probably more revealing of the role played by some identity myths than of the actual situation – bearing in mind the importance of the *school* of psychology created by Piaget himself in this small country.

6 We owe this quotation to René Castella, former chaplain of the University of Neuchâtel.

7 But even if the inter-confessional relations were stilted and the formulas dull, there were still interpersonal relations. In fact, Zundel adds: 'In my second year [at secondary school], I met a school fellow who was not a Catholic; he approached the Gospel with fresh attention; being intelligent and passionate, he was overwhelmed by the Gospel and by Pascal's *Pensées*. He was the admirable mediator who made me feel that the Gospel was not just a set of speeches and phrases, but a presence I could feel through the manner in which he read the Sermon of the Mount' (Zundel, 1976a, p. 3).

8 The author of this paper owes this quotation to Georges Panchaud who, when he was honorary professor at the University of Lausanne and guest professor at the University of Neuchâtel, wished to draw her attention to the theological sources of the Piagetian tenets.

9 Thanks are due to Jacques Méry and Luc-Olivier Pochon, mathematicians, a.k.a. Synopipe and Bromure, honorary members of the Amici Naturae, for the information about the life and spirit of this still active club. Jacques Méry allowed the author to consult these registers.

10 Thanks are due to Irena Sirotkina, who provided the reference of this interesting essay on Sabina Spielrein, who was Piaget's psychoanalyst.

11 These young women, who often (but not always) registered at the Séminaire de Français Moderne of the Faculty of Arts, were probably attracted to Neuchâtel because the area was famed for its 'good French' (i.e. French almost without dialectal interferences) and by the reputation of many tutors and nannies from the Neuchâtel area who taught in Russia (Maeder, 1993). At that time, Russian female students were actually also numerous in other Swiss universities, because they found there a freedom of speech and of study they lacked in their home towns, which were then agitated by pre-revolutionary events (Neumann 1987). Thanks are due to Rémy Scheurer, professor at the University of Neuchâtel, for these references.

12 The Bovet family has been active in Grandchamp (a village a few miles away from Neuchâtel) for several generations. At the time of Pierre Bovet, they were involved for instance in a hospital, a school, a Protestant teachers' training college and in the spiritual retreats which were to inspire the foundation of the Communauté évangélique de Grandchamp, the famous women Protestant congregation.

13 The italicised passage is emphasised by the author of this paper.

14 See Vidal (1994, p. 86) for a commentary.

15 The italicised passages are emphasised by Piaget.

16 In the same perspective and in similar circumstances, three decades later, Piaget took on a teaching assignment at the Collège de France in 1942, which he described as 'a time when academics felt the need to express their solidarity against violence, and their allegiance to permanent values' (Piaget, 1947, p. 5).

17 Thus, in 1925, in his foreword to his book *Le sentiment religieux et la psychologie de l'enfant*, Pierre Bovet wrote: 'The research on the reasoning of the child, initiated with total independence by Mr Jean Piaget and pursued by him since 1922, precisely at the Jean-Jacques Rousseau Institute, has opened new roads

for our reflections.' Here Bovet carefully stresses the autonomy of the man he has just appointed as director of research in his institute. Why does Bovet take this unusual precaution? Is it the sign of a respectful and laudatory (perhaps even patronising) attitude, or perhaps rather a mark of caution in front of the demanding attitude of this younger man who was to let his collaborators call him 'Patron' (Boss) a few years later, in this same institute?

18 Piaget acknowledged several times that he was inspired by Pierre Bovet's *results*, in particular in his work on moral judgement (Piaget, 1930a, p. 185; Piaget 1932, p. 301 in the 1957 edition). But our question concerns the enquiry *methods*.

19 Piaget was not alone in his move from the Lake of Neuchâtel to the Lake of Geneva! He actually tried to observe the adaptation processes of Neuchâtel molluscs when immersed in the waters of the Léman: did they transmit to the new generations the new characteristics they had acquired in order to adapt themselves after this delocalisation?

20 The conference was held in 1922, leading to publication in 1923.

21 My emphasis.

22 See note 12.

23 Did they perhaps leave their mark in the intellectual transactions underlying the Piagetian model? 'You give me your opinion, I give you mine, we shall value both and elaborate an agreement,' in a manner of speaking!

24 Obviously, Piaget recognised the importance of the socialisation of thought through interactions between peers. But he always had in mind the subject's own initial thought, and not 'collective inventions' or 'socio-cognitive conflicts' that must be solved. This might be the reason why the Piagetian model remains focused on the Self.

REFERENCES

Appignanesi, L. and Forrester, J. (1992) *Freud's Women*. London, Weidenfeld and Nicholson.

Barbey, L. (1982) La pensée religieuse de Jean Piaget, *Nova et Vetera* 4, 261–314.

Barrelet, J. M. and Perret-Clermont, A. N. (eds) (1996) *Jean Piaget et Neuchâtel: L'apprenti et le savant*. Lausanne: Editions Payot Lausanne, Collection Territoires.

Bovet, P. (1922) L'éducation de l'instinct social. *L'Educateur*, 48, 10, pp. 145–50.

Bovet, P. (1925) *Le sentiment religieux et la psychologie de l'enfant*. Neuchâtel, Delachaux et Niestlé.

Bovet, P. (1965) *Un siècle de l'histoire de Grandchamp*. Grandchamp, Switzerland.

Bridel, P. (1923) Le sens de la vie: Association Chrétienne d'Etudiants de la Suisse Romande, *Sainte-Croix 1922*. Lausanne, Imprimerie de la Concorde, pp. 16–37.

Bruner, J. (1990) *Acts of meaning*. Cambridge, Cambridge University Press.

Châtelain, P. Y. (1994) Les manuels d'histoire suisse dans l'école primaire neuchâteloise (1850–1900). *Musée Neuchâtelois*, 3, pp. 133–44.

Claparède, E. (1915) *Psychologie de l'enfant et pédagogie expérimentale. I: Le développement mental*. Réédition, Neuchâtel, Delachaux et Niestlé, 1946.

Donzé, M. (1980) *La pensée théologique de Maurice Zundel*. Geneva and Paris, Editions du Tricorne & Editions du Cerf.

Ducret, J. J. (1984) *Jean Piaget, savant et philosophe: les années de formation*. Geneva, Droz.

Gilliéron, C. (1985) *La construction du réel chez le psychologue*. Berne, P. Lang.

Grossen, M. and Perret-Clermont, A. N. (eds) (1992) *L'espace thérapeutique*. Neuchâtel and Paris, Delachaux and Niestlé.

Guinand, N. and Lüscher, R. (1993) Preface to *Amici Naturae: un siècle, une histoire*.

Hinde, R. A., Perret-Clermont, A. N. and Stevenson-Hinde, J. (eds) (1985) *Social relationships and cognitive development*. Oxford, Oxford University Press.

Hoyles, C. and Forman, E. A. (eds) (1995) Processes and products of collaborative problem solving. *Cognition and Instruction*, special issue, 13, 4, pp. 479–587.

Jelmini, J. P. (1996) Neuchâtel, ville natale de Jean Piaget. In: J. M. Barrelet and A. N. Perret-Clermont (eds) *Jean Piaget et Neuchâtel: L'apprenti et le savant*. Lausanne: Editions Payot Lausanne, Collection Territoires, pp. 27–38.

Lave, J. and Wenger, E. (1991) *Situated learning: legitimate peripheral participation*. Cambridge, Cambridge University Press.

Liengme, M. J. (1994) Le sens de la mesure. L'émergence d'un discours historique centré sur l'industrie horlogère neuchâteloise. *Cahiers de l'Institut d'Histoire*, 2. University of Neuchâtel.

Liengme Bessire, M. J. and Béguelin, S. (1996) De la malacologie à la psychologie: la 'conversion' de Jean Piaget s'est-elle jouée à la Faculté des lettres? In: J. M. Barrelet and A. N. Perret-Clermont (eds) *Jean Piaget et Neuchâtel: L'apprenti et le savant*. Lausanne: Editions Payot Lausanne, Collection Territoires, pp. 81–94.

Maeder, A. (1993) Gouvernantes et précepteurs neuchâtelois dans l'empire russe [1800–1890]. *Cahiers de l'institut d'Histoire*, 1. University of Neuchâtel.

Mouchet, J. P. (1967) *L'école secondaire de Boudry-Cortaillod: Grandchamp, 1876–1967*. Boudry (Neuchâtel), La Baconnière.

Neumann, D. (1987) Studentinnen aus dem russischen Reich in der Schweiz [1867–1917]. Zürich, H. Rohr.

Perret-Clermont, A. N. (1980) *Social interaction and cognitive development in children*. London, Academic Press.

Perret-Clermont, A. N. (1995) Les partenaires de l'apprentissage. *Vous avez dit . . . pédagogie*, University of Neuchâtel, 40, 10–17.

Perret-Clermont, A. N. and Nicolet, M. (eds) (1988) *Interagir et connaître*. Fribourg, DelVal.

Piaget, J. (1916) *La mission de l'idée*. Lausanne, Editions de la Concorde.

Piaget, J. (1921a) L'orientation de la philosophie religieuse en Suisse romande. *La Semaine Littéraire*, 29, 1443, 409–12.

Piaget, J. (1921b) *Introduction à la malacologie valaisanne*. Thèse présentée à la Faculté des Sciences de l'Université de Neuchâtel pour l'obtention du grade de docteur ès sciences. Sion, Imprimerie F. Aymon.

Piaget, J. (1923) La psychologie et les valeurs religieuses. Association Chrétienne d'Etudiants de la Suisse Romande, *Sainte-Croix 1922*. Lausanne, Imprimerie de la Concorde, pp. 38–82.

Piaget, J. (1925) Psychologie et critique de la connaissance. *Archives de Psychologie*, 29, 75, 193–210.

Piaget, J. (1929) Pour l'immanence. Réponse à M. J. D. Burger. *Revue de Théologie et de Philosophie*, 17, 146–52.

Piaget, J. (1930a) Immanentisme et foi religieuse. Groupe Romand des Anciens membres de l'Association Chrétienne d'Étudiants, ed. Geneva, pp. 8–54.

Piaget, J. (1930b) Les procédés de l'education morale. Rapport. *Cinquième Congrès international d'éducation morale*, Paris, Librairie Félix Alcan, pp. 182–219.

Piaget, J. (1931a) L'individualité en histoire. L'individualité: 3ème semaine internationale de snthèse Centre International de Synthèse, Paris, 15–23 May. (English translation in: *Sociological studies*. London, Routledge, 1995).

Piaget, J. (1931b) Post-scriptum à la 'Pensée philosophique en Suisse romande de 1900 à nos jours par A. Reymond'. *Revue de Théologie et de Philosophie*, 81, pp. 18–20.

Piaget, J. (1932) *Le jugement moral chez l'enfant* (réédition 1957). Paris, Presses Universitaires de France. (English translation: *Moral Judgments of the Child*. London, RKP, 1932.

Piaget, J. (1947) *La psychologie de l'intelligence*. 8th edition. Paris, Armon and Colin, 1965. (English translation: *The Psychology of Intelligence*. London, RKP, 1950).

Piaget, J. (1960) Problèmes de la psycho-sociologie de l'enfance. In G. Gurvitch (ed.) *Traité de sociologie*, vol. II. Paris, P.U.F., pp. 229–54. (English translation in: *Sociological Studies*. London, Routledge, 1995).

Piaget, J. (1965) *Sagesse et illusions de la philosophie*. Paris, Presses Universitaires de France. (English translation: *Insights and Illusions in Philosophy*. London, RKP, 1972).

Piaget, J. (1967) *Biologie et connaissance*. Paris, Gallimard. (English translation: *Biology and Knowledge*. Edinburgh, Edinburgh University Press, 1971).

Piaget, J. (1972) Discours de Jean Piaget. *Stichting Praemium Erasmianum*. Amsterdam, pp. 27–32.

Piaget, J. (1976) Autobiographie. *Revue européenne des sciences sociales*. Cahiers Vilfredo Pareto 14 (38, 39), 1–43. (See Piaget 1965/1972 for a partial English version of Piaget's autobiography).

Pontecorvo, C. (ed.) (1993) *La condivisione della conoscenza*. Firenze, La Nuova Italia.

Resnick, L., Levine, J. and Teasley, S. (eds) (1991) *Socially Shared Cognition*. Washington, American Psychological Association.

Reymond, A. (1917) Rapport du jury sur le prix de la Société académique. Département de l'Instruction Publique 1917. Première partie: Enseignement surpérieur, pp. 53–63.

Reymond, A. (1931) La pensée philosophique en Suisse romande de 1900 à nos jours. *Revue de Théologie et de Philosophie*, 81. Lausanne, pp. 5–20.

Rogoff, B. (1990) *Apprenticeship in Thinking: Cognitive Development in Social Context*. New York and Oxford, Oxford University Press.

Rougemont, G. de, Bovet, G., with Bovet, M. (1992) *La geste des Bovet de Grandchamp*. Boudry (Neuchâtel), Imprimerie Baillod.

Schaller-Jeanneret, A. F. (1996) Les premières étapes de la formation intellectuelle. In: J. M. Barretlet and A. N. Perret-Clermont (eds) *Jean Piaget et Neuchâtel: L'apprenti et le savant*. Lausanne: Editions Payot Lausanne, Collection Territoires, pp. 51–66.

Soyland, A. J. (1993) Sabina Spielrein and the hidden psychoanalysis of psychologists. *Newsletter of the History and Philosophy Section of the British Psychological Society*, 17, 5–12.

Thomann, C. (1996) L'engagement chrétien et social. In: J. M. Barrelet and A. N. Perret-Clermont (eds) *Jean Piaget et Neuchâtel: L'apprenti et le savant*. Lausanne: Editions Payot Lausanne, Collection Territoires, pp. 111–19.

Tribolet de, J. M. (1996) Arthur Piaget (1865–1952): portrait intellectuel et moral du père de Jean Piaget. In: J. M. Barrelet and A. N. Perret-Clermont (eds) *Jean Piaget et Neuchâtel: L'apprenti et le savant*. Lausanne: Editions Payot Lausanne, Collection Territoires, pp. 39–50.

Vidal, F. (1987) Piaget and the liberal Protestant tradition. In: M. G. Ash and W. R. Woodward (eds) *Psychology in Twentieth-Century Thought and Society*. New York, Cambridge University Press, pp. 271–94.

Vidal, F. (1994) *Piaget before Piaget*. Cambridge, Mass., Harvard University Press.

Vidal, F. (1996) Jean Piaget, 'Ami de la Nature' In: J. M. Barrelet and A. N. Perret-Clermont (eds) (1996) *Jean Piaget et Neuchâtel: L'apprenti et le savant*. Lausanne: Editions Payot Lausanne, Collection Territoires, pp. 95–109.

Vinh Bang (1988) *Textes choisis*. Geneva, Faculté de Psychologie et des Sciences de l'Education (reprint of *Psychologie et épistémologie génétiques*. Paris, Dunod, 1966, pp. 67–81).

Zundel, M. (1976a) La clé du royaume. *Choisir*, 200/201, 3–7.

Zundel, M. (1976b) *Quel homme et quel Dieu: retraite au Vatican*, 1972. Paris, Fayard.

6 Piaget, Vygotsky and the social dimension

Gerry P. T. Finn

From very different perspectives Gerard Duveen and Anne-Nelly Perret-Clermont provide provocative, innovative views on the social dimension to learning and thinking. The following discussion is all too brief but is also intended to be provocative: it will draw upon aspects of their accounts, but space precludes full engagement with their arguments or even a fully detailed exposition of this response. Both contributors demonstrate the necessity of forging a closer relationship between social and developmental psychologies but come to different conclusions about the significance of the social dimension in Piagetian theorising, and by implication in the Vygotskian model as well. Yet both Duveen and Perret-Clermont conclude that the contemporary images of Piaget and Vygotsky are socio-historically situated, and unhelpful: these images can be interpreted, as Duveen hints, as social representations of Piaget and Vygotsky.

Duveen approaches Piaget and Vygotsky in a different way, but still from the perspective of social representations. Building upon Moscovici's (1976, 1990) and Jovchelovitch's (1995) relatively brief discussions of Piaget's influence on the development of social representations, he proposes that social representations can reciprocate by strengthening Piaget's model. The case remains unconvincing. Duveen finds Piaget wanting on the development of gender identities. That is no surprise. Piaget's genetic epistemology deliberately excludes these topics. As Kitchener (1986: 25) explained: 'Developmental changes in sexuality, for example, are non-epistemic, and so are many kinds of personality changes'.

Duveen seems to recognise Piaget's more limited focus but argues for the addition of a social psychological subject to the psychological and epistemic subjects recognised by Piaget (Beth and Piaget, 1966). However, this additional typification would add to the confusion over the role of 'subjects' – the epistemic subject in particular – in Piagetian thinking (Kitchener, 1986). Psychological actions can be included in the activities of the epistemic subject nor, despite the common social representation of Piaget and his thinking, are psychological actions seen by Piaget to be asocial. The epistemic subject's construction of knowledge depends on *universal psycho-sociological* processes. And, as the epistemic subject is an idealised, impersonal, abstraction, neither individual nor group differences (e.g. personality factors or gender respectively) are relevant, nor would thinking based on these category differentiations be included in the epistemic subject's activities, which is the construction of universally necessary knowledge (Kitchener, 1986; Chapman, 1988; Finn, 1992; Smith, 1993).

Piaget's epistemological project was to describe the development of more advanced forms of thought, not the development of an individual's thinking (Finn, 1992). The epistemic subject is a construction representing the active development of thought itself. However, Duveen's desire to enlarge Piaget's focus returns the discussion to Perret-Clermont's warning about the dangers of misinterpreting Piaget's project and neglecting its origins in a specific socio-historical setting.

PIAGET'S IDEOLOGICAL CONCERNS

Perret-Clermont gives a rich description of the historical, socio-cultural milieu within which the young Piaget interacted and developed. She identifies the importance of locating him in his social setting to begin to appreciate Piaget's 'own quest for meaning'. However, Perret-Clermont's aims are too modest, and paradoxically too ambitious. She is too modest in denying providing an account of the social influences upon Piaget and his theorising. Inevitably her historical examination of Piaget and his social interactions does explore the social influences on him. But Perret-Clermont is too ambitious in claiming her main task to be the 'post hoc *observation*' (emphasis added) of Piaget's social interactions. Her historical approach is to be welcomed: historical dimensions to psychological phenomena are much too neglected. But retrospective observation is impossible: the use of historical sources provides *accounts*, not observations. Although Piaget did prize consistency (e.g. object constancy and conservation), that does not mean that his retrospective accounts can be taken as valid observations. Indeed, Piaget himself argued that the past was an exercise in construction and reconstituted as a function of the present (Piaget, 1976a; Piaget and Inhelder, 1973; Bringuier, 1980: 119). Autobiographical accounts, like other historical accounts, are constructions which are not psychologically neutral: the tale told serves various purposes (Finn, 1991).

Piaget (1966) accepted this case in the first updated version of his autobiography (Campbell, 1976 provides an English translation). He acknowledged autobiography to be an opportunity for the public presentation of a particular self-portrait (see also Vidal, 1994). So it is no surprise that Perret-Clermont finds intriguing omissions in Piaget's autobiographical reports. Piaget claimed only to cover 'the scientific aspects of my life' (1952: 237). Yet sometimes, here and elsewhere (e.g. Bringuier, 1980: Piaget, 1972a), Piaget refers to wider societal events. Usually the dramatic effect is to place Piaget outside the influence of any irrational societal forces. These recollections present a self-image of Piaget as the rational scientist, remote from the ideological forces swirling around him.

That image may explain the mature Piaget's embarrassment at the content of his early writings on religion, politics and science (Chapman, 1988). This embarrassment may explain his inconsistent reporting of whether he had ever re-read his earlier works (Piaget, 1952: 237; Bringuier, 1980: 10). And when the mature Piaget did acknowledge these works, it was to identify those continuities in his thinking that could be cast in a scientific form, not to comment on his religious or socio-political beliefs (cf. Vidal, 1994). Yet, as Perret-Clermont shows, Piaget's stances on social issues were important for his development. Recurrent themes in Piaget's later thinking first appear in the context of the young man's works (Chapman, 1988; Gruber and Vonèche, 1982; Vidal, 1987, 1994), which reveal a passionate Piaget, caught up in the religious and political controversies of his social milieu.

This militant, passionate Piaget damned the dominant elite in his first book: 'Cursed be the ruling classes, the orthodox, the reactionaries, the utilitarians, the sceptics' (Piaget, 1916; see Gruber and Vonèche, 1982: 28). He attacked the orthodoxy and self-satisfied hypocrisy of the Church, the complacent, self-serving cant of the bourgeoisie, and blamed politicians for the regression into the war that then engulfed Europe. Progress for Piaget was to be seen in a unity that would bring together peace, religion, science, international socialism and feminism. Rationality was equated with God and was the means to bring about this socialised Christian salvation.

Piaget rejected war. War was opposed to the true nature of humanity, which was characterised by love, cooperation and peace (Piaget, 1918: see Gruber and Vonèche, 1982). Radical Piaget's second book, *Recherche*, was a personal, philosophical essay. The leading character, the liberal Protestant Sébastien, the searcher after truth and ultimate values, was really Piaget (Piaget in Bringuier, 1980: 10). Piaget equated his own personal crisis of faith with the social crisis of the World War; the great 'contemporary disequilibrium' (Chapman, 1988: 19; see Gruber and Vonèche, 1982: 42–50). Intelligence had to be freed from the grip of passion. Orthodox theology and metaphysics were unhelpful. The search for universally immutable values and truth could only be entrusted to reason, which was now equated with science and religion. Faith remained central. Values could not be reduced to scientific phenomena. But the scientific search was itself an act of faith.

Piaget's search for meaning was to be based upon science. Science could not assess values as such. But science could show that one system of values was more evolved than another. Science also revealed that the ideal solution to the human social predicament lay in equilibrium. The process of equilibrium would restore social order. A new world order based on federalism, the equilibrium between nationalism and inter-nationalism, and socialism, the equilibrium between statist collectivism and bourgeois liberalism (and individualism), would lead to the ideal forms of socialist cooperation and world federation.

Piaget continued to advocate the superiority of his social value system. He was active within the New Education Fellowship, which denounced ethnic rivalry, nationalism and class warfare and sought to transform the world through education. At the Fellowship's sixth World Conference in 1932, Piaget (1933/n.d.) approved of the planet's increasingly inter-dependent and international society. Regrettably adults were as yet unable to grasp this global complexity but behaved 'like children faced by the grown-up world': their understanding of society was hindered by 'individual or collective self-centredness' (Piaget, n.d.: 6 and 10). However, a new education could transform children into more rational adults, a new citizenry for the future, who would then be able to conceive of the world as an interrelated and interdependent whole. The political benefits of this psycho-sociological decentering would be seen in the elimination of ethnocentrism and in the cooperative development through shared co-ordinations of socialised, logical beliefs. Again the key to progress was rationality, which Piaget argued was best exemplified by science. Education had to reject coercive practices and rely on that 'spirit of cooperation, of intellectual and moral freedom, of free research' (Piaget, n.d.: 23) found in science. The socialisation of coordinations, achieved by following the (idealised) model of the cooperative practice of science, would lead to greater tolerance. Yet Piaget's own tolerance had its limits. Perret-Clermont reports an older Piaget still active in Protestant debates and, in his own mid-thirties in the 1930s, still antagonistic to Catholicism.

So, Piaget's early beliefs cannot be dismissed as adolescent scribbles. For quite some time Piaget continued to expect to be able to demonstrate the superiority of his version of liberal Protestantism over other varieties of religious faith. Vidal (1987, 1994) has demonstrated the influence of Piaget's socio-religious values on the development of genetic epistemology and exposed Piaget's belief that his development of this science would allow the superiority of his value system to be demonstrated! Vidal's earlier account led Woodward to express alarm at Piaget's failure to separate 'objective science from subjective religion'. He noted that Piaget's identification of scientific reason with God had 'disturbing implications': it meant that there was no truly independent, critical role for science. Just as Piaget's tolerance was limited, so was his vision for science. Given its religious and socio-political origins, Woodward worried what unrecognised consequences followed the adoption of 'genetic epistemology as a basis for social or educational thought' (1987: 304) and pondered whether later Piagetian research was sufficiently removed from its roots or remained infused by its value-laden inspiration.

SOCIETY, THE SOCIAL AND THE SOCIETAL

Woodward's worries raise profound questions about Piaget's epistemo-logical research. However, Smith's (1993) careful exposition of Piaget's project provides a perspective that indicates that Piaget did not always restrict his research to epistemological questions. That does show, as Duveen implies is necessary, that Piagetian approaches can be adapted to tackle more general questions of psychological development. None the less, even if Woodward's anxieties can be allayed, the demonstration of the importance of the ideological background to Piaget's theorising supports Perret-Clermont's argument that thinking is socio-historically situated.

Piaget's developing theory emerged from his location in his social milieu. Contrary to common imagery, Piaget's theory was not only influenced by its socio-historical setting, he recognised the power of these influences in his explanations of thought (Piaget, 1995). Piaget's social dimension is even stronger than is argued by Duveen. Wisely Perret-Clermont warns of the increased potential for misinterpretation if we fail to recognise the social-historical situations in which thinking is located, but she does just this when she claims that Piaget had a 'lack of interest in social factors influencing development'.

The examples of equilibrium given earlier hint at Piaget's proposal of a social/individual parallelism. Piaget argued that logical knowledge developed through the psycho-sociological actions of the epistemic subject. Therefore there was an 'inevitable convergence of the most "general" forms of social interaction and of the co-ordination of individual actions' (Piaget, 1973b: 30). For Piaget (1972b: 36) it was:

> pointless to seek to set social logic and individual logic against one another. Logic could thus be considered, in the sense of being the final form of equilibrations, as being simultaneously individual and social: individual in so far as it is general or common to all individuals, and likewise social in so far as it is general or common to all societies.

When Perret-Clermont *et al.* (1976) argued for the priority of social over individual influences on cognitive development, Piaget countered that social and individual structures were identical, universal and 'biopsychosociological': that was what made them 'fundamentally logical' (1976b: 226). Piaget (1952: 247) did criticise his early research for being too concerned with 'the social aspect of thought'. But Piaget (e.g. 1972b) commonly used 'social' to refer only to forms of social pressure or coercion or, ironically, ideological influences, so his self-criticism may have been partially accurate (cf. Finn, 1985)! As he viewed these influences to be of no epistemological significance, this 'social' was irrelevant to his research interests.

So Perret-Clermont's criticism runs the risk of supporting the falsely individualistic image of Piaget. Yet Piaget opposed reductionism, whether individualistic or social, and advocated interdisciplinary research, based on an integrated circle of sciences, each with its own level of explanation, to advance knowledge (e.g. Piaget, 1972b, 1973a, 1973b). However, his sometimes inconsistent refusal to prioritise the social *or* the individual, but instead to assert their inevitable unity, to the neglect of their dialectical interrelationship, did limit the value of some Piagetian developmental explanations (Finn, 1985). His refusal has to be placed in its ideological context: this was Piaget's resolution of the late nineteenth-century dilemma – which he dismissed as a pseudo-problem (Piaget, 1995) – of the priority of collectivism or individualism in society. His stance has some advantages (Finn, 1992); but the resulting image of Piaget strengthens Perret-Clermont's claim that unrecognised socio-historical variations distort contemporary interpretations of earlier theorising. Piaget's theory is not asocial.

Paradoxically Vygotsky's image is false: he is overvalued as a strongly social theorist. Duveen's analysis confirms Smith's (1996) criticism of the weakness of the social dimension in Vygotsky's account of the social construction of knowledge. Inevitably Vygotsky's work was also socio-historically situated, a product of his own ideological milieu. His optimistic outlook on the new Soviet society removed the need for critical appraisal: society and the environment simply represented what was required for *continuing* advances in development (e.g. Vygotsky, 1994a, Vygotsky 1994b). Warnings about culturally based misinterpretations of Vygotsky (Van der Veer and Valsiner, 1991) have gone unheeded, only to demonstrate again how social representations form erroneous contemporary images of psychological theories. Analysis of Piagetian and Vygotskian social thinking shows the need for a more sophisticated understanding of what we mean by social – and by society.

Influences presently described simply as social are remarkably varied, and operate on a variety of levels and in very different ways. Social factors can be located at intrapersonal, interpersonal, intergroup and societal levels (Doise, 1986): distinctions need to be made and the different effects on development elaborated. Delineations of the social need careful analysis, but the dominance of 'individualism' in psychology (Farr, 1990) has hindered serious investigation of the social at all.[1] There is a unity between social and individual levels, though not quite as Piaget claimed (cf. Piaget, 1995), and it is essential that their dialectic be studied.

To do so means turning some usual questions on their head. There is some recognition of a role for society in the socialisation of individuals but the question of 'who socialises society?' (Moscovici, 1972: 54) remains ignored. In a related important reversal, Meacham (1993) asked not of the value of society for individuals but of the value of individuality, which is socially constructed, for society. He answered that it was through individuality that societies were socially reconstructed by succeeding generations, making social transformation possible. Development involves both society and individual and, as the study of both Vygotsky and Piaget demonstrates, the contribution is dialectical. As a result, a developmental psychology that truly recognises the social dimension to learning and thinking will need to evolve much more sophisticated understandings of the crudely described categories of society, social and individual, and of the complexity of their exchanges. In reply to Perret-Clermont's final set of puzzles; could these elaborations be the socio-historically situated tasks that contemporary research has now to tackle?

NOTE

1 So individualistic is contemporary psychology that a common reaction in the desperate attempt to stress that a phenomenon is social is to sprinkle the text frequently with this very adjective. It is not chance that led to this original conference session being titled 'Social collaboration and learning': yet collaboration cannot be anything other than social. But my own response has probably committed similar errors of 'social sprinkling'!

REFERENCES

Beth, E. W. and Piaget, J. (1966) *Mathematical Epistemology and Psychology*. Dordrecht: D. Riedel.

Bringuier, J. C. (1980) *Conversations with Jean Piaget*. Chicago: University of Chicago Press.

Campbell, S. F. (ed.) (1976) *Piaget Sampler: An Introduction to Jean Piaget Through his Own Words*. New York: Wiley.

Chapman, M. (1988) *Constructive Evolution: Origins and Development of Piaget's Thought*. Cambridge: Cambridge University Press.

Doise, W. (1986) *Levels of Explanation in Social Psychology*. Cambridge/Paris: Cambridge University Press/Maison des Sciences de l'Homme.

Farr, R. M. (1990) Individualism as a Collective Representation. In J. P. Deconchy (ed.) *Idéologie et réprésentations sociales*. Cousset: Delval.

Finn, G. P. T. (1985) L'intelligibilité sociale de la tâche. In G. Mugny (ed.) *Psychologie sociale du développement cognitif*. Berne: Peter Lang.

Finn, G. P. T. (1991) Social Psychology is History: History is Social Pyschology. Paper to the British Psychological Society Annual Social Psychology Conference, Guildford.

Finn, G. P. T. (1992) Piaget, Psychology and Education. *Scottish Educational Review*, 24, 125–31.

Gruber, H. E. and Vonèche, J. J. (1982) *The Essential Piaget: An Interpretive Reference and Guide*. London: Routledge and Kegan Paul.

Jovchelovitch, S. (1995) Social Representations in and of the Public Sphere: Towards a Theoretical Articulation. *Journal for the Theory of Social Behaviour*, 25, 81–102.

Kitchener, R. F. (1986) *Piaget's Theory of Knowledge: Genetic Epistemology and Scientific Reason*. New Haven: Yale University Press.

Meacham, J. A. (1993) Where is the Social Environment? A Commentary on Reed. In R. H. Wozniak and K. W. Fischer (eds) *Development in Context: Acting and Thinking in Specific Environments*. Hillsdale, NJ.: Lawrence Erlbaum Associates.

Moscovici, S. (1972) Society and Theory in Social Psychology. In J. Israel and H. Tajfel (eds) *The Context of Social Psychology*. London: Academic Press.

Moscovici, S. (1976) *Social Influence and Social Control*. London: Academic Press.

Moscovici, S. (1990) Social Psychology and Developmental Psychology: Extending the Conversation. In G. Duveen and B. Lloyd (eds) *Social Representations and the Development of Knowledge*. Cambridge: Cambridge University Press.

Perret-Clermont, A.–N., Mugny, G. and Doise, W. (1976) Une approche psy-
chosociologique du développement cognitif. *Archives de Psychologie*, 44,
135–44.

Piaget, J. (1916) *La mission de l'idée*. Lausanne: Editions de la Concorde.

Piaget, J. (1918) *Recherche*. Lausanne: Editions de la Concorde.

Piaget, J. (1933/n.d.) L'évolution sociale et la pédagogie nouvelle. In W. T. R.
Rawson (ed.) *New Education Fellowship Sixth World Conference, Nice,
MCMXXXII Full Report*. London: New Education Fellowship/*Social Evolution
and the New Education*. Education To-Morrow, no. 4. London: New Education
Fellowship.

Piaget, J. (1952) Jean Piaget. In E. G. Boring (ed.) *A History of Psychology in
Autobiography, vol. 4*. Worcester, MA: Clark University Press.

Piaget, J. (1966) Autobiographie. *Cahiers Vilfredo Pareto (Revue européene des
sciences sociales)*, 4, 129–59.

Piaget, J. (1972a) *Insights and Illusions of Psychology*. London: Routledge and
Kegan Paul.

Piaget, J. (1972b) *Psychology and Epistemology: Towards a Theory of Knowledge*.
Harmondsworth: Penguin University Books.

Piaget, J. (1973a) *Main Trends in Inter-Disciplinary Research*. London: George
Allen and Unwin Ltd.

Piaget, J. (1973b) *Main Trends in Psychology*. London: George Allen and Unwin
Ltd.

Piaget, J. (1976a) The Affective Unconscious and the Cognitive Unconscious. In
B. Inhelder and H. H. Chipman (eds) *Piaget and his School: A Reader in
Developmental Psychology*. New York: Springer-Verlag.

Piaget, J. (1976b) Postface. *Archives de Psychologie*, 44, 223–8.

Piaget, J. (1995) *Sociological Studies* (L. Smith *et al.*, trans.). London: Routledge.

Piaget, J. and Inhelder, B. (1973) *Memory and Intelligence*. London: Routledge and
Kegan Paul.

Smith, L. (1993) *Necessary Knowledge: Piagetian Perspectives on Contructivism*.
Hove: Lawrence Erlbaum Associates.

Smith, L. (1996) The Social Construction of Rational Understanding. In
A. Tryphon and J. J. Vonèche (eds) *Piaget–Vygotsky: The Social Genesis of
Thought*. Hove: Lawrence Erlbaum Associates.

Van der Veer, R. and Valsiner, J. (1991) *Understanding Vygotsky: A Quest for
Synthesis*. Oxford: Blackwell.

Vidal, F. (1987) Jean Piaget and the Liberal Protestant Tradition. In M. G. Ash and
W. R. Woodward (eds) *Psychology in Twentieth Century Thought and Society*.
Cambridge: Cambridge University Press.

Vidal, F. (1994) *Piaget before Piaget*. Cambridge, MA: Harvard University Press.

Vygotsky, L. (1994a) The Problem of the Environment. In R. Van der Veer and
J. Valsiner (eds) *The Vygotsky Reader*. Oxford: Blackwell.

Vygotsky, L. (1994b) The Socialist Alteration of Man. In R. Van der Veer and
J. Valsiner (eds) *The Vygotsky Reader*. Oxford: Blackwell.

Woodward, W. R. (1987) Professionalization, Rationality, and Political Linkages
in Twentieth Century Psychology. In M. G. Ash and W. R. Woodward (eds)
Psychology in Twentieth Century Thought and Society. Cambridge: Cambridge
University Press.

Part 3

Cognitive skills and domain specificity

7 Piaget, mathematics and Vygotsky

Peter Bryant

The mathematics that children learn is an interesting mix of universal principles, such as inferences, on the one hand, and inventions, such as counting systems, measuring systems, trigonometry and calculus, on the other. This combination is always a significant one in developmental psychology. Where there are universals, it is possible (though not necessary) that children do their learning for themselves without much help from anyone else: some of their knowledge of these universals may even be innate. Inventions, in contrast, are unlikely to be re-invented by each generation of children. They have to be communicated to the next generation: they have to be taught. So, mathematics learning is a suitable case for treatment in a book about Piaget and Vygotsky, since it raises the two central issues associated with these two giants' theories – the development of logic and the transmission from one generation to the next of cultural inventions and achievements.

The best way to begin to describe Piaget's views on children's mathematics, and also to contrast these views with Vygotsky's, is to turn first to number. Number, and number systems, are based on logical principles but also involve quite arbitrary culturally devised conventions. The base 10 system is an immensely useful cultural convention: among other things it allows us to generate numbers instead of having to remember an immensely long sequence of numbers. All one needs to remember in order to count to 99 in English is the 1–10 sequence, the odd names that we have for some of the teens (e.g. 'eleven', twelve') and for some of the decades (e.g. 'twenty', 'thirty'). The base 10 system is not in any sense necessary; there are number systems without any base system (Saxe, 1991; Saxe and Posner, 1983). So what is the nature of the children's battle with the number system which plainly goes on for several years? Is this a battle with logic or with conventions?

PIAGET ON REVERSIBILITY, CARDINALITY AND ORDINALITY

The Piagetian view is that the main constraints in human development are logical ones. It takes children a long time, he claimed, to grasp the principles of cardinal and ordinal number. Although some young children count reasonably proficiently, they do not fully understand the meaning of the number words that they produce so fluently. They have these difficulties because they lack the ability, called 'reversibility', to perceive a change and at the same time to cancel it out subjectively by imagining the opposite change. In Piaget's theory reversibility lies at the heart of the understanding of all logic, and of all mathematics.

Reversibility is needed for the understanding of cardinal number which is the understanding that any set of a given number of objects will have the same quantity of objects in it as any other set with the same number in it. This is easy to show, because there is one-to-one correspondence between any two sets of the same number. For each object in one set there is an equivalent object in the other set and vice versa. On the development of the understanding of one-to-one correspondence Piaget argues 1952, p. 89):

> The fundamental factor of this development, in my view, is the complete reversibility of the action involved in the child's procedure. The operation he performs is no longer immediately absorbed in the intuitive result obtained. Each transformation can be compensated by its inverse, so that any arrangement must give rise to any other, and conversely.

Piaget's demonstration that young children are deeply impervious to one-to-one correspondence between two spatially presented sets is still a convincing one. Their spontaneous reliance on length instead is one of the oftenest repeated and most reliable phenomena in the history of empirical psychology. Children even choose this untrustworthy cue in the face of considerable inducement not to do so: there are two studies (Piaget and Inhelder, 1971; Cowan and Daniels, 1989) in which the one-to-one correspondence cues were emphasised by lines between the objects in each row, and even here many of the children still disregarded one-to-one correspondence and went for length.

Reversibility, according to Piaget, is the key to the child's eventual discovery that one-to-one correspondence is a good cue and length a very bad one in comparisons of number. A child who has reversible cognitive processes can work out that spreading out a row has no effect on the actual number of objects in it: she can now cancel out this change for herself by imagining the inverse change and thus can realise that there has been no real change in number. Furthermore she can also see that changing the length of one of the rows does not alter the one-to-one correspondence between the two rows.

Ordinal number also causes a great deal of difficulty, according to Piaget. The relative magnitude of the words in the number sequence is represented by their order (10 follows 9 and is more than 9, 25 is later in the sequence than 22 and is duly more than 22) and so a child must grasp this relation and be able to use it if she is to understand the nature of the number system. Piaget claimed that young children find ordinality as difficult as cardinality – again because of a lack of reversibility. A child who does not possess this intellectual ability cannot, as a result, handle the quantitative relations in even a simple series. Faced with the series A>B>C, the 'irreversible' child will be able to take in at one time that A>B and at another that B>C, but simply cannot grasp these two relations at the same time. She cannot do this because she does not understand that B can simultaneously be smaller than one quantity and larger than another.

The evidence which Piaget offers for this proposition consists of the well-known seriation and transitivity studies. In the seriation experiment children are asked to put sticks of different lengths in ordered series – ordered, that is, by their size – and then to insert a new stick in the appropriate place in an already constructed series. Young children fail to do this. Children who cannot handle two-way relations should be equally out of their depth with transitive inferences. The premises in a transitive inferences take the form of two or more quantitative relations (e.g. A>B, B>C) and the inference involves combining these in order to answer a question about the relation between the two quantities which are not directly compared (A?C). Piaget and his colleagues did carry out some research on children's difficulties with inferential problems, though this evidence is rather unsatisfactory because it is mainly based on measuring problems in which children have to realise that measurement, and therefore a transitive inference, is needed (Piaget, Inhelder and Szeminska, 1960).

OTHER VIEWS ON CARDINALITY AND ORDINALITY

It would be a grand move at this point to present a Vygotskian point of view on cardinality and ordinality but that is quite difficult to do because Vygotsky never, so far as I know, concerned himself with these forms of knowledge. Are there other grounds for criticising the Piagetian ideas?

There is one reason for hesitating about Piaget's conclusion on one-to-one correspondence. It is that children often share. Sharing seems to depend on one-to-one correspondence and three studies (Miller, 1984; Desforges and Desforges, 1980; Frydman and Bryant, 1988) have shown that children as young as four share out numbers of things equally between two or more recipients rather successfully and usually do so on a repetitive 'one for A, one for B' basis. This looks like a temporal form of one-to-one correspondence.

But do they extend this understanding to number words? We (Frydman and Bryant, 1988) looked at this question in another study. In this we took a group of four-year-old children who could share quite well, and we asked them to share out some 'sweets' between two recipients. When this was done we counted out aloud the number of sweets that the child had given to one recipient, and then asked him or her how many had been given to the other recipient. None of the children straightaway made the correct inference that the other recipient had the same number of sweets even though they had meticulously shared the sweets out on a one-to-one basis: instead all of the children tried to count the second lot of sweets. We stopped them doing so, and asked the question again. Even then less than half the children made the correct inference about the second recipient's sweets.

Thus many four-year-old children fail to extend their considerable understanding of sharing to counting. We conclude from this that young children do grasp the cardinality of number and yet do not at first apply this understanding to number words. By and large this work on sharing throws some doubt on Piaget's negative views on young children's grasp of one-to-one correspondence, but it does nothing to show that they apply what they understand about cardinality to counting. That is what seems to take a long time.

There are disagreements too about ordinality, but these have mainly been about transitivity. Piaget's remarkable work on seriation has remained unscathed, though this may be because not many people have tried to scathe it yet (but see the paper in this volume by Chalmers and McGonigle). In contrast, the question about transitive inferences is one of the most vexed in studies of cognitive development. This is largely because the question imposes some formidable empirical problems for the researcher. In order to be sure that a mistake in a transitive inference task is a genuinely logical one (i.e. a failure to combine two premises to make an inferential judgement), one must be sure that the child can recall the two premises at the time that he is asked the inferential question (i.e. can remember that A>B and B>C when asked the A?C question). This was pointed out some time ago by Bryant and Trabasso (1971) and, ever since we did so, the commonest empirical solution has been to make sure that the children learn the premises thoroughly before they have to face the empirical question.

But this leads to a new problem which was originally pointed out by Perner and Mansbridge (1983). It is that the experimenter might unwittingly be teaching the child something about ordinal relations during the learning period. If a child finds it difficult to remember that A>B and that B>C because he cannot appreciate that A can have different relations to different values, maybe repeated experience with these two pairs will eventually teach him that such two-way relations are possible.

The problem intensifies when one considers the empirical connotations of another requirement for transitive inference tasks for which Bryant and Trabasso (1971) were also responsible. We made the claim that an A>B,

B>C (three value) task is inadequate. The child, we argued, could answer the eventual A?C inferential question in such tasks by remembering that A was the larger when he last saw it or that C was the smaller. Thus the child could answer the question correctly, but illogically, merely by repeating one or both of these remembered values. If, however, one has a task with four premises (A>B, B>C, C>D, D>E) three of the quantities (B, C and D) are the smaller value in one of these pairs and the larger in another. Inferential judgements based on these quantities cannot be dismissed as mere parroting.

This requirement is now generally accepted, but unfortunately it makes the problem of ensuring that children remember the initial premises a much more daunting one. It is quite difficult for a four-year-old child to learn and remember an A>B, B>C, C>D, D>E series.

One way round this difficulty is to present children with the premises at the same time as they are asked the transitive question, but this is not so easy to do without at the same time providing so much information that the need for the inference actually disappears. Ros Pears and I (Pears and Bryant, 1990) have managed an inferential task not with length but with relative position (up–down) in which no learning at all was necessary because the children could see the premises (pairs of different coloured bricks, one on top of the other) at the same time as they were asked the inferential question (the relative position of two of these bricks in a tower of five or six bricks) and we found that even four-year-old children can make respectable transitive inferences, but since this is not a dimension of much importance in children's mathematics I will not dwell on the study any further.

I will turn instead to measurement. If children need to understand transitive inferences in order to make comparisons with the help of measurement, then evidence that children can make such comparisons is also evidence that they can make transitive inferences. We (Bryant and Kopytynska, 1976) gave five-year-old children a simple measurement task in which they were faced with two blocks of wood each with a hole at the top, and were asked to compare the depths of the holes. The children also had a stick, and they used it systematically to measure these depths. Three different experiments of ours confirmed this result, and more recently Miller (1989) has reported an equivalent success with a similar, more meaningful, task (working out which hole Snoopy must be hiding in). It is hard to see how young children could manage as well as they do in these tasks unless they understood the significance of transitive inferences.

Some caution is still needed. Piaget also insisted that children must grasp logical necessity if they are to be judged as truly logical (Smith, 1993). Piaget also thought that the only way that a person can show that he understands the necessity of a logical judgement is by justifying it logically. We are faced with an empirical problem, which is how to establish not only the presence, but also the absence, of the understanding of logical necessity.

Someone who appeals to the logical necessity of a correct solution to a logical problem probably does understand logical necessity. But a child who fails to produce such a justification may not lack this understanding. She may have grasped logical necessity without being able to put it into words.

My rather hesitant conclusion about Piaget's hypothesis on ordinality and transitivity is that it is in the end rather unconvincing. Children may fumble in the seriation task, but they still seem to be able both to work out that a quantity can have more than one relative value and also to use this information in a measuring task. However, we certainly need more data on how they justify what they do in such tasks.

ONE-TO-ONE CORRESPONDENCE AND ADDITIVE REASONING

One sees Piaget at his impressive best in his ideas and his work on correspondence. Here, I believe, he shows an extraordinary freshness of observation and richness in his hypotheses, and I do not think that the world has paid this part of his work the attention that it deserves. This is partly because the world has got rather stuck with one-to-one corres-pondence and has paid scant attention to one-to-many correspondence, and partly because people do not on the whole realise how pervasive the idea of correspondence is in Piaget's theory. I take the opportunity to recommend one of Piaget's last books *Recherches sur les correspondances* (1980) which gives an exciting account of, and some convincing evidence for, his ideas about the role of action and the importance of different kinds of 'co-ordinators' in setting up correspondences.

This remarkable book, however, does not deal directly with mathe-matical understanding and I shall return for the moment to some of Piaget's original ideas. In the rest of this section I shall be following closely the argument that Terezinha Nunes and I developed in our recent book on children's mathematics (Nunes and Bryant, 1996).

How far can one take the understanding of one-to-one correspondence? We have already discussed Piaget's main claim that one-to-one corres-pondence is crucial in number comparisons. But it is also possible that one-to-one correspondence plays a significant role in two of the basic arithmetical operations – addition and subtraction. At first sight this might not seem plausible. Adding, it might be said, is just a matter of joining two quantities, and subtraction of detaching a part of a quantity: and neither action involves relating the individual members of two different sets. But there are addition and subtraction problems whose solution might directly depend on a thorough understanding of this form of correspondence. The most obvious of these are the so-called 'comparison problems' in which children have to make judgements about the difference between two static sets, e.g. 'John has 5 apples: Mary has 8 apples. How many more does

Mary have than John?' These are notoriously difficult problems for young children (Riley, Greeno and Heller, 1983; DeCorte and Verschaffel, 1987; Carpenter and Moser, 1982) and when they fail in them, which they often do even at the age of seven or eight years, it is obvious that they are not using their knowledge of one-to-one correspondence to help them. One-to-one correspondence would help a child by allowing her to realise that part of Mary's set (5 apples) corresponds to John's, that the rest of her set actually represents the difference between the two sets, and thus that the answer to the question is 8–5.

Some time ago Terezinha Nunes and I (Nunes and Bryant, 1991) set out to test this Piagetian analysis in an intervention study. If the analysis is right, we argued, a good way to help children to solve the ordinarily difficult comparison problems would be show them the significance of one-to-one correspondence in the solutions to these problems. We also had another aim in mind. We wanted to contrast spatial and temporal one-to-one correspondence. We already know about the discrepancy in the development of these two forms of correspondence and we wanted to know whether there was also some difference between them in the role that they played in children's mathematical thinking.

The study involved 180 Brazilian children in the age range five to seven years. All the children were pre- and post-tested in a set of comparison problems. Between the pre- and post-test, all children answered a series of six comparison problems and the way that these were presented differed between three groups, two of which were experimental groups and one a control group.

For both experimental groups we devised trials in which we established that the two sets were initially equal by using one-to-one correspondence. The child was asked about the static relationship immediately after this change. Then the experimenter either added some more sweets to, or subtracted some sweets from, the child's set and asked: 'How many more sweets do you have than I have?' In this way we intended to help the children to establish a connection between their knowledge of one-to-one correspondence and the idea of addition/subtraction.

These intervention trials varied between the two experimental groups in one respect. With one group the equal sets were built through a *spatial one-to-one correspondence* procedure. With the other group, the equal sets were shared out, using a *temporal one-to-one correspondence* procedure. The children in the control group simply had to answer the same six comparison problems presented to the other groups.

We found that all three groups did significantly better in the post-test than in the pre-test. However, the group that profited most was the experimental group taught with *spatial correspondence condition*. This supports the idea of the importance of one-to-one correspondence in a basic type of addition/subtraction problem. The difference between spatial and temporal one-to-one correspondence is intriguing, but difficult to interpret. At a rather superficial level one can say that the spatial type of one-to-one correspondence on which Piaget himself concentrated is more important than temporal one-to-one correspondence which is by far the easier option for young children. But why should this be so? My own view is that it is something to do with the simultaneous nature of spatial arrays (all the information is there all the time) as opposed to the successive nature of temporal one-to-one correspondence. But this is a speculation to be sorted out in further studies.

ONE-TO-MANY CORRESPONDENCE AND MULTIPLICATIVE REASONING

Anyone concerned with children's mathematics acknowledges a huge difference in the intellectual demands of additive and multiplicative reasoning. Multiplication poses more formidable problems, and one of the greatest contributions of Piaget to theories of children's mathematical understanding was to show this and to point out the differences between additive and multiplicative reasoning. However, there is a surprise here, because although Piaget did indeed show that some multiplicative tasks are difficult even for teenagers, he also pointed out that some other aspects of multiplication are well within the grasp of much younger children.

The clue to this distinction (largely neglected in most accounts of multiplicative thinking) is one-to-many correspondence. Before I explain why, I must first try to provide a framework for categorising different kinds of multiplication problem.

In our book (Nunes and Bryant, 1996) we argued that multiplication problems fall into three main categories. One category is ratio which can be solved by a one-to-many correspondence situation. A ratio is expressed not by one number but by pairs of numbers, e.g. 1:3, and one-to-many correspondence is involved because inevitably a ratio takes that form.

I will just mention the other two types of problem briefly because they will not play an important role in this paper. One is the category of co-variation problems, in which the child has to relate two variables such as the cost of sweets per kilo. On the whole the well-known proportional problems which Piaget showed to be so difficult for even quite old children were of this type. The third type of multiplicative problem involves sharing (sometimes referred to as 'splits'). There are three values in multiplicative sharing problems which are: the total, the number of recipients and the quota (or the size of the share). The quota and the number of recipients are in inverse relation to each other: as one grows, the other decreases.

Piaget (1952) reached the momentous idea of one-to-many correspondence via his analysis of one-to-one correspondence and transitive inferences. He argued that a child who understands that if $A=B$ and $C=B$, then $A=C$, should also be able to understand that if $A=2B$ and $A=C$, then $C=2B$.

His way of testing this idea was to ask children to set up one-to-one correspondence and also one-to-many correspondence between different sets of objects. He gave them some flowers and some vases, and established that there were two flowers (A) for each vase (B) and thus that (A=2B). The flowers were then set aside but the vases stayed in sight and the children were asked to pick from a box of thin plastic tubes the right number (C) of tubes for there to be one tube for each flower. The children knew that there were two flowers in each vase and only one flower was to be placed in each tube (C=A). Piaget wanted to find out whether they would understand the need to take twice as many tubes as vases (C=2B).

Several children in the five–six year range were completely stumped by this task, and Piaget's claim is that some were in difficulty because they failed to make transitive inferences and others because they could not handle one-to-many correspondence. The important point here, though, is that many did anticipate the relationships in the one-to-many correspondence very well, and Piaget suggests therefore that children as young as five to six years can already understand some aspects of multiplicative relations. Piaget emphatically claimed that these relationships are multiplicative rather than additive because the value of each new set of flowers, in this example, was being considered in relation to the basic set of vases (1×2; 1×3 etc.).

His better known and less optimistic claims about multiplicative reasoning are based on his studies of co-variation which he looked at in the context of young people's scientific concepts (Inhelder and Piaget, 1958; Piaget and Inhelder, 1975). For example, he investigated children's understanding of the proportional relations in the projection of shadows, in the understanding of equilibrium in a T-shaped balance scale and in the concept of probability. These are difficult concepts and, in his research on them, Piaget consistently reported that young people's understanding of proportional relations between variables is a relatively late achievement.

However, it is possible that children's difficulties with proportions in these problems stems from the complexity of the content of the problem rather than from the mathematical relations. The test of this idea is to give proportional problems in more familiar and thus easier contexts.

Several researchers presented students with proportional problems which had more familiar contents. The first attempts in this genre (Karplus and Peterson, 1970; Noelting, 1980a, 1980b; and Hart, 1981) seemed only to confirm Piaget's reservations about children's ability to handle co-variation problems. But some more recent work has indicated that when situations are part of everyday practices where numbers really are important and people usually do computations, children's performance seems to be considerably better. Kaput and Maxwell-West (1994), for example, observed that children's performance in price and speed problems, which in everyday life really are treated as problems that involve computation, is relatively high, and this success raises the possibility that children do understand more about the relationship between variables than Piaget gave them credit for.

There are many situations in everyday life where children readily assume that two variables change together. Bryant (1974), Muller (1978) and Van den Brink and Streefland (1978) have independently observed that young children make judgements about proportional relations in some contexts. Van den Brink and Streefland, for example, noted that, in spontaneous conversations about pictures, children use a natural framework of proportional size relations to evaluate the adequacy of pictures: they can, for example argue that one element in a picture is proportionally too big if compared to another element. Spinillo and Bryant (1991) provided more systematic evidence to support the idea that children of seven years can make judgements based on co-variation when looking at pictures. These studies do not in any way detract from Piaget's original contribution to our understanding of children's ideas about co-variation. He showed that it is a formidable problem for children – and not just for children. It was a momentous conclusion.

TURNING TO VYGOTSKY

To apply Vygotsky to children's mathematics one has to adopt, not a detailed theory, but a general approach. We have to look at the general possibility that cultures play a role in children's understanding of mathematics. The most promising move is to look for examples of the cultural inventions, mentioned earlier, on which Vygotsky laid such emphasis.

Our number system is a hierarchial structure based on decades. The decade structure makes it possible to count generatively. One does not have to remember that the next number after 149 is 150. Anyone who knows the system can generate such numbers on the basis of his/her knowledge of the structure of 10s, 100s and 1,000s.

This structure, which lies at the heart of our mathematical lives, is a cultural invention. It was invented relatively late in the history of mankind, and it is not to be found in all cultures (Saxe, 1981, 1991; Saxe and Posner, 1983). It is not something that children will learn about spontaneously. It is handed on from generation to generation, and it would disappear if it were not taught either formally or informally to successive generations. These are important points for a developmental psychologist, because they mean that the decade structure fits perfectly Vygotsky's idea of a cultural tool. Cultural tools, Vygotsky argued, are inventions which increase intellectual power, and also transform intellectual processes.

Yet we still know relatively little about the way in which children learn about the decade system or about the effects that this learning has on their mathematical understanding. The most arresting evidence is cross-linguistic. Several number systems are more regular from the linguistic point of view than ours. The Chinese, for example, say the equivalent of 'ten-one' where we say eleven: they say 'three-ten' where we say 'thirty'. It now looks as if this linguistic difference might have an effect. Miller and Stigler (1987) compared the way in which four-, five- and six-year-old Taiwanese and American children counted and found quite striking differences. For the most part the Taiwanese children did a great deal better at abstract counting (i.e. just producing the numbers in the correct sequence) and there was a striking difference between the two groups in the counting of the teens which gave the American children a great deal more difficulty than it did the children from Taiwan. When the two groups counted objects, there was absolutely no difference between them in terms of their success in counting each object once but again the Taiwanese children did a great deal better in producing the right number words in the right order.

Miller and Stigler attribute the differences to the regularity of the Chinese system. One cannot rule out the possibility of differences in other factors, such as motivation, playing a part, but the Miller and Stigler explanation looks plausible and receives considerable support from subsequent comparisons by Miura *et al.* (1988) of Japanese and American children's performance in simple mathematical tasks and by reports from Fuson and Kwon (1992a, 1992b) of the considerable achievements of Korean children in complex addition tasks (the Japanese and the Korean number words are a great deal more regular than the English ones).

The differences originally reported by Miller and Stigler go far beyond success in counting. We (Lines, Nunes and Bryant, unpublished paper) recently compared groups of Taiwanese and British children in a shop task which involved money. This shop task was originally devised by Carraher and Schliemann (1990), who asked children to buy certain objects and charged them certain amounts of money. In some cases the children could pay in one denomination (ones or tens), and in others they had to mix denominations (ones and tens) in order to reach the right sum. The condition which mixed denominations was easily the harder of the two, and Carraher and Schliemann rightly argued that this demonstrated that the children were having some difficulty in using the decade structure to solve mathematical problems, at any rate as far as money is concerned.

The Carraher/Schliemann study made an interesting developmental point about growth in the understanding of the decade structure, and our more recent project (Lines, Nunes and Bryant, unpublished paper) suggests that the nature of the linguistic system may have a considerable effect on the way that children become able to use the decade system. For we found not only that British children were worse at counting than Taiwanese children (a replication of Miller and Stigler) but also that, in the shop task, the Taiwanese/British difference in the mixed denominations condition was particularly pronounced. The Taiwanese were no better than the British children when the task was to pay for the purchases in ones, and not much better than the British group when they had to pay in tens. But when the children had to pay in a mixture of tens and ones (10p and 1p or $10 and

$1) the superiority of the Taiwanese children was very striking indeed. It seems that the linguistic advantage helps the Chinese-speaking children not just to count more proficiently but also to grasp the relations between different levels of the decade structure and to use these relations to solve simple problems. The number system becomes a cultural tool far earlier for them than for English-speaking children.

So the nature of the cultural tool affects the way that children learn about it, and so does the context in which they learn about this tool. Children learn about the decade sructure at school but also outside it. The fact that money and other measures are organised in decades means that all children are bound to receive a significant amount of informal instruction about decades outside the classroom.

CONCLUSION

Between them, but in very different ways, Piaget and Vygotsky set the scene for much of the work that has been done over the last twenty years or so on children's mathematical understanding. Piaget's emphasis on logical universals, and Vygotsky's on cultural tools, provide two of the main themes in this research. They are not the only themes, by the way, and not even the only important themes. But they are an immense contribution, and their complementarity, and not just the coincidence of the two men being born in the same year, are a good enough reason for putting them together in one paper.

REFERENCES

Bryant, P. (1974) *Perception and Understanding in Young Children*. London: Methuen.

Bryant, P. and Kopytynska, H. (1976) Spontaneous measurement by young children. *Nature*, 260, 773.

Bryant, P. and Trabasso, T. (1971) Transitive inferences and memory in young children. *Nature*, 232, 456–8.

Carpenter, T. P. and Moser, J. M. (1982) The development of addition and subtraction problem solving. In T. P. Carpenter, J. M. Moser and T. A. Romberg (eds) *Addition and Subtraction*, pp. 10–24. Hillsdale, NJ: Lawrence Erlbaum Associates.

Carraher, T. N. and Schliemann, A. D. (1990) Knowledge of the numeration system among pre-schoolers. In L. P. Steffe and T. Wood (eds) *Transforming Children's Mathematics Education*, pp. 135–41. Hillsdale, NJ: Lawrence Erlbaum Associates.

Cowan, R. and Daniels, H. (1989) Children's use of counting and guidelines in judging relative number. *British Journal of Educational Psychology*, 59, 200–10.

DeCorte, E. and Verschaffel, L. (1987) The effect of semantic (structure on first graders' solution strategies of elementary addition and subtraction word problems. *Journal for Research in Mathematics Education*, 18, 363–81.

Desforges, A. and Desforges, G. (1980) Number-based strategies of sharing in young children. *Educational Studies*, 6, 97–109.

Frydman, O. and Bryant, P. E. (1988) Sharing and the understanding of number equivalence by young children. *Cognitive Development*, 3, 323–39.

Fuson, K. and Kwon, Y. (1992a) Korean children's understanding of multidigit addition and subtraction. *Child Development*, 63, 491–506.

Fuson, K. and Kwon, Y. (1992b) Learning addition and subtraction: effects of number words and other cultural tools. In J. Bideaud, C. Meljac and J.-P. Fischer (eds) *Pathways to number*, pp. 283–306. Hillsdale, NJ: Lawrence Erlbaum Associates.

Hart, K. (1981) *Children's Understanding of Mathematics 11–16*. London: John Murray.

Inhelder, B. and Piaget, J. (1958) *The Growth of Logical Thinking from Childhood to Adolescence*. New York: Basic Books.

Kaput, J. and Maxwell-West, M. (1994) Missing-value proportional reasoning problems: factors affecting informal reasoning patterns. In G. Harel and J. Confrev (eds) *The Development of Multiplicative Reasoning in the Learning of Mathematics*, pp. 237–92. Albany, NY: State University of New York Press.

Karplus, R. and Peterson, R. W. (1970) Intellectual development beyond elementary school II: ratio, a survey. *School Science and Mathematics*, 70, 813–20.

Lines, S., Nunes, T. and Bryant, P. E. (unpublished paper) Number naming systems in English and Chinese: linguistic effects on number understanding and basic mathematical skill.

Miller, K. (1984) The child as the measurer of all things: measurement procedures and the development of quantitative concepts. In C. Sophian (ed.) *Origins of Cognitive Skills*, pp. 193–228. Hillsdale, NJ: Erlbaum.

Miller, K. (1989) Measurement as a tool for thought: the role of measuring procedures in children's understanding of quantitative invariance. *Developmental Psychology*, 25, 589–600.

Miller, K. and Stigler, J. W. (1987) Counting in Chinese: cultural variation in a basic skill. *Cognitive Development*, 2, 279–305.

Miura, I. T., Kim, C. C., Chang, C. and Okamoto, Y. (1988) Effects of language characteristics on children's cognitive representation of number: cross-national comparisons. *Child Development*, 59, 1445–50.

Muller, D. J. (1978) Children's concepts of proportion: an investigation into the claims of Bryant and Piaget. *British Journal of Educational Psychology*, 48, 29–35.

Noelting, G. (1980a) The development of proportional reasoning and the ratio concept, Part I: Differentiation of stages. *Educational Studies in Mathematics*, 11, 217–53.

Noelting, G. (1980b) The development of proportional reasoning and the ratio concept, Part II: Problem-structure at successive stages: Problem-solving strategies and the mechanism of adaptive restructuring. *Educational Studies in Mathematics*, 11, 331–63.

Nunes, T. and Bryant, P. (1991) Correspondencia: un esquema quantitativo basico (one-to-one correspondence as a basic quantitative scheme). *Psicologia: Teoria e Pesquisa*, 7, 273–84.

Nunes, Y. and Bryant, P. (1996) *Children Doing Mathematics*. Oxford: Blackwell.

Pears, R. and Bryant, P. (1990) Transitive inferences by young children about spatial position. *British Journal of Psychology*, 81, 497–510.

Perner, J. and Mansbridge, D. G. (1983) Developmental differences in encoding length series. *Child Development*, 54, 710–19.

Piaget, J. (1952) *The Child's Conception of Number*. London: Routledge and Kegan Paul.

Piaget, J. (1980) *Recherches sur Ies correspondances*. Paris: Presses Universitaires de France.

Piaget, J. and Inhelder, B. (1971) *Mental Imagery in the Child*. London: Routledge and Kegan Paul.

Piaget, J. and Inhelder, B. (1975) *The Origin of the Idea of Chance in Children*. London: Routledge and Kegan Paul.

Piaget, J., Inhelder, B. and Szeminska, A. (1960) *The Child's Conception of Geometry*. London: Routledge and Kegan Paul.

Riley, M., Greeno, J. G. and Heller, J. I. (1983) Development of children's problem solving ability in arithmetic. In H. Ginsburg (ed.) *The Development of Mathematical Thinking*, pp. 153–96. New York: Academic Press.

Saxe, G. (1981) Body parts as numerals: a developmental analysis of numeration among the Oksapmin in Papua New Guinea. *Child Development*, 52, 306–16.

Saxe, G. (1991) *Culture and Cognitive Development: Studies in Mathematical Understanding*. Hillsdale, NJ: Lawrence Erlbaum Associates.

Saxe, G. and Posner, J. K. (1983) The development of numerical cognition: cross-cultural perspectives. In H. Ginsburg (ed.) *The Development of Mathematical Thinking*, pp. 292–318. New York: Academic Press.

Smith, L. (1993) *Necessary Knowledge*. Hove: Lawrence Erlbaum Associates.

Spinillo, A. and Bryant, P. (1991) Children's proportional judgements: the importance of 'half'. *Child Development*, 62, 427–40.

Van den Brink, J. and Streefland, L. (1978) Ratio and proportion in young children (6–8). Osnabruck: Paper presented at the annual conference of the International Group for the Study of the Psychology of Mathematics Education.

Vygotsky, L. (1986) *Thought and Language*. Cambridge, MA: MIT Press.

8 Socializing intelligence

Lauren B. Resnick and Sharon Nelson-Le Gall

At this conference celebrating the births of Piaget and Vygotsky, we want to explore a conception of intelligence that is founded in part on the cultural and developmental theories of Vygotsky but that can find full expression only through joining with the constructivist lines of epistemological theory, for which we are indebted to Piaget. We argue for a view of *intelligence as social practice*, a conception rooted at least as much in theories of social development and social competence as in theories of cognitive development. It is also grounded in our efforts to make sense of and actively contribute to educational programmes aimed at raising the overall cognitive competence and academic achievement of the least educationally advantaged populations of children in our formal educational systems.

Our argument addresses one of the central social and political, as well as scientific, debates of our time: what intelligence is, who has it, and the role of social institutions in developing and sustaining it. *Intelligence* is one of the great constructs of scientific psychology. Perhaps no concept has garnered as much attention from psychologists. Yet after a century of fundamental and applied research on intelligence, there is no single definition of the construct to which all psychologists would agree. And, in the USA at least, fierce battles continue to rage concerning the social and political implications of differences in measured intelligence, without adequate attention to what the measurements mean and how intelligence actually functions in the world (Herrnstein and Murray, 1994).

We present our argument in four parts. First, we argue that interpreting intelligence as a social practice requires a critical expansion of the definition of the construct to include not just the cognitive skills and forms of knowledge that have classically been considered the essence of intelligence, but also a cluster of social performances such as asking questions, striving to master new problems and seeking help in problem solving. One's likelihood of engaging in these social practices of intelligence, furthermore, is as much a matter of how one construes his or her rights, responsibilities and capabilities as of purely cognitive capacities. To put it in oversimplified form (we elaborate later), if you believe that you are *supposed* to be asking questions and learning new things all the time, you *will* ask lots of questions and strive to keep learning.

Second, we show that important individual differences exist in people's beliefs about intelligence and that these beliefs are related to people's tendency to engage in the social practices of intelligence that we define in the first section. Perhaps the most important differences, we argue, relate effort and ability – whether people believe that effort can actually create ability or only compensate for limitations in ability. There are also important differences in what *kind* of effort people put out under conditions of challenge, depending in great part on their beliefs about the nature of intelligence.

Third, we argue that the beliefs and habits that constitute the social practice of intelligence are acquired through processes more akin to what developmentalists have studied as *socialization* than to what they have studied as either cognitive development or learning. Vygotsky's (1978) theory of cognitive development as a process of internalizing socially shared actions and of the role of language in enabling and constraining overall cognitive development forms a point of contact between our notion of intelligence as socialized and the more traditional views of intelligence as a purely cognitive competence.

Fourth, we ask how schools and other institutions charged with promoting human development might function to socialize intelligence as we define it here. In the concluding section, we lay out a set of hypotheses that go well beyond individual development to embrace concepts of social design and mechanisms of cultural change.

(RE-)DEFINING INTELLIGENCE

We begin this section by briefly reviewing several major strands of psychological theorizing about intelligence, from individual difference and mental measurement theorists through Piaget. We then present our own definition of intelligence as social practice, a view that extends Vygotsky's interpretation of learning and cognitive development as inherently social and builds on more recent sociocultural theories as well.

Intelligence as individual mental abilities

Individual difference psychologists – from Binet to modern psychometricians – can be roughly divided into two camps. One, launched by Binet (Binet and Simon, 1905) himself, defines intelligence very loosely and pragmatically: some people seem to learn more quickly and behave more adaptively than others. Rather than trying to define precisely the mechanisms that make for this adaptive capacity, Binet collected a broad band of questions that children might be expected to learn to answer as they grew up. He used the collection as a whole, scaled according to empirically derived age expectations, to compare the relative intelligence of children. This general knowledge criterion, presumably reflecting speed and ease of learning, was carried into pencil-and-paper intelligence testing by Terman (1916, 1919) and others who developed measures of *general intelligence*, which largely became known as IQ.

Historically, IQ was understood to point to differences in mental ability, not to social competence or performance (although many intelligence tests do contain some items that test knowledge of appropriate social behaviour). It was also assumed to be largely determined genetically and to set firm limits on how much learning could be expected of an individual. This question of intelligence as limiting learning is an issue to which we return later. For now, what is important to note is that measurers of general intelligence essentially gave up on defining intelligence, except to insist that it is a mental capacity of some kind.

Another group of individual difference psychologists – for example, Thorndike (1926), Thurston (1938), Carroll (1966), Guilford (1967), Sternberg (1977) – kept looking for differentiated components of intelligence, often using increasingly sophisticated techniques of factor analysis and cluster analysis. For the most part, this research has focused on purely cognitive capabilities, but there have been persistent efforts to broaden the concept of what counts as intelligent, as in Howard Gardner's (1993) concept of 'multiple intelligences', which encompass such abilities as music and the visual arts. Some theorists have also expanded the term *intelligence* to cover more social competencies, for example, Robert Sternberg's efforts to define, measure and even teach 'practical intelligence' (Sternberg and Wagner, 1986). Even these theories, however, treat intelligence as an attribute of the individual, not as a set of practices in which individuals adapt and tune their behaviours to immediate contexts of performance.

Intelligence as structures for reasoning

Piaget's interest in human intelligence was entirely different in kind from any of the mental measurers. Uninterested in individual differences, he focused an entire research career on the question of what underlay the adaptive mental capacities of the human species (Piaget, 1960, 1970a, 1970b). His answer, well known to participants at this conference, was that humans are biologically prepared to develop certain logico-deductive structures. Piagetian theory holds that each individual develops these structures, along with certain fundamental mathematical and scientific concepts for which the logical structures are essential, through interactive engagement with the world. Piaget himself was never very clear about the nature of this interaction. Some 'social Genevans' (e.g. Doise and Mugny, 1984; Perret-Clermont, 1980) have argued that social interaction, especially the cognitive conflict created by certain forms of disagreement with peers, is an essential engine of the development of intelligence. For most of these theorists, however, intelligence itself remained an essentially individual, biologically founded construction.

Intelligence as acquisition of cultural tools and practices

Vygotsky is the first modern theorist of cognitive development to place social interaction at its heart. In fact, many of Vygotsky's interpreters (e.g. Cole and Scribner, 1974; Rogoff, 1990; Wertsch, 1985), along with other theorists of *situated cognition* (e.g. Lave, 1988; Suchman, 1992; see also Resnick *et al.*, in press), have argued that learning and cognitive development are a matter of absorbing appropriate cultural practice through (scaffolded) participation in activities important in the society.

Vygotsky (1978, p. 88) proposed that the development of human mental functioning 'presupposes a specific social nature and a process by which children grow into the intellectual life of those around them'. In each sociocultural context, children participate in both formal and informal instructional exchanges that bring about their adaptive functioning within those contexts. Through reciprocal processes of social interaction, children develop a system of cognitive representations as interpretive frameworks and make a commitment to the common value system and sets of behavioural norms promoted in their sociocultural context. This process of socialization thus incorporates the acquisition and use of knowledge, ways of representing that knowledge, and ways of thinking and reasoning with that knowledge. These, along with language, are the 'cultural tools' that might be said to constitute intelligence.

Intelligence as habits of learning

The idea of cultural tools for reasoning and thinking takes us part of the way towards the redefinition of intelligence that we are seeking. We would like to go further, though, to connect the cultural practice conception with the notion of general intelligence as the ability to learn well and easily. This is important, we believe, because *our* culture particularly rewards certain patterns of learning – those connected with success in school and other closely related institutions – and provides socially and economically disfavoured places in society for those who do not engage in these favoured ways of learning. It is for these social justice reasons, as well as the hope of confirming theories of what makes people good learners (i.e. 'smart'), that the prospect of *teaching intelligence* has fascinated many psychologists.

Different theorists of intelligence have tried teaching the cognitive skills that have been central in their theories: the skills that are directly tested on IQ tests, such as techniques for recognizing or generating analogies (e.g. Pellegrino and Glaser, 1982), Piagetian logical structures (e.g. Shayer and Adey, 1981) and metacognitive strategies (see Brown *et al.*, 1983). There is a repeated pattern in the results of these experiments. Most of the training experiments were successful in producing immediate gains in performance on the kinds of tasks taught. But, with the exception of the recent Shayer and Adey work (which involved a much more extended and ambitious intervention than the laboratory training studies), subjects in the studies ceased using the cognitive techniques in which they had been trained as soon as the specific conditions of training were removed. In other words, they became *capable* of performing the skill that was taught, but they acquired no general *habit* of using it and no capacity to judge for themselves when it was useful.

This repeated finding is just what one would expect from an intelligence-as-cultural-practice perspective. Cognitive activity and intelligent behaviour occur in a socially organized environment. Culturally organized environments produce constraints on what affordances can be utilized by whom and when (Goodnow, 1990a, 1990b; Reed, 1993). The objects and situations experienced in an environment provide affordances because they possess specific characteristics or properties. These particular properties are not intrinsic; rather, they are properties that exist with respect to agents who will perceive or utilize them. Reed (1993) observes that learning affordance properties of objects, events and places requires practice and experience that are typically gained through consistent encouragement and even instruction from other individuals.

Subjects in the cognitive skill training experiments learned to engage in a particular practice (e.g. rehearsing, forming mnemonics) in a particular environmental situation. In a new situation, the learned practices appeared to have no relevance. The practices were tuned to the affordances and environmental presses of the training situation. When those affordances and presses were not perceived in the new situation, the learned practices disappeared.

This analysis suggests that, if we want to see a general 'ability to learn easily' develop in children, we need a definition of intelligence that is as attentive to robust *habits of mind* and how they are nurtured as it is to the specifics of thinking processes or knowledge structures. As we show in the next section, there is reason to believe that people's habits of thinking are heavily influenced by their beliefs about intelligence. For now, we want to propose a working definition of intelligence that will structure the remainder of our paper.

Intelligence as a social construction

Our definition of intelligence treats intelligence as a social construction, as much a matter of how individuals construe themselves and their action in the world as of what specific skills they have at a given moment. *People who are intelligent-in-practice*:

- *believe they have the right (and the obligation) to understand things and make things work*. Goodnow (1990a, 1990b) observes that people do not merely acquire knowledge, cognitive skills and strategies, or learn to apply that knowledge or skill in problem solving. They also learn that we are expected to acquire some pieces or forms of knowledge and skill and that some domains of knowledge or skill 'belong' more to some people than to others. Our intelligence-as-cultural-practice view of intelligence treats acquiring knowledge and new skills as the responsibility of each individual.

- *believe that problems can be analysed, that solutions often come from such analysis and that* they *are capable of that analysis.* This belief in one's efficacy to acquire valued knowledge and skills and to use these in solving valued problems can be socialized through the tacit messages embedded in the routines of daily practices.
- *have a toolkit of problem-analysis tools and good intuitions about when to use them.* These might be metacognitive skills, analogical reasoning skills, quantitative analysis skills or a host of other specific learnable capabilities.
- *know how to ask questions, seek help and get enough information to solve problems.* In this definition of intelligence, making use of the social environment is an integral part of the understanding process.
- *have* habits of mind *that lead them to actively use the toolkit of analysis skills and the various strategies for acquiring information.* None of the cognitive skills and social strategies that are elements of intelligence-in-practice are functional unless the individual routinely uses them and seeks occasions to use them.

PATTERNS OF BELIEF AND BEHAVIOUR: RELATING EFFORT AND ABILITY

We are concerned in this section with habits of mind, the tendency to use one's toolkit of analysis skills and one's strategies for gathering information. We turn to a body of research that has been examining the factors that seem to shape these habits, factors that have much to do with people's beliefs about the relations between effort and ability. People differ markedly in these beliefs, and their beliefs are closely related to the amount and above all to the kinds of effort they exert in situations of learning or problem solving.

Most research on these differences has been carried out by social developmentalists interested in *achievement goal orientation.* Different kinds of achievement goals can affect not only how much effort people put into learning tasks but also the *kinds* of effort. Several classes of achievement goals have been identified that are associated with different conceptions of success and failure and different beliefs about the self, learning tasks and task outcomes (Ames, 1984; Dweck and Leggett, 1988; Nicholls, 1979, 1984). Two broad classes of goals have been identified: *performance-*

oriented and *learning-oriented* (these are the terms used by Dweck and her colleagues; Nicholls used the terms *ego-involved* and *task-involved*).

People with performance goals strive to obtain positive evaluations of their ability and to avoid giving evidence of inadequate ability relative to others. Performance goals are associated with a view of ability as an unchangeable, global entity that is *displayed* in task performance, revealing the individual either to have or to lack ability. This view of ability or aptitude has sometimes been termed an *entity theory of intelligence.*

In contrast, people with learning goals generally strive to develop their ability with respect to particular tasks. Learning goals are associated with a view of aptitude as something that is mutable through effort and is *developed* by taking an active stance towards learning and mastery opportunities. Learning goals are associated with a view of ability as a repertoire of skills continuously expandable through one's efforts. Accordingly, this view of aptitude has been labelled an *incremental theory of intelligence* (Dweck and Leggett, 1988).

People who hold incremental theories of intelligence tend to invest energy to learn something new or to increase their understanding and mastery of tasks. But brute energy alone does not distinguish them from people with entity theories. Incremental theorists are particularly likely to apply self-regulatory, metacognitive skills when they encounter task difficulties, to focus on analysing the task and trying to generate and execute alternative strategies. In general, they try to garner resources for problem solving wherever they can: from their own store of cognitive learning strategies and from others from whom they strategically seek help (Dweck, 1988; Nelson-Le Gall, 1990; Nelson-Le Gall and Jones, 1990). In general, these individuals display continued high levels of task-related effort in response to difficulty. Thus performance goals place the greater effort necessary for mastering challenging tasks in conflict with the need to be regarded as already competent, whereas learning goals lead to adaptive motivational patterns that can produce a quality of task engagement and commitment to learning that fosters high levels of achievement over time.

The achievement goals that individuals pursue also appear to influence the inferences they make about effort and ability. Performance goals are associated with the inference that effort and ability are negatively related in determining achievement outcomes; so high effort is taken as a sign of low ability (Dweck and Leggett, 1988). Learning goals, by contrast, are associated with the inference that effort and ability are positively related, so that greater effort creates and makes evident more ability.

This body of research on achievement goal orientation shows that the beliefs and the habits of mind that we have defined as the practices of intelligence are associated. It shows, furthermore, that there are individual differences in beliefs about the nature of intelligence and, therefore, in associated practices. Where do these beliefs come from? How are the habits of practice acquired? We address these questions in the next section.

ACQUIRING HABITS OF MIND THROUGH SOCIALIZATION

Persistent habits and deeply held beliefs about the self and human nature in general are not the kinds of things that one learns from direct teaching and certainly not from school-organized lessons. They are, instead, acquired through the processes that developmentalists usually call *social-ization*. The term *socialization* refers to the incorporation of the individual as a member of a community. As soon as a child is born, adults and other knowledgeable individuals begin to contribute to the child's socialization by arranging the environment and the tasks encountered in it and by guiding the child's attention to and participation in the community's valued practices. Socialization is the process by which children acquire the standards, values and knowledge of their society.

Socialization proceeds not so much through direct formal instruction of the young or novice individual, although there are instances in which direct instruction or tutoring occurs. Rather, it proceeds via social interaction, through observation and modelling, cooperative participation and scaffold-ing. It depends, furthermore, on the negotiation of mutual expectations, that is, intersubjectivity. We readily acknowledge the socialization process, its function and products in informal, everyday out-of-school settings such as the family. But, with few exceptions, psychologists fail to recognize its role in intellectual functioning in more formally organized contexts such as schools.

Individual differences in beliefs about effort and ability are, we assume, socialized by different patterns of family belief and practice. But there are also broad societal differences. In the USA, most adults recognize ability as an inherently stable characteristic of individuals, one that is unequally distributed among the human population and not subject to being increased by personal or environmental influence (Nicholls, 1984; Weiner, 1974). Most also tend to hold the view that effort and ability are distinct, negatively related causes of achievement outcomes. In other words, the dominant cultural norm in the USA is an entity theory of intelligence.

These assumptions about ability and effort are shared throughout our society and promulgated by our societal institutions (Howard, 1991); it is not surprising, therefore, to see them clearly manifested in most tradi-tionally structured formal schooling settings. In such classrooms, direct comparisons of one student's work and learning outcomes with another's are frequent and often public. Teachers and students find it 'normal' that some students do not learn what is taught and do not achieve as well as others. When the emphasis in the classroom or the school is on relative ability and (presumptively associated) performance outcomes, and when instructional policies and practices seek to sort students by aptitude, students and teachers alike are more likely to focus on *performance* than on *learning* goals.

In other cultures, however, effort and ability are not viewed as independent dimensions. It has been reported, for example, that, in several Asian cultures (e.g. Chinese and Japanese), people are typically socialized to espouse and act on the belief that high effort and perseverance are the keys to successful performance; indeed, perseverance is even a moral obligation. The positive orientation towards hard work and effort that Japanese people are socialized to adopt conveys a shared belief that ability can be changed and that it refines and enhances the self (Holloway, 1988; Peak, 1993; Stevenson and Lee, 1990). People in such cultures behave as if they pursue learning goals. This alternative view about the relation of effort and ability is likewise reflected in these societies' educational philosophies and is promulgated by their educational institutions.

In their extensive comparative studies of US, Japanese and Chinese education systems, Stevenson and Stigler (1992) have described in substantial detail a very different pattern of beliefs and practices in Chinese and Japanese schools than in ours. Differences in organization, expectation and practice can be detected as early as preschool (Peak, 1986, 1993; Tobin, Wu, and Davidson, 1989). These differences in motivational orientation and their associated institutional support may have much to do with the generally higher academic achievement in these countries.

In Japan, folk beliefs place more emphasis on social competence as a component of intelligence than is the case for laypersons in the USA (Holloway, 1988). Being an effective speaker and listener, being good at getting along with others and taking another person's point of view are all aspects of social competence that tend to be viewed as controllable by the individual. This emphasis on the quality of interactions and relations between individuals and their social environment reinforces the development of a sense of connectedness and collective identity that is important, in that failure in performance becomes a failure for others as well as the individual.

INSTITUTIONAL DESIGNS FOR SOCIALIZING INTELLIGENCE

In this final section, we consider how schools might be organized to deliberately socialize learning goal orientations in children. We focus our attention on American schools – the only ones we know well, the ones in which we have an opportunity to test the hypotheses that we outline here.

The possibility that effort actually creates ability, that people can become smart by working hard at the right kinds of learning tasks, has never been taken seriously in America (Resnick, 1995). Certain educational initiatives and programmes have instantiated some aspects of a learning-oriented motivational design, a design in which practices assume that well-directed effort can create ability and not just reveal its limits. For example, Edmonds and his associates (1979) described characteristics of schools in which poor and minority students were succeeding beyond normal expectations. Among the features of these schools were the setting of high expectations for achievement and frequent assessment of children against these expectations. Jaime Escalante, a mathematics teacher in Los Angeles, succeeded in teaching advanced placement calculus to some of the poorest and, supposedly, most difficult to teach students in California's schools (Escalante and Dirmann, 1990).

Jaime Escalante, educators working within the Effective Schools movement and others who have been able to raise achievement levels among traditionally low-achieving populations of students, worked on motivational characteristics of teaching and learning. They did this by changing fundamental institutional norms, expectations and practices (in Escalante's case, within a classroom; in Effective Schools, within a whole school). Working with students judged by others, and often by themselves, as weak or even candidates for remediation, they placed students in honours programmes or held out expectations for above-normal achievement. Although the organizers of these programmes did not speak explicitly to theories of personal motivation, they all implicitly depended on changes in the mediating motivational characteristics of students. That is, the greater the level of effort invested by students in all programmes, their persistence in courses that were – at least initially – difficult for them, and the subsequent greater learning and achievement that they showed were presumably partly a function of changes in their motivational orientations.

Each of these programmes and others like them, however, have had to work against beliefs widely held in American society and influential in its educational institutions: namely, that what individuals can learn and what schools can teach are largely determined by ability, and that ability is largely unalterable by effort or environmentally offered opportunities (Howard, 1991, 1995). The existence of cultures that appear to promote overall tendencies to learning rather than to performance raises a fundamental question for American schooling: might we, by systematically altering some of our schooling practices, create more learning-oriented motivational patterns and, thereby, higher achievement?

American researchers have typically studied different goal orientations as if they were individual dispositions, whereas the role of the schooling environment as contextual influences on achievement goal orientations is relatively unstudied. We know that learning goals can be elicited and made differentially salient by situational or instructional demands (e.g. Ames, 1992; Jagacinski and Nicholls, 1984). Several structures of the classroom environment have been found to have an impact on student motivation and are largely controlled by teachers (Rosenholtz and Simpson, 1984). Included among these are the design of academic tasks and activities, the evaluation practices employed and the distribution of authority and responsibility in the classroom (Ames and Archer, 1988; Nelson-Le Gall, 1992, 1993; Resnick, 1995).

The belief that institutional demands and rewards can change psychological belief structures is held intuitively by many educators and lay people. The effects of such institutional features on individual motivational orientations, however, have not been examined directly. Similarly, although research has shown that certain motivational orientations raise performance on particular tasks, it has not shown that these orientations raise overall academic achievement. Working in collaboration with the educators in a number of schools that have decided to try to implement an overall school programme that promotes learning goal orientations and that treats effort, rather than aptitude, as the primary determinant of learning results, we are planning a research programme that will examine four interrelated hypotheses that derive from the arguments we have developed here.

First, we will seek evidence that instructional environments can be created that systematically and in a sustained way evoke learning goals and their associated behaviours. Such environments would, by our hypothesis, be those in which there is a continuous press for all students to engage in strategic learning behaviours, such as testing their own understanding, developing arguments and explanations, providing justifications and adhering to discipline-appropriate standards of evidence and reasoning. Furthermore, an instructional environment that evokes learning goals is likely to be one in which beliefs in each student's capacity to engage in these strategic learning behaviours are communicated both explicitly and implicitly. Finally, an environment that evokes and supports learning goals is likely to be one in which expectations of accomplishment are clear, students understand the evaluative criteria and often judge their own work, and there is clear feedback to students about how they are progressing towards a public standard of accomplishment. Working with our school-based collaborators, we will be building a set of tools for analysing the extent to which these features are present in classrooms throughout the school. These tools will be used both to produce structured observational research data and as a basis for training teachers in ways of organizing their own and their students' work to maximize these features.

Second, we will test the hypothesis that long-term participation in environments that evoke learning goals also changes students' beliefs about what it takes to succeed academically. In our collaborating schools and classrooms, we will measure student beliefs and motivational orientations at several different times during their participation in classrooms that make learning goals salient. This means following students for at least a whole school year and preferably longer. It also makes it desirable to study schools in which entire faculties are creating environments that make learning goals salient. Students would then be spending a greater proportion of their time in such environments, and it would be more likely, therefore, that fundamental belief changes would occur.

Third, we surmise that teachers' capacity to initiate and maintain incremental environments is partly a function of their beliefs about their students' capacities for learning and about their own efficacy as teachers. Using interviews and questionnaires, we will examine teachers' beliefs at different stages of their participation in our collaborative programme. We will then relate teachers' beliefs to their observed instructional activity and to interactions with students in their classrooms.

Fourth and finally, all of these motivational factors are of interest as mediators of student achievement. This means that we must examine a number of indicators of student achievement (e.g. standardized test scores, performance assessments, portfolio results, teacher grades) and relate differences and changes in these indicators to all of the motivational and behavioural data on schools, classrooms, teachers and students.

This is a form of research in which no sharp lines can be drawn between development and research, between our collaborative work with school staffs in developing new school environments and our joint evaluation of their effects. The research is planned as a series of iterative development and study cycles in which social and institutional design principles are actively merged with psychological theory and empirical research methods. Only in such long-term, institutionally based design experiments will it be possible to evaluate possibilities for a radical rethinking of the nature of intelligence and its relation to social beliefs and practices of our society.

REFERENCES

Ames, C. (1984). Competitive, cooperative, and individualistic goal structures: A motivational analysis. In R. Ames and C. Ames (eds), *Research on Motivation in Education* vol. 1, pp. 177–207. San Diego, CA: Academic Press.

Ames, C. (1992). Classrooms: Goals, structures, and student motivation. *Journal of Educational Psychology*, 84, 261–71.

Ames, C. and Archer, J. (1988). Achievement goals in the classroom: Students' learning strategies and motivation processes. *Journal of Educational Psychology*, 80, 260–7.

Binet, A. and Simon, T. (1905). The development of intelligence in children. *L'Année Psychologique*, 163–91. Also in T. Shipley (ed.) (1961). *Classics in Psychology*. New York: Philosophical Library.

Brown, A. L., Bransford, J. D., Ferrara, R. A. and Campione, J. C. (1983). Learning, remembering, and understanding. In J. Flavell and E. M. Markman (eds), *Handbook of child psychology* (4th edn), vol. 3, *Cognitive Development*, pp. 515–629. New York: Wiley.

Carroll, J. B. (1966). Factors of verbal achievement. In A. Anastasi (ed.), *Testing Problems in Perspective*. Washington, DC: American Council on Education.

Cole, M. and Scribner, S. (1974). *Culture and Thought*. New York: Wiley.

Doise, W. and Mugny, G. (1984). *The Social Development of the Intellect*. Oxford: Pergamon Press.

Dweck, C. S. (1988). Motivation. In R. Glaser and A. Lesgold (eds), *Handbook of Psychology and Education*, pp. 187–239. Hillsdale, NJ: Erlbaum.

Dweck, C. S. and Leggett, E. L. (1988). A social-cognitive approach to motivation and personality. *Psychological Review*, 95, 256–73.

Edmonds, R. (1979). Effective schools for the urban poor. *Educational Leadership*, 37, 15–23.

Escalante, J. and Dirmann, J. (1990). The Jaime Escalante math program. *Journal of Negro Education*, 59, 407–23.

Gardner, H. (1993). *Multiple Intelligences: The Theory in Practice*. New York: Basic Books.

Goodnow, J. J. (1990a). The socialization of cognition: What's involved? In J. W. Stigler, R. A. Shweder and G. Herdt (eds), *Cultural Psychology: Essays on Comparative Human Development*, pp. 259–86. Cambridge: Cambridge University Press.

Goodnow, J. J. (1990b). Using sociology to extend psychological accounts of cognitive development. *Human Development*, 33, 81–107.

Guilford, J. B. (1967). *The Nature of Human Intelligence*. New York: McGraw-Hill.

Herrnstein, R. J. and Murray, C. (1994). *The Bell Curve: Intelligence and Class Structure in American Life*. New York: Free Press.

Holloway, S. (1988). Concepts of ability and effort in Japan and the U.S. *Review of Educational Research*, 58, 327–45.

Howard, J. (1991). *Getting Smart: The Social Construction of Intelligence*. Lexington, MA: Efficacy Institute.

Howard, J. (1995). You can't get there from here: The need for a new logic in education reform. *Daedalus*, 124, 85–92.

Jagacinski, C. and Nicholls, J. (1984). Conceptions of ability and related affects in task involvement and ego involvement. *Journal of Educational Psychology*, 76, 909–19.

Lave, J. (1988). *Cognition in Practice: Mind, Mathematics and Culture in Everyday Life*. Cambridge: Cambridge University Press.

Nelson-Le Gall, S. (1990). Academic achievement orientation and help-seeking behavior in early adolescent girls. *Journal of Early Adolescence*, 10, 176–90.

Nelson-Le Gall, S. (1992). Perceiving and displaying effort in achievement settings. In T. Tomlinson (ed.), *Motivating Students to Learn: Overcoming Barriers to High Achievement*, pp. 225–44). Berkeley, CA: McCutchan Publishing.

Nelson-Le Gall, S. (1993). Children's instrumental help-seeking: Its role in the social construction of knowledge. In R. Hertz-Lazarowitz and N. Miller (eds), *Interaction in Cooperative Groups: The Theoretical Anatomy of Group Learning*, pp. 49–68. New York: Cambridge University Press.

Nelson-Le Gall, S. and Jones, E. (1990). Cognitive-motivational influences on children's help-seeking. *Child Development*, 61, 581–9.

Nicholls, J. (1979). Quality and equality in intellectual development: The role of motivation in education. *American Psychologist*, 34, 1071–84.

Nicholls, J. (1984). Achievement motivation: Conceptions of ability, subjective experience, task choice and performance. *Psychological Review*, 91, 328–46.

Peak, L. (1986). Training learning skills and attitudes in Japanese early education settings. In E. Fowler (ed.), *Early Experience and the Development of Competence*, pp. 111–23. San Francisco: Jossey-Bass.

Peak, L. (1993). Academic effort in international perspective. In T. Tomlinson (ed.), *Motivating Students to Learn: Overcoming Barriers to High Achievement*, pp. 41–59. Berkeley, CA: McCutchan Publishing.

Pellegrino, J. W. and Glaser, R. (1982). Analyzing aptitudes for learning: Inductive reasoning. In R. Glaser (ed.), *Advances in Instructional Psychology*, vol. 2, pp. 269–345. Hillsdale, NJ: Erlbaum.

Perret-Clermont, A.-N. (1980). *Social Interaction and Cognitive Development in Children*. New York: Academic Press.

Piaget, J. (1960). *The Psychology of Intelligence*. Peterson, NJ: Littlefield, Adams.

Piaget, J. (1970a). Piaget's theory. In P. H. Mussen (ed.), *Carmichael's Manual of Child Psychology*, vol. 1. New York: Wiley.

Piaget, J. (1970b). *Genetic Epistemology*. New York: W. W. Norton.

Reed, E. (1993). The intention to use a specific affordance: A conceptual framework for psychology. In R. Wozniak and K. Fisher (eds), *Development in Context*, pp. 45–76. Hillsdale, NJ: Erlbaum.

Resnick, L. B. (1995). From aptitude to effort: A new foundation for our schools. *Daedalus*, 124, 55–62.

Resnick, L. B., Saljo, R., Pontecorvo, C. and Burge, B. (in press). *Discourse, Tools, and Reasoning: Situated Cognition and Technologically Supported Environments*. Heidelberg: Springer-Verlag.

Rogoff, B. (1990). *Apprenticeship in Thinking: Children's Guided Participation in Culture*. New York: Oxford University Press.

Rosenholtz, S. and Simpson, C. (1984). The formation of ability conceptions: Developmental trend or social construction. *Review of Educational Research*, 54, 31–63.

Shayer, M. and Adey, P. (1981). *Towards a Science of Science Teaching: Cognitive Development and Curriculum Demand*. London: Heinemann.

Sternberg, R. J. (1977). Intelligence, information processing, and analogical reasoning: The componential analysis of human abilities. Hillsdale, NJ: Erlbaum.

Sternberg, R. J. and Wagner, R. K. (1986). *Practical Intelligence: Nature and Origins of Competence in the Everyday World*. Cambridge: Cambridge University Press.

Stevenson, H. and Lee, S. (1990). Contexts of achievement: A study of American, Chinese, and Japanese children. *Monographs of the Society for Research in Child Development*, 55, 1 and 2, serial no. 221.

Stevenson, H. and Stigler, J. (1992). *The Learning Gap: Why our Schools are Failing and What we can Learn from Japanese and Chinese Education*. New York: Summitt Books.

Suchman, H. (1992). *Plans and Situated Actions: The Problem of Human–Machine Interaction*. Cambridge: Cambridge University Press.

Terman, L. M. (1916). *The Measurement of Intelligence*. Boston: Houghton Mifflin.

Terman, L. M. (1919). *The Intelligence of School Children: How Children Differ in Ability*. Boston: Houghton Mifflin.

Thorndike, E. L. (1926). *Measurement of Intelligence*. New York: Teachers College, Columbia University.

Thurstone, L. L. (1938). Primary mental abilities. *Psychometric Monographs*, 1 (whole no.).

Tobin, J., Wu, D. and Davidson, D. (1989). *Preschool in Three Cultures: Japan, China, and the United States*. New Haven, CT: Yale University Press.

Vygotsky, L. S. (1978). *Mind in Society: The Development of Higher Psychological Processes* (M. Cole, V. John-Steiner, S. Scribner and E. Souberman, eds). Cambridge, MA: Harvard University Press.

Weiner, B. (1974). *Achievement Motivation and Attribution Theory*. Morristown, NJ: General Learning Press.

Wertsch, J. V. (1985) *Vygotsky and the Social Formation of Mind*. Cambridge, MA: Harvard University Press.

9 Expertise and cognitive development
Seeking a connection

Robin N. Campbell

This session was supposed to be about cognitive skills and domain specificity. I confess that when I agreed to be a discussant I was unsure what was intended by this designation. My knowledge of Piaget persuaded me that he was interested both in domain-specific thinking and in the domain-general structures and processes that support such thinking. Throughout his many and mighty works there was a pattern of studying development across a range of specific domains – distinguished by *content* – followed by a synthesis of these separate developmental progressions in a general theory of development. 'Domain specificity' is now generally used as a buzz-phrase for the sort of results reported by Chi (e.g. Chi, 1978; Chi and Koeske, 1983); namely that if motivated to acquire expertise in some domain – for example, dinosaur taxonomy – very young children will seem to do so, so much so that they come to function in that domain much as an adult expert would. I wonder, though, if Chi has the courage of her convictions? Would she eat a dish of wild mushrooms picked and prepared by a four-year-old expert in the taxonomy of the large fungi? But leaving questions of validity aside, it is difficult to make a connection between these findings and the products of Piaget's usual methods. After all, in all but his earliest work he took considerable pains to present children with unfamiliar tasks – tasks in which no expertise had been accumulated, no doubt for the excellent reason that he wanted to be sure that he was studying *thinking* rather than well-grooved habits and heuristics executed without effort or reflection (see Campbell and Olson, 1990).

A bizarre example of an attempted connection between these types of work would be to suggest that obsessive pre-school dinosaur experts might show more understanding of number conservation or quantification of class-inclusion if the standard tasks were put to them using dinosaurs rather than the usual beads or counters! But this *gedanken*-experiment – I assume imprudently that no facilitation would occur – only serves to expose the ambiguities of the word 'domain' and the limits of this sort of expertise. Probably the notion of expertise is only applicable to certain domains and not to others. What would it mean to be an expert in the domain of 1–1 correspondence or even in conservation? It seems likely that the all-or-nothing character of these achievements precludes the application of the concept of expertise.

I also gave some thought to the question of whether and how the notion of domain specificity could be applied to Vygotsky's work. One of the most remarkable passages in all Vygotsky occurs on the first page of *Thought and Language* and it seems to declare a clear interest in the linkages between domains and the development of such links, rather than in the development of the particular domains themselves (Vygotsky, 1962, p. 1):

> [In the old psychology] it was taken for granted that the relation between two given functions never varied; that perception, for example, was always connected in an identical way with attention, memory with perception, thought with memory. As constants, these relations could be, and were, factored out and ignored in the study of the separate functions. Because the relations remained in fact inconsequential, the development of consciousness was seen as determined by the autonomous development of the single functions. Yet all that is known about psychic development indicates that its very essence lies in the change of the interfunctional structure of consciousness. Psychology must make these relations and their developmental changes the main problem, the focus of study.

Vygotsky then moves on to argue that this shift of focus is necessary for productive study of the relation between speech and thought. But these domains – attention, perception, memory, thought – are distinguished not by content but by *process*. That is, Vygotsky's prescription offers nothing specific to the study of the development of reasoning about dinosaurs or any other content-defined domain. Rather, it is a general prescription to be applied to the development of any field in which we express our understanding and mastery by means of language.

My final preliminary thought about the topic was that perhaps what was intended was an examination of the propositions (1) that all *thinking* might be domain specific; (2) that different domains might require different thinking skills; and (3) that these different skills might not be supported by any domain-independent structures and processes of the sort outlined by Piaget. At least there is some meat in this idea (cf. Carey, 1985), even if it seems excessively radical. We do find islands of apparently thoughtful competence in some special populations or cases, and the appeal to horizontal décalage to link together achievements which seem to involve the same thinking skills can come to seem absurd when the décalage spans ten years or more – as it does in the case of loss of egocentricity, for example. However, from a phenomenological point of view one kind of thinking feels much like another, and our whole educational system is based on the idea that teaching subjects are not cognitive islands. It seems likely that an eclectic position embracing both domain-general and domain-specific processes will prevail here (cf. Sternberg, 1989)

That, then, was the outcome of my preliminary thinking about our topic for this session. I was relieved that I was to be a mere discussant rather than obliged to offer a main paper, since it was not at all obvious to me how to deal with the topic.

When I came to examine the two papers, however, I was somewhat perplexed by their contents. To take the paper by Resnick and Le Gall first, I found it rather difficult to make any comment on it at all. It seemed to have nothing much to say about Piaget or Vygotsky, and it displayed no obvious connection to the issues associated with domain specificity. On the positive side, it made some suggestions about how educational practice might be improved, but this is unfortunately a domain in which *I* have no expertise! I suppose that their proposal that certain general habits of mind might be acquired by particular regimes of socialization and education amounts to a rejection of the idea that there are no domain-independent thinking skills. And their proposals might be relatable in a more specific way to Vygotskian concepts: for example, they make the reasonable claim that any individual's potential for learning – or 'zone of proximal development' – is as much a function of these regimes of social-ization and education as of the constitution of the individual. However, I have to say that I find the distinction which they draw between 'perfor-mance goals' and 'learning goals' elusive. Certainly, they associate some personality traits with the pursuit of the one, and others with the pursuit of the other, but what defines the difference between these two sorts of goal is unstated and surely tenuous. So too is the distinction between 'entity' and 'incremental' theories of intelligence. If I were a head teacher and you advised me to 'deliberately socialize learning goal orientation', I would of course murmur that as a mere head teacher I had no powers to determine curriculum or teaching methods, but I would also wonder what on earth you had in mind. On the other hand, perhaps if I really was a head teacher I would know what Resnick and Le Gall meant by this advice.

Turning to Bryant's paper, here at least I encountered more familiar ground, though the ground I think is *arithmetic* rather than the *mathematics* claimed by the title. There is surely a difference, and one possibly relevant to our topic, since mathematics is domain-independent or general while arithmetic is firmly linked to the domains of quantity and measurement.

I was greatly encouraged to read, throughout the paper, many statements drawing attention to the value and perspicacity of Piaget's work on arithmetic and measurement. It is unfortunate that influential books published by Bryant (1974) and by my own teacher Donaldson (1978) – who were both at that time admirers of Piaget and who had certainly read Piaget thoroughly and carefully – consisted mainly of criticisms of Piaget's results and conclusions. There is little doubt that these criticisms went too far (see Gold, 1987). Indeed, it seems to me that the general treatment of Piaget's work by psychologists in Britain and America has often been rather reprehensible. In the worst cases, convenient opinions of that work are casually constructed from the reading of a few pages of one of his books, or worse, from some second-hand account. These opinions, often flawed and superficial, lead to crude experiments designed to refute them, and naïve or complaisant editors publish yet another paper proving a wholly inadequate version of 'Piaget's theory' to be wrong. Contempt for Piaget scholarship is particularly strong in Britain, and a potent sign of this contempt is the unavailability of Piaget's books. When I last looked, the only Piaget book in print from a British publisher was *Sociological Studies*, published by Routledge. So low is the demand for his work that even the excellent compendium by Gruber and Vonèche (1977) is long out of print. If the Piaget centenary is to amount to anything more than a token obeisance, then it must lead to a re-evaluation of the worth of Piaget's work, to greater awareness of the value of actually reading it, and to wider availability of the books.

In his oral presentation Bryant remarked that Piaget's books are long and often rather hard to finish. This is not because they are dull, but because they are densely illustrated and argued and apt to finish with lengthy and intricate analyses of concepts and of developmental transitions – of theory, in a word. But reading them to a conclusion is often repaying, as Bryant pointed out in relation to the work on one–many correspondence, which is presented late in Piaget (1952). I read *Play, Dreams and Imitation* to the end a few years ago and discovered the following amazing passage (Piaget, 1951, ch. 8, sect. 4):

> Representative assimilation begins as a process of centration . . .
> Confronted by various objects which he compares in order to arrange
> them into classes . . . the child who is on the threshold of the represen-
> tative realm is incapable of putting at the same level present data and
> the earlier data to which he assimilates them. According to his interests
> and the object that drew his attention at the starting point of his actions,
> he centres this . . . and assimilates the others to it.
>
> Moreover, precisely because one of the elements is centred as a
> prototype or representative sample of the set, the schema of this
> set, instead of achieving the abstract state that characterizes a concept,
> continues to be linked to the representation of this typical individual,
> i.e. to an image.

There, and in the passages surrounding it, Piaget described in 1945 the kind of prototype-based structure for early concepts 'independently' reconstructed by Rosch and others in the middle 1970s (e.g. Rosch *et al.*, 1976).

So far as the work reported in Bryant's paper is concerned, it is certainly not anti-Piagetian. Rather, his intriguing and clever experiments complement and clarify Piaget's analysis of the development of arithmetic principles. Indeed, I think that this was true of Bryant's early work too, even if his conclusions at that time were more aggressively stated.

I have a few observations about these experiments.

1 The interesting manipulation in the Frydman and Bryant (1988) sharing experiment which led to better performance from four year olds may have gone further than necessary. A double yellow brick is one thing and also two things. But the 'two-ness' of a double yellow brick may not be salient to these younger children. Perhaps the manipulation using blue and yellow bricks in singles and doubles succeeded not so much because it made the correspondence vivid at every step of the sharing process, but because the use of two colours made the 'two-ness' of the double brick more salient.

2 Although Bryant tends to discount this, I think that Trabasso was right to worry that the outcome of the lengthy training required in their ingenious experiments on transitive inference was the construction of an image of the sticks correctly seriated. The main evidence for this outcome is that latencies to respond on critical inference trials are shorter than latencies to the premise trials – which premises compose these inferences. Surely if something is to count as 'making an inference', then the converse relation of latencies should obtain. Of course, the construction of the seriated image depends on transitive inference but this simply reinforces the point made by Perner and Mansbridge, conceded by Bryant, that the training procedure – for those children equipped to survive it – trains inference as well as securing premise recall.

3 There is a fairly obvious problem in comparing Bryant and Kopytynska's measurement task with Piaget's task. In the latter it is unlikely that a child would pick up a stick and raise it alongside a tower unless she had the intention to measure. But if a child is offered a block with a hole in it and a stick that fits the hole it seems *highly* likely that the stick will be put in the hole! I would expect even a two year old to do this within seconds, and of course with no thought of measurement. An older child might well insert the stick spontaneously and only *then* notice the potential opportunity for measurement. It may be that the various controls and alternative ways of assessing performance in Bryant and Kopytynska's study eliminate this sort of explanation but the data in the original report leave this possibility somewhat open to further investigation. It might be, too, that Piaget's analysis of measurement as an application of transitive inference deserves some reflection. Is the relation between measuring stick (or a part of it) and tower properly regarded as one of *equality* or might it not be better thought of as a relation of *representation* of the tower's height or the hole's depth? I am not sure whether this analysis makes measurement a more or less complicated achievement than the standard analysis, but at least there may be some difference between measurement and more straightforward applications of transitive inference.

4 Finally, and desperately seeking a connection to our advertised topic, the long history of research on transitive inference is an excellent

demonstration of the application of a set of domain-specific cognitive skills. What I have in mind here are those tactical moves mapped out in Smedslund (1969). That paper presented itself as a sort of list of factors that must be considered if a cognitive-developmental diagnosis is to be made accurately. Neglect of certain factors in experimental procedures – such as memory load or difficult verbal instructions – could lead to errors of underestimation of ability; neglect of other factors – such as perceptual solutions, cueing or guessing – could lead to errors of over-estimation of ability. In fact, the paper was used as a handbook for Piaget-'bashing', notably by Smedlund himself! And it has been used effectively by Piaget-defenders too, There is no doubt that the critical analysis of developmental experiments using Smedslund's intellectual toolkit, with several more recent supplements, is a skill at the heart of the experimental skirmishing that goes on around the body of Piaget's work, and it is the study of transitive inference that we have to thank – if that is the right word – for this lively state of affairs!

REFERENCES

Bryant, P. E. (1974). *Perception and Understanding in Young Children*. London: Methuen.

Campbell, R. N. and Olson, D. R. (1990). Children's thinking. In R. Grieve and M. Hughes (eds) *Understanding Children: Essays in Honour of Margaret Donaldson*, pp. 189–209. Oxford: Blackwell.

Carey, S. (1985). Are children fundamentally different kinds of thinkers and learners than adults? In S. F. Chipman, J. W. Segal and R. Glaser (eds) *Thinking and Learning Skills*, volume 2: Research and Open Questions, pp. 485–517. Hillsdale, NJ: Lawrence Erlbaum Associates.

Chi, M. T. H. (1978). Knowledge structures and memory development. In R. S. Siegler (ed.) *Children's Thinking: What Develops?*, pp. 73–96. Hillsdale, NJ: Lawrence Erlbaum Associates.

Chi, M. T. H. and Koeske, R. D. (1983). Network representation of a child's dinosaur knowledge. *Developmental Psychology*, 19, 29–39.

Donaldson, M. C. (1978). *Children's Minds*. London: Fontana.

Frydman, O. and Bryant, P. E. (1988). Sharing and the understanding of number equivalence by young children. *Cognitive Development*, 3, 323–39.

Gold, R. (1987). *The Description of Cognitive Development: Three Piagetian Themes*. Oxford: Clarendon Press.

Gruber, H. E. and Vonèche, J. (1977). *The Essential Piaget*. London: Routledge and Kegan Paul.

Piaget, J. (1951). *Play, Dreams and Imitation in Childhood*. London: Routledge and Kegan Paul.

Piaget, J. (1952). *The Child's Conception of Number*. Routledge and Kegan Paul.

Rosch, E., Mervis, C., Gray, W., Johnson, D. and Boyes-Braem, P. (1976). Basic objects in natural categories. *Cognitive Psychology*, 3, 382–489.

Smedslund, J. (1969). Psychological diagnostics. *Psychological Bulletin*, 71, 237–48.

Sternberg, R. J. (1989). Domain-generality versus domain-specificity: the life and impending death of a false dichotomy. *Merrill-Palmer Quarterly*, 35(1), 115–30.

Vygotsky, L. S. (1962). *Thought and Language*. Cambridge, MA: MIT Press.

Part 4

Measurement of development

10 Measuring development
Examples from Piaget's theory

Trevor G. Bond

Influential critiques (e.g. Brown and Desforges, 1977; Lawson *et al.*, 1978; Case, 1991) have discounted the validity of Piaget's theory of intellectual development specifically on the grounds of the poor psychometric evidence that existed for the relationships amongst tests of concrete and of formal operational thinking. It would be straightforward to demonstrate that such claims are, at most, marginal to Piaget's epistemology, given the gulf between the explicit philosophical foundations of Piaget's theory in rationalism and structuralism and the implicit empiricist orientation of the criticisms. However, given that Piaget's theory has been popularised as one informing educational (and psychological) assessment and intervention, it would be avoiding the issues to argue that the theory should be evaluated strictly on its own philosophical terms (see Bond and Jackson, 1991; Smith, 1993). But it does not seem unreasonable to require of any psychometric evaluation of Piagetian theory that, at least, the psychological or educational tests being used must interpret Piaget's theory in its own terms, and the statistical analyses must be sensitive to the expressly developmental nature of Piaget's explanatory account.

This paper interrelates the findings of two recently reported major investigations (Bond, 1995b; Bond and Bunting, 1995) along with that of more recently completed research to address important issues relevant to the measurement of cognitive development, particularly as they impact on Piagetian theory, and by implication on their application to the theory of Lev Vygotsky. While this paper presents self-contained detailed psychometric evidence about the development of formal operational thought in particular, the commentary provided on the validity and utility of Piaget's ideas is especially timely in the context of the success of the CASE interventions in the UK, based largely on Piagetian theory (Adey and Shayer, 1994). While the content of the paper is explicitly Piagetian, in keeping with my long-standing commitment to Piagetian research, the attention paid to aspects such as test construction, sample selection and data analysis techniques should make the paper relevant to all those interested in the measurement of development and learning.

THE TESTS

The research projects reported here make use of three widely used but quite disparate tests of operational thinking. They include a careful replication of the 'Genevan' method used by Inhelder and Piaget, a pencil and paper version of the same task that was developed in the UK and a multiple-choice test that was constructed in Australia. While the tests/tasks that follow adopt a wide range of testing and evaluation strategies, they share a commitment of the investigators to develop methodologies that are directly and explicitly derived from Piagetian theory, especially as it is reported in detail for the development of formal thought in *The Growth of Logical Thinking* (*GLT*) (Inhelder and Piaget, 1958). For these researchers it is taken as given that tests claiming to measure the development from concrete to formal thought should adhere as far as it is possible to the relevant parts of the Piagetian account.

The PRTIII (pendulum)

The Piagetian Reasoning Test III – Pendulum of Shayer *et al.* (Wylam and Shayer, 1978) is one of a set of demonstrated class-tasks designed specifically to address the elicitation of the problem-solving behaviour revealed by the use of the Inhelder tasks as reported in *GLT*. An important criterion used in the development of the tests was that in each test each child should have two separate opportunities to display each of the critical behaviours described in GLT for that particular task. Furthermore, the original scoring procedures for the PRTIII – Pendulum were designed to impose on each child's performance one of Piaget's classificatory ordering levels (early concrete, late concrete, early formal etc.) based on the Piagetian criteria taken directly from Chapter 4 of *GLT*.

The BLOT

Unlike any other test which purports to measure formal operational thinking, Bond's Logical Operations Test (Bond, 1976) was designed to represent each and every one of the logical schemata of the formal operations stage. In *GLT*, Piaget's recourse to a mathematical model based on his interpretation of principles drawn from symbolic logic was explicated in chapter 17, 'Concrete and Formal Structures' (pp. 272–333). The BLOT consists of thirty-five items in multiple choice format which are designed as instantiations of the calculus of the sixteen binary operations of truth functional logic and the INRC four-group of operations from Piaget's logical model (Piaget, 1949, 1953; Inhelder and Piaget, 1955/1958; Bond, 1978, 1980).

The *méthode critique* (pendulum)

Aspects of the Genevan investigative technique, variously called the clinical method, the *méthode clinique* or the *méthode critique*, depending on the age and source of the reference, are described in a number of Genevan sources (Piaget, 1963; Vinh-Bang, 1966; Inhelder, 1989). Few sources, or users, outside of the Genevan group based around Inhelder, her assistants and students, seem to consider the large set of philosophical and psychological underpinnings of the method (see in particular Bond and Jackson, 1991, as well as commentary in Bideaud, Houdé and Pedinelli, 1993 and in Smith, 1992). Even the title can be misleading; the more recent Genevan label, *méthode critique*, both more completely represents Inhelder's method of critical exploration and serves to distinguish it from the less rigorous techniques often alluded to in the secondary literature. Suffice it to say that those who have not worked to adhere closely to the Genevan guidelines or who have not looked through some of the thousands of '*procès-verbal*' housed in the Archives Jean Piaget, Geneva where the original *De la logique de l'enfant à la logique de l'adolescence* (*LELA*, Inhelder and Piaget, 1955) (and other) interviews are reported in their entirety, would be at a distinct and serious disadvantage in attempting to replicate the Genevan methods in their own research. The development of investigatory and analytical techniques adopted by the researcher in the *méthode critique* administration of the pendulum task reported below relied heavily on the most detailed and exhaustive reading of Chapter 4 in *GLT* and in *LELA* and the corresponding unpublished protocols and analyses housed in Geneva.

The samples

In the research on formal operations, the issues of sample size and sampling method apparently require some attention. Lawson (1985, pp. 574–5) noted that careful subject selection is critical to valid investigations of operational ability in group test situations:

> Three criteria should be met. First, subjects should be in a narrow age range to avoid the possibility that performance is influenced by other age related variables. Second, subjects should be ones that demonstrate a wide range of performances on the tasks in question . . . subjects should be old enough so that a portion of them will score at the 3B level on each of the tasks. Third, subjects should be ones at which formal reasoning is, for the most part, still developing or has already reached equilibrium.

For the BLOT *v.* PRTIII investigation, children who comprised the whole of the third-year draft of a rural secondary school in England made up the sample. As a consequence, all subjects were aged in their fifteenth year (ages 15.0–15.11 years). Complete data sets exist for 150 subjects (N = 150). In the PRTIII *v. méthode critique* (pendulum) comparison, the total tested sample consisted of fifty-eight adolescent students (aged 12.5 to 15.9 years) from a very large public secondary school in Townsville, Australia, drawn from three science classes across grade 8 (n = 20), grade 9 (n = 18) and grade 10 (n = 20).

In both studies, the classes used in the study were carefully selected by the science teachers at the school to ensure that a wide range of ability levels would be obtained.

THE ANALYTICAL TECHNIQUE

Rasch analysis (Rasch, 1960; Wright and Stone, 1979; Wright and Masters, 1982; Wilson, 1985; Adams and Khoo, 1993) is held to be the most appropriate for this purpose because it addresses the unidimensionality of the collected data and is sensitive to the explicitly developmental nature of Piagetian (and other) accounts. The details of the argument are more thoroughly canvassed by Bond (1995a) along with detail of relevant Continental (rather than UK and US) research reports. It is important to note that each of the data collecting techniques used in the research reported in this chapter was developed without Rasch analysis to guide in its development, that the testing procedures were developed independently (in Switzerland, Britain and Australia) and that they adopt remarkably different formats and require significantly different marking schemes.

Scoring

For the BLOT, the scoring procedure is as straightforward as one could expect of a multiple choice test; minimal judgement is required of the investigator and students are scored '1' for each correct answer (and '0' for each incorrect response). The PRTIII requires implementation and evaluation by a trained assessor (science teachers are routinely trained in the implementation and evaluation procedures) and specific written guidelines are provided whereby the investigator makes qualitative judgements to determine whether the appropriately sophisticated reasoning has been revealed in the written answer to each particular question. Although the original PRTIII guidelines contain detailed guidelines about deriving overall stage allocations based on the qualitative patterns of responses, for these (and other recent) investigations, students' answers were scored '1' where they were judged to meet the criteria and '0' where they failed to do so.

For the *méthode critique* investigation a set of descriptive criteria was prepared, extracted directly from the content of chapter 4 in *GLT* (pp. 67–79). Subsequent elaboration and refinement of these descriptions produced a set of eighteen performance criteria, ranging from the gross to the minute and covering behaviours from the preoperational (I) to late formal operational (IIIB) levels of ability (Bond and Bunting, 1995). In the scoring of performances, the wealth of descriptions provided in *GLT* suggested that while a simple dichotomous yes/no (1,0) procedure would be appropriate for some of the identified behaviours, that would not provide sufficient detail for other areas of performance. Rather, an ordinal scale was used to allow for the inclusion of items with three or more graded values for these behaviours so that a total of thirty-four criteria against which performance on the pendulum task could be assessed. This method allowed for a more sensitive evaluation of performances, reflecting lesser or greater operational ability. Each of the individual interviews was completely transcribed from video recordings and then scored so that the eighteen scores represented the presence of any or all of the thirty-four *GLT* criteria (see Bond and Bunting, 1995).

A brief introduction to Rasch analysis

There are a number of features that make Rasch analysis a highly appropriate technique for the analysis of developmental data (Wilson, 1985; Bond, 1995a). Firstly, it provides an estimation of the *unidimensionality* of the data set under analysis (unidimensionality is an idea somewhat related to the unifactorial solution entailed in factor analytical approaches). However, Rasch analysis is sensitive to the incremental nature of developmental acquisitions and provides estimates of item difficulty and person ability along a single developmental continuum wherein the *probability* of any person's success on any test item is read directly from the developmental distance between the person's ability and the item's difficulty.

The basis of Georg Rasch's model (Rasch, 1960) is an algorithm which expresses the *probabilistic* expectations of *item* and *person* performance when one *latent trait* (a single ability or competence) is held to underlie the developmental sequence represented by an observation schedule. For the purpose of illustrating some key Rasch principles, Figure 13 contains a selected data matrix (just twelve persons and twelve items) from the responses of a group of forty primary school children to a developmental test of the ability to solve twenty-nine problems based on the mathematical concept of area (Bond, 1996; Bond and Parkinson, 1996; Parkinson, 1996). Children's responses **A–L** are represented in the **rows** and the test items **1–12** are represented in **columns**; e.g. the ✓ in box B4 indicates that child B succeeded on item 4, while the X in H10 indicates failure by child H on item 10 of this sub-set. For convenience of illustration, the **persons** are ordered from *most able*, **A** at the top to *least able*, **L** at the bottom of the data set; the *easiest item*, **item 1** is in the left-hand column, while responses to **item 12**, the *most difficult item*, are in the right-hand column. Raw scores indicating **person's ability** on this twelve-item test are totalled

	1	2	3	4	5	6	7	8	9	10	11	12	Ability	n/N
A	✔	✔	✔	X*	✔	✔	✔	✔	✔	X	✔	✔	10	.83
B	✔	✔	✔	✔	✔	✔	✔	X	X	✔	✔	X	9	.75
C	✔	✔	X*	✔	✔	✔	✔	X	✔	✔	X	X	8	.67
D	✔	✔	X*	✔	✔	✔	✔	X	✔	✔	X	X	8	.67
E	✔	✔	✔	✔	✔	✔	X	✔	X	X	X	X	7	.58
F	✔	✔	✔	✔	✔	✔	X	✔	X	X	X	X	7	.58
G	✔	✔	✔	✔	X	X	✔	X*	✔*	X	X	X	6	.50
H	✔	✔	✔	✔	✔	✔	X	X	X	X	X	X	6	.50
I	✔	✔	✔	✔	X	X	✔	X	✔*	X	X	X	6	.50
J	✔	✔	✔	✔	X	X	X	✔*	X	X	X	X	5	.42
K	✔	✔	✔	X	X	X	X	✔*	X	X	X	X	4	.33
L	✔	X	✔	✔	X	X	X	X	X	X	X	X	3	.25
Facility	12	11	10	10	7	7	6	5	5	3	2	1		
n/N	1.0	.93	.83	.83	.58	.58	.50	.42	.42	.25	.17	.08		

Figure 13 Selected data matrix for twelve persons (A–L) on twelve items (1–12) for the purpose of introducing Rasch principles (Parkinson, 1996)

Notes

ITEMS:

Showing strict developmental orderliness (i.e. over fit): item 2 (failed by least able person, L, only), Item 12 (passed by most able person, A, only), Item 11, (only A & B pass).

Showing acceptable developmental orderliness (i.e. over fit): item 10 has only one 'unexpected' response (from the most able person A).

Showing lack of developmental orderliness (i.e. poor fit): item 8 is obviously problematic; more able persons (B, C & D) fail, while less able persons (J & K) pass. This needs investigation because this item seems to involve attributes other than just the ability revealed by the test items as a group.

PERSONS:

Showing strict developmental orderliness (i.e. over fit): person H passes the six easiest items and fails the six hardest (exactly predictable from *ability* of 6/12 or .50).

Showing acceptable developmental orderliness (i.e. over fit): persons E & F fail item 8 but pass item 7 (with *ability* of 7/12 or .58); but items 7 (.50) and 8 (.42) have similar *facilities*. Note that patterns of persons G & I are more misfitting than responses of person H (all have ability of .50).

Showing lack of developmental orderliness (i.e. poor fit): person A is obviously problematic: A's failure of item 10 is a little unexpected but failure on item 4 is completely out of line with A's overall high *ability*. This needs investigation because this performance pattern seems to involve attributes other than just the ability revealed by the persons as a group.

SHADING: Apparently irregular performance is more probable for recently acquired abilities.

ASTERISK: ✔* X* : This irregular performance is relatively improbable given the ability of the person and the facility of the item.

as **Ability** and expressed as a decimal fraction (n/N) in the adjacent column. The total number of correct responses to each item is listed in a row as **Facility** and expressed as the corresponding fraction (n/N) in the next row.

For data that adheres to the Rasch model, the total (n) of correct responses is the necessary and sufficient summary of item facility and person ability in each case. The simple calculation of item facilities and person abilities (n/N) reveals the *ordinal* relationships amongst abilities on the one hand and amongst difficulties on the other. (The ordering is revealed in decreasing size of the n/N decimal fraction.) These of course are merely *orderings* of the *nominal* categories (✓ – correct and X – incorrect) and, as such, are not sufficient for the inference of *interval relationships* between the frequencies of observations.

By their very nature, *developmental* theories predict both a substantial variation in the presence of the targeted ability in the sample as well as a considerable variation in the difficulty of the items representing observation schedule. In this data set, the (ordered) developmental nature of the observations is obvious – presences of the ability (✓s) change to absences of ability (Xs) along the line of increasing difficulty of the items (**1–12**) and along the line of the decreasing ability of the persons (**A–L**).

For experienced researchers or teachers, the arrangements of some points in the table will provoke reflection on the nature of the development made evident by these empirical manifestations of the underlying theoretical ideas. Of only passing concern is the small zone of unpredictability (shaded area) routinely associated with the intersection of the patterns of 'ability' and 'facility'; it is only reasonable that recently acquired or yet to be consolidated developmental abilities might not be fully reliable in display.

More attention must be paid to the relatively 'unexpected' incidences of ✓ or X (marked *) which seem markedly out of place; they are of greater concern to the underlying theoretical model. Indeed, they are of *more* or *less* concern depending on their *number*, *location* and *pattern* in the data matrix (see Figure 13 notes). Persons who score well on difficult items in spite of low overall total scores might have done so by guessing or cheating. Similarly, poor scores on easy items in spite of high overall total scores might indicate lack of concentration or guessing. Poorly conceptualised or constructed items result in less predictable performance patterns of *items* and *persons*. Of course, the presence of other idiosyncratic circumstances, including particular person/item interactions, is always a possibility.

However, given the premise that the items are the empirical expression of a theoretical description of some particular aspect of development which should tap the presence of that ability in the target population, then the crucial problem addressed by Rasch analysis concerns the possibility of judging to what extent the pattern of the data is supportive of the key propositions that:

1 person performance patterns should reflect both person abilities and item difficulties;
2 item performance patterns should reflect both item difficulties and person abilities;
3 and, that the *probability* of any occurrence/observation (any item for any person) is a *function* of the difficulty of that item *relative* to the ability of the person.

Firstly, the Rasch analytical process performs a logarithmic transformation on the item and person summary data (the n/N fraction) to convert the ordinal data to yield interval data along a *logit* scale which represents the 'gaps' in ability and difficulty detected in the data set – actual item and person performance determine the interval sizes, they are not introduced as *a priori* assumptions of the investigator or the analytical algorithm. Logit scales are used in Figures 14 and 15 to represent the *facilities* of items of the BLOT and PRTIII tests – items to the right of the logit scale are more difficult. In a corresponding fashion, logarithmic transformations of the n/N *ability* fractions for persons may be plotted on the same logit scale to represent estimates of *person ability* on these same tests, with locations of *persons* rather than of *items* displayed along the logit scale. In Figure 16 ability estimates on the BLOT are plotted against PRTIII ability estimates for each person to form the basis of the graph comparing BLOT and PRTIII abilities.

Figure 14 Item difficulties for the BLOT located on a logit scale (the gradation of early concrete to late formal items is read from left to right; error bands show the imprecision of each item location)

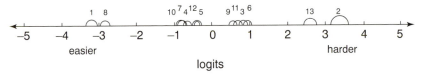

Figure 15 Item difficulties for the PRTIII–Pendulum located on a logit scale (the gradation of early concrete to late formal items is read from left to right; error bands show the imprecision of each item location)

Secondly, the analysis then *compares* the distribution of the set of *actual observations* to Rasch's mathematical modelled distribution of *expectations*. Notwithstanding the possibility of occasional errors of ability or facility estimation due to carelessness, fatigue or guessing, estimates of *fit* that

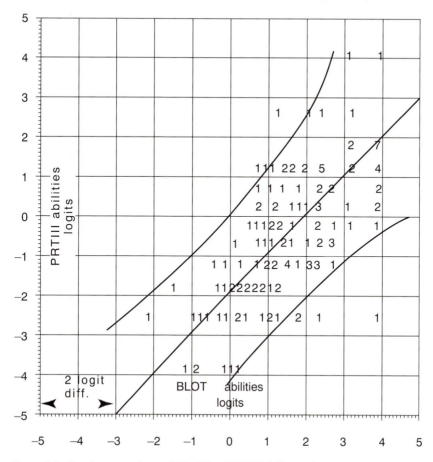

Figure 16 Rasch comparison of BLOT v PRTIII ability estimates for each person (each location is a plot of that person's BLOT performance against PRTIII performance, each located on the same logit scales used in Figures 14 and 15; on average the PRTIII is 2 logits more difficult than the BLOT)

accompany Rasch analysis estimate the variation between the Rasch model expectations and the pass/fail, ✓/X patterns evident in the data. The notes that accompany Figure 13 attempt to identify qualitatively, for illustrative purposes, the relative importance of the *misfits* evident in the sample data. Of course real data sets for Rasch analysis are considerably larger than the excerpt used in Figure 13 and misfit patterns are calculated across the whole person/item array. Of course all 'real' data will deviate to some lesser or greater extent from Rasch's idealised mathematical model. Data is held to be unidimensional when the *fit* between actual and modelled distributions is adequate. Under these conditions, the claim might be made that a single difficulty/ability continuum is sufficient to explain the item/person performances.

THE RESULTS

The accompanying figures summarise the detailed quantitative descriptions of concrete and formal operational thought that are remarkably congruent with expectations derived directly from Piaget's explanatory account in *LELA/GLT*. In the first instance, the location of test items are plotted in Figure 14 for the BLOT and Figure 15 for the PRTIII. In each case the items are located on a logit scale with the easier items to the left and the more difficult items to the right. The item difficulty locations are derived from the Rasch logarithmic transformation of the item facility ratio (n/N) mentioned above. Each item location is indicated by an *error* band which estimates the *precision* of that location. The thirty-five BLOT items span about 5 logits of difficulty, with considerable overlap in the mid-range, while the PRTIII has many fewer items (fourteen) which span a larger developmental range with fewer items, leaving correspondingly larger gaps. Detailed discussion of these results (Bond, 1989; Bond, 1995b) reveals that the order and placement of the BLOT and the PRTIII items closely correspond to the stage ordering expectations derived from the descriptions of Inhelder and Piaget (1955/1958).

Rasch analyses routinely address the extent to which any test (or combination of tests) may be held to measure behaviours relating to a single underlying psychological construct (the concepts of *unidimensionality* and *fit* outlined above). In the case of Piagetian research, a high degree of inter-relatedness of task/test performance might be held as evidence of the *structure d'ensemble* that is fundamental to the Genevan conception of cognitive development.

The BLOT v. the PRTIII

For the BLOT and the PRTIII tests, the detailed output of the Rasch analysis (see Bond, 1995b) reveals that each test is substantially *unidimensional*, with generally unremarkable estimates of *misfit* for almost all of the test items – i.e. by and large, each test may be regarded as consisting of a group of highly interrelated items that measure a single underlying trait. More particularly, when the results from the two tests are analysed together they are demonstrably unidimensional, i.e. they measure the *same* single underlying trait. The technique of *common-person equating* used here is the strictest test of test equivalence envisaged under Rasch analysis techniques. Each of the adolescents in the sample had two test results – one for the BLOT and one for the PRTIII. Following the Rasch process each *person ability location* (transformed n/N) can also be located on the logit scales shown in Figures 14 and 15. Then, Figure 16 reveals the locations of all of the *person abilities* on the BLOT and PRTIII when they are plotted against each other – each numeral indicates the number of persons at each location. The straight line models the unattainable 'perfect' linear relationship between the two tests computed from Rasch's model, while the two curved control lines represent the 'error' of measurement – when the data conform to the Rasch model, 95% of observations fall within this band. The graph in Figure 16 shows, however, that the PRTIII is considerably more difficult than the BLOT (by 2 logits). Given the claims of critics who rely on evidence derived from correlational and factor analytical techniques (see Brown and Desforges, 1977; Lawson *et al.*, 1978; Case, 1991), the value of this analytical technique starts to become obvious.

The PRTIII v. The *méthode critique*

While some might claim that statistical analysis of pencil and paper tests of operational thinking does not get to the very core of the Piagetian *oeuvre*, recent adoption of Partial Credit analysis (based on the Rasch model) and the most detailed development of performance criteria from *LELA* and *GLT* have provided the first meaningful psychometric analyses of the Genevan data collection technique, the *méthode critique* (Bond and Bunting, 1995). The Partial Credit model (Wright and Masters, 1982) provides for the simultaneous analysis of dichotomous and polychotomous response formats, making it appropriate for the results of the sorts of decisions routinely made by those who make hierarchical stage-wise classifications of interview data using Piaget's qualitative criteria – while some performances are rated '0-1', 'X-✓' or 'no-yes', others are rated '0-1-2' (none-some-all *or* some-more-most), '0-1-2-3' (none-preoperational-early concrete-late concrete) or '0-1-2-3-4' (preoperational-early concrete-late concrete -early formal-late formal).

Again the analysis reveals that item and subject characteristics are substantially unidimensional – i.e. measure a single underlying ability trait. The details of the statistical location of task items (*item difficulties* in logits) provide a substantial quantitative corroboration of Piaget's stage and substage criteria which, Inhelder and Piaget claim, were based purely on Piaget's logico-mathematical analysis (Bond and Bunting, 1995). This is a remarkable correspondence given the geographical, language and methodological gulfs between the original adolescent research of Inhelder in the 1940s and this attempt at verification of the basic theoretical and empirical principles half a century later.

Subsequently, further Rasch analysis (Bunting, 1993) which included PRTIII performance data from the same sample of adolescents, revealed the *conjoint unidimensionality* of the *méthode critique* administration of Inhelder's pendulum problem and the written class-task version of that pendulum task developed by Shayer and his colleagues for the CSMS research of the 1970s in the UK. Interestingly, the PRTIII is considerably more difficult than the *méthode critique* version (again by 2 logits). Admittedly, not all the quantitative item placements correspond to those predicted by Piaget's qualitative analyses; further empirical data and theoretical analyses need to be focused on those discrepancies.

DISCUSSION

It is claimed here that Rasch analysis of carefully constructed and implemented tests illuminates a number of apparently intangible and intractable Piagetian ideas. In the first place, it examines (and verifies) the unitary nature of operational thought; the Brown and Desforges criticism, and that of Lawson and of Case, focused exactly on this apparent inadequacy of Piagetian theory. The evidence presented here would suggest that the question of the validity of central Piagetian constructs was closed prematurely and based, unfortunately, on inappropriate analytical techniques. With the less imperfect vision of hindsight, it seems naïve to expect that ability on any aspect (test) of operational thinking could exactly represent the intellectual development of any child or that these skills should immediately and completely transfer to any new learning (testing) situation. The Piagetian concept of 'horizontal *décalage*' generally seems to be regarded as a *post hoc* modification to Piaget's ideas designed primarily to protect the theory from falsification. But the evidence gained from these analyses is not only theoretically informative but practically useful as well. The BLOT is more sensitive to the onset of formal operational thinking and gives a more finely graded assessment of it. However, the PRTIII does not have the 'ceiling effect' evident in BLOT performance. A concern about the 2 logit difference between the PRTIII and the other two tasks requires further consideration.

The item difficulty plots for each of the tests give some evidence of the stage-like nature of the ability under examination. This is most obvious for the PRTIII where four clusters of items, representing different Piagetian levels, are clearly evident. While the evidence is more equivocal in the case of the item plots for the BLOT and the *méthode critique* plots, dense groups of closely associated items are separated by areas with few or no item locations. Moreover, Bond (1995b) and Bond and Bunting (1995) discuss the correspondences between these quantitative results and Piaget's qualitative findings. Rasch analysts with interest in stage-like development (e.g. Wilson, 1989; Wilson and Draney, 1995; Mislevy and Verhelst, 1990) are working on quantitative techniques to investigate discontinuity (rather than continuity) in developmental constructs.

The quantitative evidence apparently supports the claim that the PRTIII measures the same ability as does the *méthode critique* technique on the same Piagetian problem – the pendulum – even if one requires intensive training, individual implementation and expert evaluation and the other can be successfully implemented and evaluated by a school teacher with general training in science and Piagetian ideas. Again the PRTIII is more difficult than is the *méthode critique* administration (by the same amount as was estimated in the BLOT *v*. PRTIII comparison) but the disadvantage is not uniform: there are some students in both comparisons for whom the PRTIII facilitates (rather than inhibits) the display of formal operational thought. This highlights an important and fundamental competence/ performance distinction and will not come as any surprise to those who know that Piaget was quite aware of the potential for a variety of strategies to elicit empirical data more or less sensitively, as well as more or less accurately. Indeed Piaget held that standardisation of the *méthode critique* risked damage to the very qualities of Genevan method that he found most advantageous (Piaget and Szeminska, 1941; Bond and Jackson, 1991).

These results provide strong psychometric evidence that three markedly different tests apparently measure the same underlying psychological trait – the development of formal operational thinking. The preliminary finding that the PRTIII routinely underestimates the presence of formal operational thinking (compared to the BLOT and the *méthode critique*) requires further investigation. But given that the results of the CASE project show a close interrelation between cognitive development elicited in written responses by the PRTs and GCSE results in science, maths and language, also collected in written examination form (see Shayer, this volume), perhaps it is more a matter of making informed test choices which keep in mind the intentions of the teacher or researcher.

De Ribaupierre (1993) has carefully argued how, in the Piagetian tradition of developmental research, we must first define structural invariants across tasks before we start examining individual differences, and disarms those critics who confuse the Piagetian claim for structural invariance with their own mistaken demand for developmental synchrony across tasks as the empirical consequence. The results presented in this paper show that Rasch analysis is appropriate for the quantitative estimation of structural invariance amongst tasks while *at the same time* providing for the detailed description of individual differences in performance. In that light, the Piagetian conception of 'horizontal *décalage*' is not read as some inadequate explanatory device but as a qualitative description of a feature of development which will require theoretical explanation when the *décalages* between tasks and between individuals have been more systematically investigated and quantified.

Current research projects in Australia provide detailed quantitative support for the validity and utility of the PRTII – Volume and Heaviness (which focuses more closely on the development of concrete operational constructs of conservation) and the Piagetian description of development of time-based concepts of speed and rate following the most detailed empirical investigation of these concepts in a sample of teacher education students in a developing country. Several projects focus on the links between formal operational thinking and achievement in secondary school science. At the pre-matriculation level, high correlations between science achievement and BLOT scores have been uncovered. The BLOT is also being used in the junior secondary school to detect ceiling effects in school achievement associated with pre-formal levels of cognitive development. The first of these projects reveals that children at the concrete operational

180 *Trevor G. Bond*

level of thought have very little chance of scoring above about 60% on traditional school-based assessment instruments in science while the second reveals that the sophistication of the science concepts developed by children in constructivist learning environments appears predictable from cognitive development scores on the BLOT. Two longitudinal projects attempting to plot the course of cognitive development during adolescence in quantitative terms are now in their third year of data collection.

The received view is that significant aspects of Piagetian theory have not survived the falsificationist tests of the seventies and eighties. The continuing success of the CASE project in the UK and the detailed results discussed here suggest that the operationalisations of Piagetian theory and/or the statistical techniques adopted in the disconfirming studies are worth closer scrutiny. While developmental and educational psychologists now tend to adopt qualitative approaches to the evaluation of Vygotsky's ideas, the guidelines adopted in this current presentation have obvious relevance. Rasch analysis appears to be a quantitative analytical method ideally suited to the estimation of the development of learners through the zone of proximal development. One interesting project might address the question of whether the results of 'supported' and 'unsupported' testing were sufficiently different to warrant the term 'zoped'. The very same Rasch technique for estimating item difficulties (as was used for the Piagetian investigation above) could be used to help determine whether problems in the 'zoped' were sufficiently in advance of the child's current developmental level to represent a real 'potential for learning'. The Rasch test of underlying unidimensionality could help us to infer whether those results were sufficiently related to each other to be represented as a genuine developmental trait of the child – 'zoped' abilities that were not so related to the child's current developmental patterns might then be regarded as merely an artefact of teacher intervention. Given confirmation of the Vygotskian position on each of those questions, that 'zoped' abilities are both related to the child's current development and are sufficiently in advance of that development to be the focus of new learning experiences, Rasch analysis could then be used to provide detailed maps of the learning and teaching sequences revealed in the 'zoped' and then to estimate the extent to which learning and development actually take place for any individual or a group of individuals as a result of teaching.

REFERENCES

Adams, R. J. and Khoo, S. T. (1993). *Quest: The Interactive Test Analysis System.* Hawthorn: Australian Council for Educational Research.
Adey, P. and Shayer, M. (1994). *Really Raising Standards.* London: Routledge.
Bideaud, J., Houdé, O. and Pedinelli, J.-L. (1993). *L'homme en developpement.* Paris: PUF.
Bond, T. G. (1976). *BLOT: Bond's Logical Operations Test.* Townsville: TCAE.

Bond, T. G. (1978). Propositional logic as a model for adolescent intelligence: additional considerations. *Interchange*, 9, 2, 93–100.

Bond, T. G. (1980). The psychological link across formal operations. *Science Education*, 64, 1, 113–17.

Bond, T. G. (1989). An investigation of the scaling of Piagetian formal operations. In P. Adey (ed.) *Adolescent Development and School Science*. New York: Falmer Press, pp. 334–41.

Bond, T. G. (1995a). Piaget and measurement I: the twain really do meet. *Archives de Psychologie*, 63, 71–87.

Bond, T. G. (1995b). Piaget and measurement II: empirical validation of the Piagetian model. *Archives de Psychologie*, 63, 155–85.

Bond, T. G. (1996). Confirming ideas about development: using the Rasch model in practice. Invited Address, Human Development and Psychology Colloquium Series, Harvard Graduate School of Education, January, videotape.

Bond, T. G. and Bunting, E. M. (1995). Piaget and measurement III: reassessing the *méthode critique*. *Archives de Psychologie*, 63, 231–55.

Bond, T. G. and Jackson, I. (1991). The GOU protocol revisited: a Piagetian contextualization of critique. *Archives de Psychologie*, 59, 31–53.

Bond, T. G. and Parkinson, K. (1996). Quantitative analysis of the *méthode clinique* II: the child's conception of area. Poster presented at the Annual Symposium of the Jean Piaget Society, June.

Brown, G. and Desforges, C. (1977). Piagetian psychology and education: time for revision. *British Journal of Educational Psychology*, 47, 7–17.

Bunting, E. M. (1993). *A Qualitative and Quantitative Analysis of Piaget's Control of Variable Scheme*. Thesis. Townsville: James Cook University of North Queensland.

Case, R. (1991). *The Mind's Staircase*. Hillsdale, NJ: Erlbaum.

Inhelder, B. (1989). Bärbel Inhelder. In G. Lindzey (ed.) *A history of psychology in autobiography*, vol. VII, pp. 208–43. Stanford: Stanford University Press.

Inhelder, B. and Piaget, J. (1955/1958). *De la logique de l'enfant à la logique de l'adolescent/The Growth of Logical Thinking from Childhood to Adolescence: An Essay on the Construction of Formal Operational Structures*. Paris: Presses Universitaires de France/London: Routledge and Kegan Paul.

Lawson, A. E. (1985). A review of research on formal reasoning and science teaching. *Journal of Research in Science Teaching*, 22, 7, 569–617.

Lawson, A. E., Karplus, R. and Adi, H. (1978). The acquisition of propositional logic and formal operational schemata during the secondary school years. *Journal of Research in Science Teaching*, 15, 6, 465–78.

Mislevy, R. J. and Verhelst, N. (1990) Modelling item responses when different subjects employ different solution strategies. *Psychometrika*, 55, 195–215.

Parkinson, K. (1996). *Children's Understanding of Area: A Comparison between Performance on Piagetian Interview Tasks and School-based Written Tasks*. Thesis. Townsville: James Cook University of North Queensland.

Piaget, J. (1949). *Traité de logique: essai de logistique opératoire*. Paris: Colin.

Piaget, J. (1953). *Logic and Psychology*. Manchester: Manchester University Press.

Piaget, J. (1963). *Le jugement et le raisonnement chez l'enfant* (5th edn). Neuchâtel: Delachaux and Niestlé.

Piaget, J. and Szeminska, A. (1941). *La genese du nombre chez l'enfant*. Neuchâtel: Delachaux and Niestlé.

Rasch, G. (1960/1980). *Probabilistic Models for Some Intelligence and Attainment tests*. Copenhagen: Danmarks Paedogogiske Institut/Chicago: University of Chicago Press.

de Ribaupierre, A. (1993) Structural invariants and individual differences: on the difficulty of dissociating developmental and differential processes. In R. Case and W. Edelstein (eds) *The new structuralism in cognitive development: theory and research on individual pathways. Contributions in Human Development*, vol. 23, pp. 11–32. Basel: Karger.

Smith, L. (1992). *Jean Piaget: Critical Assessments*. London: Routledge.

Smith, L. (1993). *Necessary Knowledge*. Hove: Erlbaum.

Vinh-Bang (1966). La méthode clinique et la recherche en psychologie de l'enfant. In F. Bresson and M. de Montmollin (eds) *Psychologie et épistémologie génétiques*, (pp. 67–81) Paris: Dunod.

Wilson, M. (1985). *Measuring Stages of Growth*. Hawthorn: Australian Council for Educational Research.

Wilson, M. (1989). Saltus: a psychometric model of discontinuity in cognitive development. *Psychological Bulletin*, 105, 276–89.

Wilson, M. and Draney, K. (1995). Partial Credit in a developmental context: a mixture model approach. Paper presented at the annual meeting of the National Council for Measurement in Education, San Francisco, April.

Wright, B. D. and Masters G. N. (1982). *Rating Scale Analysis*. Chicago: MESA Press.

Wright, B. D. and Stone, M. H. (1979). *Best Test Design*. Chicago: MESA Press.

Wylam, H. and Shayer, M. (1978). *CSMS science reasoning tasks*. Windsor: NFER.

11 Capturing dynamic structuralism in the laboratory

Margaret Chalmers and Brendan McGonigle

For Piaget, it all began with measurement. Taking the twentieth century's new slide-rule for assessing mental capacity 'psychometrically', he turned it into an instrument of diagnosis and explanation. It was in the course of administering the Binet-Simon intelligence tests, using the usual criteria (the age at which 50% of children could pass a given test), that Piaget became aware that 'mistakes' – patterned and interpretable – were as measurable as correct answers and the reasoning behind the child's response became as important as correctness *per se*. The measure was no longer a score, but a typical pattern of responding; a typical mode of explanation and justification of the answer. Based now on theoretical rather than on actuarial grounds, new tests specifically designed to amplify and explore these responses were generated by Piaget and his colleagues and were later represented in the major domain-dedicated works on number, space, geometry, logic and so on (Piaget and Szeminska, 1952; Piaget and Inhelder, 1956; Piaget *et al.*, 1960; Inhelder and Piaget, 1964). Thus, for example, the original three-term reasoning test adapted directly from Burt (1919), *Edith is fairer than Suzanne; Edith is darker than Lili; Which is the fairest/darkest of the three*? (Piaget, 1928), became elaborated subsequently into a set of tests designed to capture the grasp of transitive relations at their earliest point of emergence in the child's thinking. These were 'concrete' tasks such as the famous measuring problem (Piaget, *et al.*, 1960) in which children are required to build a tower equal in size to one which is spatially remote from the one under construction. This relies on the grasp of the principle: if A = B and B = C then A = C, and thus is similar in its formal requirements to the three-term reasoning task. The fact that the concrete task is typically solved at around seven years (by 50% of the group sampled) whilst the linguistic version is solved at around twelve/thirteen years (Piaget, 1928) was less significant than the fact that both reputedly measured the same underlying principle of relation co-ordination. In this way the test battery was augmented by an explanatory principle which was as much an interpretation of the tests themselves as it was of the child. 'Measurement' of intellectual development would never mean the same thing again. The schism was born between the laboratory, with its task analysis, and the 'field' of educational and clinical practice with its batteries of tests.

It is not the purpose of this paper to evaluate these two approaches in relation to one another (but see e.g. Elkind, 1971). Measurement of the real individual in relation to the group will always be necessary. The very practice of test administration over large populations, furthermore, allows them to be revised, fine-tuned and factor-analysed into broad categories such as 'performance IQ', 'spatial' and 'verbal' intelligence, and so on. Through judicious item replacement and repeated use alone, they can be made into ever better instruments of fast assessment and statistical prediction, whatever the explanatory principles (or lack of them) uniting the tests themselves. Their future is guaranteed.

But now on the cusp of the next century, and with a large part of this one devoted to the measurement of what we might now regard as the *theoretical* child, it might be fitting to ask how far we have progressed with this task, and what, if anything, is now left for the laboratory. Does anything of significance remain to be measured that would cast further light on the developmental process itself? What new questions remain to be derived directly from this majestic theory? In this paper we shall offer the view that the axiomatic nature of Piaget's theory in fact stood critically in the way of measurement, that it has guided experimental work in developmental cognition in the wrong direction, and that as a result, some of the major, original questions still remain to be answered. In particular, we suggest that an exaggerated structure/process distinction has arisen from failures to instantiate Piaget's axiomatically derived structures in experimental tasks, and that this in turn has had the effect of severing the measurement of cognitive growth from the behavioural regulations on which it depends. Turning to what we believe to be the central and enduringly important proposition in Piagetian theory – that knowledge is acquired through a dynamic interaction between the child and a structured, potentially informing environment, we shall argue on the basis of epigenetic type paradigms developed within our own research programme, that complex cognitive structures can be exposed using behaviour-based paradigms which explicitly provoke cognitive regulation. We propose that such paradigms, which are essentially non-verbal in character, offer a real possibility of measuring cognitive development in terms completely congruent with the concept of cognitive epigenesis through dynamic self-regulation.

PIAGET, MEASUREMENT AND THE LOGICAL MOTHER STRUCTURES

The key concept in Piaget's (structural) account of development which, we shall argue, has had a negative influence on developmental cognition is *relational reversibility*. Influenced by the way in which the Bourbaki group provided structures within mathematics which could unify number theory, calculus, geometry and topology, Piaget sought 'mother-structures' in children's thinking which would explain, with equal parsimony, how basic scientific, mathematical and logical principles come to be grasped (see e.g. Inhelder and Piaget 1964; Piaget, 1970). Of the three mother-structures he identified, two were united through the common property of relational reversibility. Of these, one is an algebraic principle, characterised by the concept of inversion (operation p multiplied by the inverse operation, p to the minus 1, equals zero). Thus $+A-A = 0$. This first structure is implied in the understanding of class inclusive relations. That is, the partitioning of a class B composed of say two sub-classes, e.g. A and A', requires that the knowing agent can move intellectually from class to sub-class by means of inversion ($A+A' = B$ and $B-A = A'$ etc.).The second is an order structure in which reversibility is expressed as reciprocity: $A = B$ is equivalent to $B = A$. This structure is the one involved in the understanding of transitivity and other order relations. (The third principle is a topological one and applies to the understanding of space and the development of geometry.) The grasp of reversibility supposedly 'frees' the subject from the ties of immediate time and space. An operational subject can conserve the quantity of a liquid under visual transformation, because the transformation can be reversed *in principle* (Piaget and Inhelder, 1956). At this stage too (at around seven/eight years), the subject might perceive that an object (A) is larger than another (B), but will be simultaneously appreciative of the fact that B is smaller than A (Inhelder and Piaget, 1964). Relational reversibility liberates the child into a new world of schematic combinations. Reciprocal relations allows items to be seriated into larger structures ($A > B > C > D$, etc.) and their transitivity to be apprehended (A is bigger than C) and so on. Mobility within these structures, referred to by Piaget as 'anticipation' and 'hindsight', is the by-word of operationality and is the key to cognitive equilibrium (Inhelder and Piaget, 1964).

Thus the concept of stable logical structures for organising knowledge formed the template for Piaget against which he matched the child's behaviour. Development was characterised by a slow and gradual differentiation of logical from empirical knowing, a process which becomes increasingly private owing to the growing interiorisation of actions, the semiotic instruments of thought. What was measured directly was the emergence of landmark behaviours – the *consequences* of structural growth. Enriched beyond correctness *per se*, this now included (in the case of reasoning tasks, for example) the verbal justifications offered by the child for the answer given. Those which were 'devoid of logical necessity' (Piaget, 1928, p. 234) were typical of the pre-operational child whose justifications were based instead on piecemeal or unco-ordinated bits of information. But for the logical (necessary) connections to become fully articulable, the child had to have progressed well beyond the first appearance of the mother structures at the level of concrete operations (such as seriation and class-inclusion), to the stage of formal operations where s/he has access to the 'logic of propositions' (Piaget, 1970, p. 39). Thus the formal operational child should make explicit allusion during the three-term series test to the necessity of the outcome in terms, e.g. '*If* Edith is fairer than Suzanne *and* Edith is darker than Lili *then* Suzanne *must be* darkest.' But at the pre-formal, non hypothetico-deductive levels, the mapping of behaviour against the template of the mother-structures had to be explored at the level of overt non-verbal behaviour (as in e.g. seriation and measurement) and, where verbal judgement and decision-making was used, in relation to a concrete perceivable reality (as in e.g. class-inclusion and conservation). Specially designed tasks and carefully documented case studies were thus generated in awesome profusion by Piaget and his colleagues and did indeed appear to illustrate how these core mother-structures emerge as a result of private acts of discovery in the context of almost every sphere of human knowing – even into those areas of science and mathematics which others have reserved for more socio-culturally based explanations (Vygotsky, 1962). A vast amount has been measured in the name of Piagetian structuralism in terms of these paradigms, and the fund of new knowledge acquired through the innovations of the Genevan laboratory is now legendary. This outstanding achievement is one of the things we celebrate in this anniversary year.

Whilst theoretically grounded, however, the 'new' measures of cognitive growth were not designed in the spirit of 'null hypothesis' testing. The structures motivating growth were there at the outset – they were never up for refutation. As Inhelder and de Caprona (1987) have described it, 'Genetic psychology is adult-centred, indeed scientist-centred. It starts from the end, the final stage, and reconstructs its construction.' Whilst Piaget was open to theoretical innovations in contemporary mathematics which could further develop his formal characterisation of the end-state, as in the case of the concept of 'correspondence' which he used to augment his earlier concept of rule-based 'transformation' (Beilin, 1980), develop-ments in psychology had little impact, no real place or relevance. This was not because structure was favoured over process (the more usual remit of psychological theory). Piaget's attention to regulatory devices of assimi-lation and accommodation during what some have called his 'functionalist' phase (Inhelder and de Caprona, 1987) testifies to that. But process in Piagetian theory has always been derived directly from his structural account. The process of equilibration, for example, achieves stability in the sense that it can explain how certain skills emerge, such as searching for objects which have been visibly displaced, counting up to ten and sorting objects by their properties. But these processes always contain the seed of further re-organisation and re-integration into yet more sophisticated skills (e.g. searching for objects which have been invisibly displaced, enumeration and hierarchical classification) and are on an inevitable growth trajectory until the structures become realised at least in the 'epis-temic' subject. This seed is the structurally defined end-state which Piaget argues to be the ultimate cognitive motive and the biological imperative (Piaget, 1971) and *its* existence proof is in logic and mathematics. In short, the interactive dynamics postulated by Piaget have never been used to discover *what the structures might be*. As we review below, this was also largely true of the experimental tradition which followed on the heels of the Genevan programme.

THE EXPERIMENTAL PROGRAMME AND THE STRUCTURE/PROCESS DISTINCTION

As we pay homage to the man so must we recognise those who have followed in his tradition. Whether taken in the spirit of confirmation (e.g. Youniss and Murray, 1970) or refutation (e.g. Braine, 1959), a huge corpus of supplementary data on age of emergence (e.g. Bryant and Trabasso, 1971), task synchrony (e.g. Kingma, 1984) and teachability (e.g. Smedslund, 1963) of Piagetian skills has been amassed in an experimental endeavour inspired by Piaget's own findings and measurements. However, despite such arduous efforts to subject the original tasks to interpretative and implementational qualification, two things have failed to materialise. One is any proof or instantiation of the mother-structures as far as reversibility is concerned (see e.g. Gladstone and Palazzo, 1974; Leiser and Gilliéron, 1990). The other is an *alternative* characterisation of cognitive structures with both the generality and specificity offered by the Piagetian one. The latter is related to the reluctance with which the failure of the first has been acknowledged. Thus, for example, the transitivity debate has been concerned more with the reasons why children might not 'use' operatory mechanisms in the context of particular versions of the task (see e.g. Grieve and Nesdale, 1979) than with *whether* operatory mechanisms are the best characterisation of transitive choice mechanisms in the first place (McGonigle and Chalmers, 1992). But rather than abandon some of the background assumptions of the Piagetian agenda and perhaps change its theory of measurement, a Kuhnian type raft-clinging has occurred where, in the absence of alternative characterisations of intelligent systems on a similar scale, there has been a tendency to hunt even harder for the operatory structures, the more elusive they have become.

Such single-mindedness was perhaps first registered in the overwhelming indifference (by developmentalists) to the discoveries in the 1960s that adults often fail to implement *logical* solutions to simple three-term series task like the Edith/Lili/Suzanne test. Such failures were not of the 'imperfect reasoner' variety that Piaget could have easily have ascribed to implementational failure, furthermore – for these performances could not simply be described as a 'shortfall' from perfect accuracy – but suggested instead a psychological structuration of the task entirely different from one based on reversibility. Typically, human adults reason in ways which show unidirectionality of processing (Huttenlocher, 1968), partiality of access to logically derivable solutions (de Soto *et al.*, 1965) and a lack of sensitivity to logical indeterminacy (Clark, 1969; McGonigle and Chalmers, 1986). In subsequent decades, the ubiquity of reaction time phenomenon during reasoning tasks administered to adults and known as the 'Symbolic Distance Effect', showed the existence of linear search structures (see e.g. Potts, 1972), but no direct evidence of logical constructions based on reversible operations.

The discovery by Trabasso (Trabasso *et al.*, 1975) of similar phenomena in the error and reaction time profiles of children at every age tested (four to nine years), forced developmentalists to take notice (see also McGonigle and Chalmers, 1986). But now the distinction between structure and process came to the aid of those still cleaving to the Piagetian agenda, and 'new' data based on RT and error profiling was soon re-cast as 'information processing' (Breslow, 1981). Surely what was emerging, the argument went, was a sharper distinction between the real-time processes as revealed under the microscope of modern experimental techniques, and the more general structural principles which link performances on related tasks 'in much the way that linguistic deep structures link together various surface structure manifestations of language' (Breslow, 1981, p. 348). The implication remained that one would ultimately be 'mappable' onto the other if the time and trouble was taken to effect such a mapping. Yet at least one recent and highly detailed attempt to explicitly converge Piagetian structural principles with an information processing analysis of performance (on the Piagetian task of seriation) has failed dramatically to achieve this and resulted in the conclusion that the 'unexpected slack in the relation between structures and procedures . . . demands serious attention' (Leiser and Gilliéron, 1990, p. 173).

One riposte to this from Piaget's defenders is well articulated by Smith (1993), who contends that to expect such task-based instantiation of structural principles in any case is to fail to understand the theory! The assessment, he argues, is not co-extensive with the structural account. 'Assessment tasks alone provide an insufficient unit of analysis in support of this commitment to matching' (Smith, 1993, p. 97). Our concern, however, is less with the means by which behaviour is 'matched' against hypothesised operational structures, than with the fact that this exercise itself seems to have distorted and fractionated the original Piagetian thesis. In particular it appears to have forced apart the cognitive structures from the behaving-in-the-world environment from which they are supposed to emerge – a disjunction and divergence which is surely anathema to Piaget's own position. In an atmosphere where the structural principles were becomingly increasingly isolated from behaviour as measured in information-processing based programmes, greater efforts have been made latterly to recover 'representation' and 'understanding' from mere 'behaving' (see Karmiloff-Smith, 1992, and Halford, 1993, for two recent examples). It is quite easy to see how events have led to this. For the greatest excitement in the experimental attempts to validate Piagetian doctrine was generated by the 'early competence' claims which attended new studies of class-inclusion, conservation and transitivity (see e.g. Light, 1988, and Thayer and Collyer, 1978). Competences found by Piaget with seven to eight year olds were sought after in four and five year olds. In this climate, the burden of exposing operational understanding in 'pre-operational' children led investigators to highlight the representational aspects of the solution by minimising the concrete givens in the task. Thus, of the original measures and paradigms, as used by Piaget, those with a predominately perceptual and behavioural content have been the subject of the greatest revision by those who have followed. Whereas Piaget allowed his subjects to *see* the towers in the measurement experiment, and to *compare* two sticks in his 'concrete' transitivity tasks, it appears accepted wisdom nowadays to reject such conditions as allowing a 'perceptual' solution (Adams, 1978; Perner *et al.*, 1981). In seriation, the classic task explicitly requires the subject to place in order of size a visible, touchable, liftable, placeable, set of elements – a requirement which has made success on this task one of the most robust of all Piagetian tasks in terms of its correlation with chronological age. Yet investigators have gone to extreme lengths to reduce direct perceptual encounters with the objects in seriation, by using 'invisible' or 'imagined' versions which ostensibly demand a 'representational' solution (Baylor *et al.*, 1973; Leiser and Gilliéron, 1990).

A further consequence of the tendency to focus on 'representation' has been the heavy reliance on verbal judgement as an experimental measure even with relatively young children. Despite a widespread awareness of the dangers of over-interpreting failure at the linguistic level (McShane, 1991), the majority of contemporary Piagetian-derived tasks are instantiated in the form of an exchange of referring expressions, such as 'Are there more (Xs) or (Ys)?'; 'Is there more here or here?'; 'Are they the same or different?', etc. Yet if explicit verbal justifications are not seen as a trustworthy access to the child's representations of the world, owing to the question-begging issues they raise on the relationship between language and thought (Smith, 1993), then verbally mediated judgments are little better, especially with young children. For linguistic judgment, even when accurate and supported by logical justifications, is by nature more *qualitative* and *indeterminate* than the real-world states which such judgement is supposed to reflect. In conservation of quantity and other two-state based tasks, this might not be obvious, as there is a one-to-one correspondence between the visible state of the objects (less/more/same) and the referring expressions. But in the case of tasks with high upper levels of complexity and determination, such as classification, to what extent can answers to binary questions such as 'are there more daisies than flowers?' possibly capture, by themselves, the ontological and organisational complexities of such a structure, its nesting relations, asymmetries, and so on, especially in subjects where such structural complexity is precisely that which is under test? Whilst 'articulated representative regulations' such as 'increasing articulations of classifications, relations of order, etc.' (Piaget, 1974, p. 58) might indeed be a product and even a part of structural development, do such language-based measures afford appropriate indices by themselves? Piaget thought not: 'These large total structures outdistance the subject's language and could not even be formulated with the sole aid of current language' (1974, p. 120), arguing by contrast that: 'the roots of logical thought are not to be found in language alone . . . but are to be found more generally in the co-ordination of actions which are the basis of reflective abstraction' (Piaget, 1970, pp. 18 and 19).

As this typical comment also illustrates, however, there is another essential component of 'understanding' in Piaget's analysis, and it is this component which seems to have become lost. Grounded in the real world, and forged by emerging structures directly abstracted from behaviour itself, which 'does not include an abstraction based on the characteristics of the object but an abstraction based on the actions affecting these objects' (Piaget, 1974, p. 106), these are the *regulatory* functions which, whether in structural or in functional mode (Inhelder and de Caprona, 1987), he has never failed to emphasise. As he put it, 'between the ages of seven and twelve . . . we observe a long period characterised by concrete operations (categories, relations, numbers) *linked to the manipulation of objects themselves*' (Piaget, 1974, p. 116, our emphasis).

It is the great paradox of the neo-Piagetian movement that it is precisely this link that is missing in much of modern experiment. The hunt for operational structure, whether an explicit goal or simply the implicit context for developmental cognition, has resulted in a retreat from the study of the wellsprings of those action-based regulatory processes which dynamic structuralism is *committed to revealing* if it is to be taken seriously as a scientific theory of cognitive growth.

A NEW BEHAVIOUR-BASED APPROACH: COMBINATORICS VERSUS LOGIC IN THE ANALYSIS AND MEASUREMENT OF COMPLEXITY

In our own work, we have wholeheartedly endorsed the need for a Piagetian style epigenetic analysis to unravel the dynamics of cognitive structuration in complex systems. Rather than map behaviour onto *a priori* structures, however, our goal is to discover what these structures might be by setting up laboratory-based microworlds designed to assess the regulatory relationships between the subject and task environments of increasing complexity. In the absence of pre-hoc structures like Piaget's which define the motive for growth from an end-state perspective, we have introduced adaptive pressures on the subject from the most central feature of all behaviour-ordering, and the combinatorial problems which such behaviours necessarily generate (McGonigle and Chalmers, 1996, 1997).

As in language production, and other forms of production based on actions, this pressure to organise is seen in the fact that combinatorial explosion occurs beyond four or five constituents of action. Thus in any four-constituent sequence, for example, twenty-four combinations are possible: with an increase of a single unit, the possibilities leap geometrically to 120. As such action sequences and combinations are the basic currency of survival (Tinbergen, 1951), we believe that the action-as-genesis problem raised by Piaget can be restated here as a problem of *sequential constraint* where, in the case of simple animals, evolutionary engineering takes care of the problem through a simple chaining mechanism (Schneirla, 1959). This illustrates a *path restriction policy*, which in the case of fixed action sequences avoids the combinatoric problem at the expense of plasticity. For more complex agents such control is achieved through autonomous regulation. Here the agent must discover for itself path restriction policies which are adaptive and economy preserving, through inductive procedures which allow it to discover these empirically. To obtain a window on the emergence of such procedures, we have investigated the ways in which complex agents such as human and non-human primates derive these constraints through their executive control of sequences.

New paradigms have enabled us to translate challenging cognitive tasks into explicitly sequential ones, using touch-screen apparatus in which the general requirement is that subjects touch every icon within a set in an exhaustive and non-reiterative order. In training versions of such tasks, redundant economy-preserving sequences can be contrasted directly with less economic routes through the same set of items, to see when and to what extent there is an advantage for the former, and when such an advantage expresses itself as a generalised principle. Thus, in seriation (training), using novel procedures which we first initiated in 1988, five- and seven-year-old children learned to order a set of size icons on the screen which varied both in number and in sequential characteristics. The number of items is an important variable here because, viewed from the combinatorial standpoint, small changes, for example from five to seven items, produces a geometrical expansion of possible sequences from 120 to 5,040! Confronted with this combinatorially explosive problem, one adaptive response would be to evolve search structures which exploit constraints inherent in size as a property. Only monotonic series (biggest to smallest and *vice-versa*) have such an economy-preserving characteristic, as these enable the subject to search according to one direction of change, and describe each item correspondingly at a low level of description (e.g. next biggest). The directional rule has itself, however, to be regulated by forward scanning to determine the size and regularity (or otherwise) of the interval difference. Thus these computations are by no means independent; for failure to abide by the interval or metrical requirements will affect the application of the iterative relational rule. For example, 'jumping' or neglecting an interval or two of difference when searching from smallest to biggest will ultimately leave the subject with residual items which cannot be searched and incorporated without back-tracking and repair. So monotonic searches can provide a highly economy-preserving and data-reducing control device. Such data reduction possibilities do not extend to the other possible size sequences, however, which derive permutatively from the same set of items. In contrast, non-monotonic sequences based, for example, on the choice of middle size first, then second smallest, then biggest, etc. will demand very high levels of item description and low levels of prediction, given the uneven serial contour which such series feature. Under these conditions, the only choice the subject has to secure high prediction, is to repeat and rehearse such sequences over and over again.

Whilst all subjects from the age of five years onward show a training advantage for monotonic sequences of five elements over non-monotonic ones in our experiments (McGonigle and Chalmers, 1993a), their detection of serial constraints afforded by such sequences was partial. One index of this is that they showed no significant difference in the acquisition of monotonic sequences from the speed and accuracy with which they learned entirely arbitrary sequences based on five individual colours, themselves devoid of any inherent sequential structure. In addition, five year olds failed to transfer immediately to a seven-item version of the monotonic sequence, which they found much more difficult, and indeed some even failed to learn it at all. Seven year olds, by contrast, acquired monotonic size sequences rapidly, showed a superiority over the colour-based arbitrary sequence, and coped without any apparent 'costs' with the expansion of the monotonic sequence to seven items. However, even these subjects found non-monotonic sequences difficult, and the majority failed to acquire the seven-item version (see Figure 17).

As an overall measure, such procedures yield an age by task structure and task complexity difference which suggests that the seven year old may have reached an asymptotic level of redundancy detection in the case of size relations. However, the generality of this competence for other series even within a visual modality, such as relative brightness, remains to be assessed.

Such data show that it is orders with the *lowest computational demands* which emerge over development. One implication of this is that children improve as they get older by making tasks easier! A second implication is that in so far as cognitive growth is autonomous and self-regulatory, economy provides one rationale for such growth. If so, complex, *autonomous*, agents must have some means of selecting economic procedures other than those based solely on explicit environmental arbitration, in this case in the form of response by response feedback. Whilst valuable in the assessment of upper limits on task-achieving competences, traditional training methods can obscure these regulatory processes.

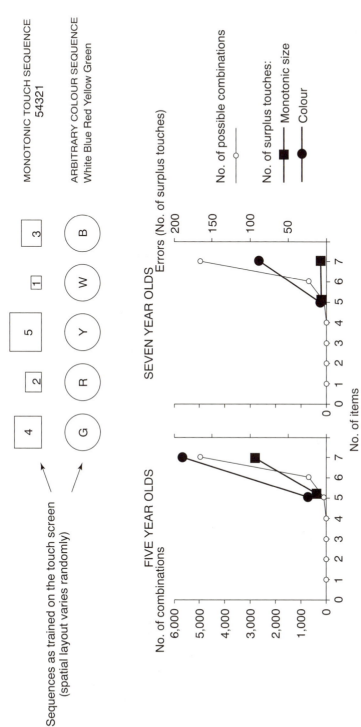

MONOTONIC TOUCH SEQUENCE
54321

ARBITRARY COLOUR SEQUENCE
White Blue Red Yellow Green

Sequences as trained on the touch screen
(spatial layout varies randomly)

SEVEN YEAR OLDS

FIVE YEAR OLDS

No. of possible combinations

No. of surplus touches:
■ Monotonic size
● Colour

Errors (No. of surplus touches)

No. of items

No. of combinations

Figure 17 Paradigm and results showing age-related change in the exploitation by children of (linear) economy-preserving constraints on sequencing

Until now, we have been unaware of paradigms dedicated specifically to assess self-regulation of this sort. Accordingly we have devised a variety of new procedures designed to put (task-inspired) pressure on the subject to self-organise, and have also introduced free search procedures into our training paradigms (e.g. McGonigle *et al.*, 1992, 1994; McGonigle and Chalmers, 1993b). In particular these have been designed to evaluate the extent to which subjects *classify* and *search* hierarchically to compensate for the increasing cognitive load demanded by having to order progressively longer sequences.

To manipulate this load on the agent, we first require the subject to order icons on the touch screen which come from putatively different categories as in A (square), B (circle), C (triangle), D (diamond), etc. arranged within spatial arrays which vary randomly from trial to trial. In this phase the string length can be extended (up to at least twenty-five icons) but is without any compensating structural possibilities – if the subject is to search exhaustively without reiteration, a routinised arbitrary sequence must be rehearsed. The crucial contrast is provided by having the same subjects order items which demand seriation of the same length of sequence; however, the compositionality of the set to be seriated has now been altered. In this latter condition, multiple exemplars of the A class, the B class, etc. are provided; again spatial layout of items is at random. Failure to classify would result in strings of unorganised units such as ABBBACCBC etc., and the limits on string length that could be controlled (without reiteration or omission) would be similar to those recorded under arbitrary sequence conditions, which can only be learned by brute force memory and rehearsal. However, if classification and chunking is used, strategically organised strings such as A1 A2 A3 B1 B2 B3 etc. would be produced, and more extended sequence control should be expected as a consequence. With these procedures we have found that young children and monkeys (*Cebus apella*) execute much longer than those previously reported; monkeys, for example, can now achieve twelve-item seriation where there are opportunities for classification such as in a three-class by four-exemplar string (see Figure 18), and we have not reached the upper limits of their performance. However, if not structured, six or so independent items seems around their limit. Analyses of the time it takes to respond to each item in turn within the sequence, furthermore, shows strong classification effects.

In this way we can now help determine within a *behavioural* paradigm how subjects may compensate for combinatorially complex and progressively unmanageable search tasks by devising data reducing, informationally efficient strategies. As each of the categorical exemplars is also subject to ordering requirements, and these in turn can be differentiated to provide yet further layers of exemplars, there is now a real chance that the paradigms which we have devised will enable us to assess the levels of *hierarchical* management which subjects can achieve without requiring the

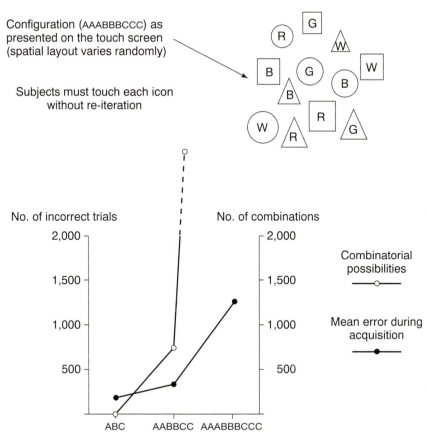

Figure 18 Paradigm and results showing the exploitation by monkey (*Cebus apella*) of classificatory structure in the control of a sequencing task requiring exhaustive search

language-based tests of Piaget. Figure 19 shows how principled nesting can allow a very large number of items to be controlled in the course of a single serial production. It also enables us to combine assays of size seriation and hierarchical organisation within the same paradigm and, crucially, with the same measures.

In this way the conditions for regulation, its goals and its consequences for structural elaboration are provided for within this programme. Thus our combinatoric/sequential approach offers a highly gradable series of tasks with respect to complexity and executive control without requiring that the experimenter moves to linguistic input to tap into levels of understanding which only those with semiotic instruments can engage in. It offers both a common currency in an evolutionary context as well as identifying some of the important cognitive regulators – based on the relationship between

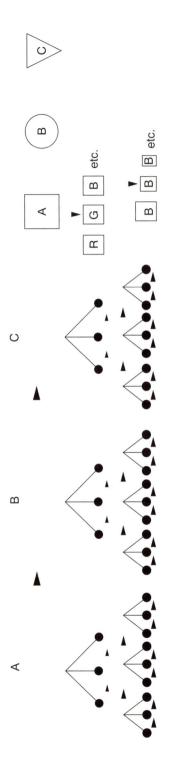

etc. . . . .

Figure 19 Hierarchical architecture for efficient search and executive control of items presented for seriation on the touch screen

cognitive load and its compensation by the agent designed to purchase the most executive control for the least cognitive effort or expenditure of resource.

Based on real time production, moreover, our procedures aid in the process of better determination of the agent as it executes a particular task. In addition, we can also assess the emergence of cognitive structuration as it may elaborate and develop over a protracted time period. Taking these two aspects together enables us to assess how the agent may move from weak to strong as a consequence of dynamic cognitive re-organisation. Routines which are forged first in relatively simple tasks are later assessed in situations where sequences are extended, the items replaced and the compositionality of the set to be searched is subject to experimental variation. The development of strong inductive procedures over time can thus be laid bare both in transfer measures and through an analysis of principled 'interpretations' of error, well beyond the 'shuttlings', 'fumblings' and 'gropings' so beloved by Piaget. That is, in an informationally rich context in which the error space can be vast, 'mistake' is rarely the obverse of a 'correct' response. For it has already become clear from our learning analysis that error interpretation has to be learned through the acquisition first of successful sub-routines – which then allow error to be defined as its derivation. In this way the errors which Piaget found so characteristic of different stages of cognitive growth can now be explicitly incorporated into the measurement of the inductive procedures leading to such growth.

For these reasons, an epigenetic stance is still, we believe, a highly viable approach to the question of knowledge gain in both evolution and development. However, revisions are necessary. First, we suggest replacing Piaget's logical-axiomatic based currency as the formal motive of inductive systems with an informatic-based combinatoric approach. In this, reversibility and the achievement of logical impartiality is replaced by the idea that cognitive complexity derives from the roots of ordering and derives its strength from the selectivity and privileged representations of order (see McGonigle and Chalmers, 1986). This contrasts with the more democratic implications of a logic-based system where the various forms of relational expression, for example, are seen to be 'equivalent'. In this equivalence, the power and generality of operatory structures is to be found. But the only economy of resource management that it can possibly lead to is a recombinative one where structures become reintegrated at *new levels* of functioning through the deployment of ever more 'powerful' solutions (in the inclusive sense) (Halford, 1993; Cellérier, 1987). Whilst we do not repudiate such a principle as an explanation of how domain independence might be achieved, the fact remains that the dynamics of domain-specific solutions have to be *first* made transparent in order to understand how they may (in some cases at least) become re-synthesised or generalised.

THE FUTURE

Now laid bare for future scientific development is one of the great unresolved issues of this century – the mapping relationship between language and cognitive structure. In the past, the confounds inherent in the accessing of complex cognitive operations by means of linguistic tasks have made it difficult if not impossible to factor out the cognitive from the linguistic. Now, we believe it is possible, given new paradigms and new technology, to provide transparent measures of the cognitive profiling rich enough to establish when and if linguistically expressed knowledge understates, overstates or introduces something different into competences assessed independently with behaviour based procedures.

As for action itself, as Beilin (1980, p. 256) has argued, 'even though Piaget's theory makes much of the interaction between subject and object . . . he rarely, if ever, specifies what in experience stems from action'. With our new procedures which allow subjects to manipulate and rearrange icons on a screen, and thus alter the *state* of the array in addition to merely searching items within a predetermined spatial layout, it is now possible to evaluate, in perhaps a more focused way, the role of specific actions in the genesis and construction of cognitive structures (McGonigle and Chalmers, 1993b). For what might be a crucial evolutionary advantage for the human agent – the adroit manipulation of objects – will now be evaluated, not simply as an index of success (as in the spatial ordering of items in a seriation task), but as the externalisation of successful search procedures, now in the form of self-produced state-based feedback which may well constitute a separate layer of competence with a powerful potential role in the growing interaction between agent and world.

In short, if, as Vygotsky has suggested, complex functions are fossilised in the cognitive competences of human adults, then we need a major onslaught on the behaviour-based fractionation of such competences whilst maintaining, crucially, a *common currency of measurement* over the evolutionary and developmental landscape. Given the large canvas that these programmes demand, moreover, such agendas will surely continue to be inspired by the great landmark questions raised by Piaget in his celebrated and imaginative attempts to reveal the embryology of mind.

REFERENCES

Adams, M. J. (1978) Logical competence and transitive inference in young children. *Journal of Experimental Child Psychology*, 25, 477–89.

Baylor, G. W., Gascon, J., Lemoyne, G. and Pothier, N. (1973) An information processing model of some seriation tasks. *The Canadian Psychologist*, 14, 2, 167–96.

Beilin, H. (1980) Piaget's theory: refinement, revision or rejection? In R. H. Kluve and H. Spada (eds) *Developmental Models of Thinking*, pp. 245–61). London: Academic Press.

Braine, M. D. S. (1959) The ontogeny of certain logical operations: Piaget's formulation examined by nonverbal methods. *Psychological Monographs*, 73, 5 (whole issue).

Breslow, L. (1981) Reevaluation of the literature on transitive inferences. *Psychological Bulletin*, 89, 2, 325–51.

Bryant, P. E. and Trabasso, T. (1971) Transitive inferences and memory in young children. *Nature*, 232, 456–8.

Burt, C. (1919) The development of reasoning in school children. *Journal of Experimental Pedagogy*, 5, 68–77 and 121–7.

Cellérier, G. (1987) Structures and functions. In B. Inhelder, D. de Caprona and A. Cornu-Wells (eds) *Piaget Today*, pp. 1–14. Hove: Lawrence Erlbaum.

Clark, H. H. (1969) Linguistic processes in deductive reasoning. *Psychological Review*, 76, 387–404.

de Soto, C. B., London, M. and Handel, S. (1965) Social reasoning and spatial paralogic. *Journal of Personality and Social Psychology*, 2, 513–21.

Elkind, D. (1971) Two approaches to intelligence: Piagetian and psychometric. In D. R. Green, M. P. Ford and G. B. Flamer (eds) *Measurement and Piaget*. Proceedings of the CTB/McGraw-Hill Conference on Ordinal Scales of Cognitive Development.

Gladstone, R. and Palazzo, R. (1974) Empirical evidence for reversibility by inversion. *Developmental Psychology*, 10, 6, 942–8.

Grieve, R. and Nesdale, A. R. (1979) Observations on a test of transitive inference in children. *Australian Journal of Psychology*, 31, 1, 43–8.

Halford, G. S. (1993) *Children's Understanding: The Development of Mental Models*. Hillsdale, NJ: Lawrence Erlbaum.

Huttenlocher, J. (1968) Constructing spatial images: a strategy in reasoning. *Psychological Review*, 75, 550–60.

Inhelder, B. and de Caprona, D. (1987) Introduction to B. Inhelder, D. de Caprona and A. Cornu-Wells (eds) *Piaget Today*, pp. 1–14. Hove: Lawrence Erlbaum.

Inhelder, B. and Piaget, J. (1964) *The Early Growth of Logic in the Child*. London: Routledge and Kegan Paul.

Karmiloff-Smith, A. (1992) *Beyond Modularity: A Developmental Perspective on Cognitive Science*. London: MIT Press.

Kingma, J. (1984) Task sensitivity and the sequence of development in seriation, ordinal correspondence, and cardination. *Genetic Psychology Monographs*, 110, 2, 181–205.

Leiser, D. and Gilliéron, C. (1990) *Cognitive Science and Genetic Epistemology*. New York: Plenum.

Light, P. (1988) Context, conservation and conversation. In K. Richardson and S. Sheldon (eds) *Cognitive Development to Adolescence*. Hove: Lawrence Erlbaum.

McGonigle, B. and Chalmers, M. (1986) Representations and strategies during inference. In T. Myers, K. Brown and B. O. McGonigle (eds) *Reasoning and Discourse Processes*. London: Academic Press.

McGonigle, B. and Chalmers, M. (1992) Monkeys are rational! *The Quarterly Journal of Experimental Psychology*, 45B, 3, 189–228.

McGonigle, B. and Chalmers, M. (1993a) an experimental analysis of ordering skills in children. ESRC Project grant final report (British Library).

McGonigle, B. and Chalmers, M. (1993b) Assessing the role of ordering skills in cognitive growth. ESRC project grant proposal.

McGonigle, B. and Chalmers, M. (1996) The ontology of order. In L. Smith (ed.) *Critical Readings on Piaget*. London: Routledge.

McGonigle, B. and Chalmers, M. (1997) *The Growth of Intelligence in Complex Systems*. MS in preparation for MIT Press.

McGonigle, B., Lillo, C. de and Dickinson, T. (1992) Serial order induced search in children and monkeys. Paper presented at the 5th European Conference on Developmental Psychology, Seville, Spain.

McGonigle, B., de, C., Lillo, T., and Dickinson, (1994) Classification to order: a comparative analysis of categorical seriation in monkey and man. Paper presented to the XVth Congress of the International Primatological Society, Bali, Indonesia.

McShane, J. (1991) *Cognitive Development: An Information Processing Approach*. Oxford: Blackwell.

Perner, J., Steiner, G. and Staehlin, C. (1981) Mental representation of length and weight series and transitive inferences in young children. *Journal of Experimental Child Psychology*, 31, 177–92.

Piaget, J. (1928) *Judgment and Reasoning in the Child*. London: Routledge and Kegan Paul.

Piaget, J. (1970) *Genetic Epistemology*. New York: Columbia University Press.

Piaget, J. (1971) *Biology and Knowledge*. Edinburgh: Edinburgh University Press.

Piaget, J. (1974) *The Child and Reality*. London: Muller.

Piaget, J. and Inhelder, B. (1956) *The Child's Conception of Space*. London: Routledge and Kegan Paul.

Piaget, J. and Szeminska, A. (1952) *The Child's Conception of Number*. London: Routledge and Kegan Paul.

Piaget, J., Inhelder, B. and Szeminska, A. (1960) *The Child's Conception of Geometry*. London: Routledge and Kegan Paul.

Potts, G. R. (1972) Information processing strategies used in the encoding of linear orderings. *Journal of Verbal Learning and Verbal Behaviour*, 11, 727–40.

Schneirla, T. C. (1959) An evolutionary and developmental theory of biphasic processes underlying approach and withdrawal. In M. R. Jones (ed.) *Nebraska Symposium on Motivation*, VII. Nebraska: University of Nebraska Press.

Smedslund, J. (1963) The acquisition of transitivity of weight in five-to-seven-year-old children. *Journal of Genetic Psychology*, 102, 245–55.

Smith, L. (1993) *Necessary Knowledge: Piagetian Perspectives on Constructivism*. Hove: Lawrence Erlbaum.

Thayer, E. S. and Collyer, C. E. (1978) The development of transitive inference: a review of recent approaches. *Psychological Bulletin*, 85, 1327–43.

Tinbergen, N. (1951) *The Study of Instinct*. London: Oxford University Press.

Trabasso, T., Riley, C. A. and Wilson, E. G. (1975) The representation of linear and spatial strategies in reasoning: a developmental study. In R. Falmagne (ed.) *Reasoning: Representation and Process in Children and Adults*, pp. 201–29. Hillsdale, NJ: Lawrence Erlbaum.

Vygotsky, L. S. (1962) *Thought and Language*. Cambridge: MIT Press.

Youniss, J. and Murray, J. P. (1970) Transitive inference with nontransitive solutions controlled. *Developmental Psychology*, 2, 2, 169–75.

12 Why measure development?

James Ridgway

> If 90 psychologists take 90 minutes to test 9 classes, how long will 45 psychologists take?
>
> If 90 musicians take 90 minutes to play Beethoven's 9th symphony, how long will 45 musicians take?

Whenever psychologists use mathematics and statistics for theory building or analysing data, they make assumptions about the phenomena being investigated. In the question about musicians, the humour arises because one is invited to apply a particular mathematical model (here, proportional reasoning) to a situation where it violates one's implicit theory of the phenomenon (here, the duration of symphonies). The argument can be generalised; whenever psychologists choose statistical tools and research methods, they make assumptions about the phenomena they are studying. The choice of research methods, and the choice of method of analysis, provides an insight into the psychological assumptions being made. Theories themselves are constructed for some purpose, and have a likely domain of application; theorists make choices about the things they want to explain, and make choices (albeit implicitly) about the sort of generalisations which are likely to result from their work. For example, both Piaget and Vygotsky turned away from psychometric work early in their careers. The main objective of this early psychometric work was the classification of individuals on the basis of some ill-defined 'ability' in order to allocate persons to treatments (in this case, to identify people unlikely to benefit from conventional education); this contrasts directly with a detailed theoretically based analysis of performance on individual tasks in order to say something about the development of underlying mental processes.

In education, measures of development are used for a whole variety of purposes (Ridgway and Passey, 1993). In this paper, just three purposes will be considered: evaluating theories of development; guiding classroom practices; and engineering educational reform. The paper argues that these different purposes lead to quite different sorts of measurement. In each, the role of the psychologist is to develop and validate coherent theories and measures which match each purpose.

Piaget's theory has its roots in biology, and has three distinct elements; first is a large body of evidence collected from children of different ages on a range of reasoning tasks; second is a classification system to describe the behaviours that were observed (e.g. descriptions of concrete, pre-operational and formal operational thinking); and third, a theory to explain the observed patterns (in terms of interaction and co-ordination between cognitive structures and the environment).

Piaget argued that:

- development occurs through an invariant hierarchy of stages
- each stage has a unity of operation, and applies to all intellectual skills
- the key process of development is equilibration.

As an approach to theory building, one can see that Piaget's primary focus is on modelling – that is to say, the creation of a psychological story which provides an account of a large assembly of evidence. This can be contrasted with an approach to theory building based on hypothesis testing, where alternative explanations are created, and tested against each other until one can be rejected. Of course, this characterisation of modelling versus testing is a great oversimplification, but it illustrates something of the philosophical gap between Piaget and some of his critics.

Much of the work in the Piagetian tradition has been confirmatory – data are collected which are seen to be consistent with his work, or which lead to some refinement of his ideas. This can be contrasted with the work of his critics, such as Bryant (e.g. 1974, 1995), who looked for alternative explanations of phenomena such as the problems that eight year olds have with transitive inference. Bryant was able to show that some of the problems experienced by younger children actually reflect memory limitations, rather than problems of inference, and that there are considerable improvements in performance when these (irrelevant) limitations are side-stepped. The key question is how one deals with this new evidence from a theoretical viewpoint. A Popperian is likely to reject the whole theoretical framework; a modeller is likely to adjust the theory a little.

What of Piaget's central notion of intellectual stages? The idea of a stage depends on some sort of unity of function (despite appeals to décalage). Studies have shown low correlations between performances on different measures of the same operation (Pascual-Leone, 1970; Hamel, 1974); low test-retest scores (average 0.4) on the same Piagetian tests taken at different times during a longitudinal study (Neimark, 1975); low correlations between tests which measure competencies which are supposed to develop together, such as combinations and permutations; and large differences in the facilities of tasks with the same logical structure (Wason and Johnson-Laird, 1972). Brown and Desforges (1977) looked at the correlations amongst tests supposed to measure concrete and formal operational thinking. They concluded that, because the correlations were weak, Piaget's notions were wrong.

It is unfortunate that many of the criticisms of Piaget's theory are based on low correlations between performances on different tasks. Correlation assumes that variables are linearly related; while it is common knowledge in the psychological community that correlation provides a poor fit to curvilinear data, there seems little awareness that correlation also fails to provide a good fit to data which are hierarchically ordered. A simple correlational analysis will not reveal hierarchies, even if the data fit Piaget's model perfectly. This argument might seem obscure, but is sufficiently important to be worth illustrating with a concrete example.

Table 5 Invented hierarchical data

	item 1	item 2	item 3	item 4	item 5	item 6	Test Score 1	Test Score 2
child 1	1	0	0	0	0	0	1	0
child 2	1	1	0	0	0	0	2	0
child 3	1	1	1	0	0	0	3	0
child 4	1	1	1	1	0	0	3	1
child 5	1	1	1	1	1	0	3	2
child 6	1	1	1	1	1	1	3	3

Table 5 shows invented data: a score of 1 means that an item has been answered correctly, and a score of 0 means that an item has been answered incorrectly. Children and tasks are perfectly ordered; child 1 has a total score of 1; child 6 has a total score of 6. Items are perfectly ordered, too; item 1 is the easiest item; item 6 is the hardest item. No child is successful on a later item without having succeeded on every easier item. It is clear that if one knows the score of a child, one can state exactly those items which have been answered correctly and incorrectly.

Test Score 1 is calculated by adding the scores from the easiest items; Test Score 2 is calculated by adding the scores from the most difficult items. Inspection by eye shows that the correlation between Test Score 1 and Test Score 2 will be low. The calculated value is $r = 0.57$ (repeating the analysis for twenty items and twenty children produces $r = 0.60$). This value is misleadingly high, if one wishes to claim that r^2 shows the percentage of predictable variance, as one can see by imagining the scatter plot of the Test Score 1 against Test Score 2.

The same argument applies to the use of simple factor analysis. Factor analysis seeks to model the interrelations between test items via a linear combination of factors; it places no restrictions on the dimensionality of the space, and does considerable violence to artificial data constructed to show a pronounced developmental sequence. Any developmentalist who uses such techniques to evaluate a hierarchical theory is certain to find evidence against stages and hierarchies. The situation is strictly analogous to the example of the musicians – the mathematical model being used to judge the success of the theory is completely inappropriate for the purpose.

Trevor Bond has used Rasch scaling to develop measures of developmental progress, and reports an analysis of data from three independently developed measures of developmental progress, each developed to reflect Piagetian stages. A great strength of Bond's paper is the triangulation of different measures of operational thinking: Bond's Logical Operations Test (BLOT) (Bond, 1976) – a multiple choice test; the Piagetian Reasoning Test III – Pendulum (PRTIII) (Wylam and Shayer, 1978) – which requires written responses, trained observers and assessors; and the *méthode clinique* version of Inhelder's (1989) pendulum task – which, in the version used here, requires grades to be assigned to videotapes of performance on each of eighteen performance criteria. It should be noted that while both PRTIII and BLOT are developed from Inhelder's (1989) account in *The Growth of Logical Thinking*, they were developed independently from each other. All three measures showed evidence of hierarchical development; all were strongly interrelated and all related strongly to educational attainment.

Bond reports a strong relationship between BLOT scores and achievement in secondary school science:

> The BLOT is also being used in the junior secondary school to detect ceiling effects in school achievement associated with pre-formal levels of cognitive development . . . children at the concrete operational level . . . have very little chance of scoring above about 60% on traditional school-based assessment instruments in science . . . the sophistication of the science concepts developed by children in constructivist learning environments appear predictable from cognitive development scores on the BLOT.

He reports the evidence from the Cognitive Acceleration in Science Education (CASE) research (Adey and Shayer, 1994) that PRTIII scores are strongly correlated with performance on GCSE examinations in science, mathematics and language.

The work which Bond reports has direct relevance to theories of development, and has something to say about the principles of educational design – most obviously, that students are unlikely to learn if they face tasks which require them to function at intellectual levels which are beyond them. The major theme that a theory must be evaluated using appropriate methods and tools permeates Bond's work.

There is a stark contrast between behavioural descriptions relevant to the evaluation of theories of development, and descriptions of the micro structure of learning, or prescriptions about how classroom interactions might best be managed. For this, one needs studies conducted at the appropriate grain-size.

McGonigle and Chalmers (1996) argue that the axiomatic nature of Piaget's theory has guided experimental work in developmental cognition in the wrong direction. In particular, they argue, the measurement of cognitive growth has become divorced from the behavioural regulations on which it depends. McGonigle and Chalmers attempt to understand the nature and development of cognitive structures by watching them develop in laboratory based micro worlds (notably where participants are involved in ordering objects). Multiple comparisons between objects lead to a combinatoric explosion as the number of objects in the set increases, and so constraints must be applied to the problem if it is to be solved even partially. Many adaptations can be used to solve the problem, from chaining (biologically wired) responses, to the use of search strategies under conscious control, which can be expressed verbally. Their experimental paradigm allows experimenters to look at the reuse of cognitive structures in progressively more difficult problems. McGonigle and Chalmers want to replace Piaget's axiomatic system with one based on information processing, where the nature of the problems shape the emergence of cognitive structures based on the efficiency of different structures to solve real problems for the user. Efficient resource management will require old solutions to be reworked into new ones, and later represented in some abstract form.

McGonigle and Chalmers (1977, 1984) have done a good deal of work exploring the similarities and differences in the performances of non-verbal subjects – notably monkeys – on seriation tasks. Such tasks are interesting because they allow one to see the development of competence which is not mediated by language, and to compare the development of performance in non-human primates with the development of performance in children. The development of cognitive structures can be explored directly by behaviourally based paradigms; their work shows that the development of these structures need not depend on verbal mediation. McGonigle and Chalmers (1992) conclude from a set of experiments exploring transitive inferences made by monkeys that the development of transitive inference is a response to an environmental demand for a decision about how to act, not (as Piaget would have it) a result of a need to decide how to think, and that it is the result of processing constraints (i.e. the need to handle the combinatoric explosion as the number of items to be ordered increases) not the unfolding of a pre-specified intellectual flower.

Their paper makes no reference to Vygotsky, yet the views expressed are recognisably Vygotskian. According to Vygotsky's cultural-historical theory:

- specific functions are not given at birth, but are provided via social and cultural patterns
- in different historical and cultural periods, different sorts of individual development will take place
- development depends upon social activity
- development can be seen as the internalisation of social activities

- systems of signs and symbols are crucial to this development
- development is a life long process.

The work of McGonigle and Chalmers makes a contribution to our understanding of the micro structure of some of these processes. Their work
underlines the key themes of this paper – that the methods and measures
used by researchers are an integral part of their theories; that theories are
constructed for some purposes.

Vygotsky's distinction between higher order and lower order mental
functions (e.g. Vygotsky, 1981) has direct relevance to current educational
debates. Lower order mental functions are inherited, unmediated,
involuntary and isolated from other mental functions. Higher order mental
functions come about as a result of learning; they are mediated by signs and
other tools, such as literacy and mathematics; they are under voluntary
control; and they are integrated with other mental functions.

If one brings a Vygotskian framework to the measurement of development, one must move towards the assessment of higher order functioning,
and away from the assessment of isolated skills. This message is completely
coherent with many of the recent reforms in educational measurement.
Educational measurement is attracting a great deal of attention world wide,
and from a wide range of constituencies. A dominant political message is
that economies in the developed world can no longer depend on mass
production to support low skill, high wage economies (as in the car industry
in the 1960s); global competition and the easy export of capital and jobs will
ensure that high wages will flow only in high skill economies. Educational
goals are shifting to emphasise higher order skills, despite a 'back to basics'
backlash. These political and economic pressures have had an impact on
curricula world wide (e.g. Australian Education Council, 1990 and National
Council of Teachers of Mathematics, 1989). It remains to be seen if the
educational community can respond by developing ways to assess these
new skills (e.g. the work of the Balanced Assessment project, discussed by
Ridgway and Schoenfeld, 1994), and if new methods of teaching can
promote the development to facilitate these skills. Again, the key issue is to
ensure that measurement is appropriate to the functions it is to serve.

We are in the midst of a sea of educational reforms, and these reforms
imply changes at many levels, from the microstructure of learning episodes
through to the evaluation of educational reforms. All actions contain some
implicit theories (and sometimes explicit theories) of the phenomena, and
of the change processes themselves. Educational reform buys into theories
of intellectual development, and into theories of how to bring about
change. When we look at current assessment tools in education, we have a
window into closet theories of development and pedagogy. The heartland
of psychology is the exploration of such theories; psychologists are well
placed to make a contribution to the thoughts and actions of a number of
different groups – politicians and policy makers, teachers and curriculum

designers, educational researchers and other psychologists. It is essential that our approaches to measurement and research methodologies are appropriate to the theoretical debates they seek to inform, and to the practical actions which might result.

REFERENCES

Adey, P. and Shayer, M. (1994). *Really Raising Standards: Cognitive Intervention and Academic Achievement*. London: Routledge.

Australian Education Council (1990). *A National Statement on Mathematics for Australian Schools*. Carlton, Victoria: Curriculum Corporation.

Bond, T. G. (1976). *BLOT: Bond's Logical Operations Test*. Townsville: TCAE.

Bond, T. G. (1995). Piaget and measurement I: the twain really do meet. *Archives de Psychologie*, 63, 71–87.

Bond, T. G. (1995). Piaget and measurement II: empirical validation of the Piagetian Model. *Archives de Psychologie*, 63, 155–85.

Bond, T. G. and Jackson, I. (1991). The Gou Protocol revisited: a Piagetian contextualization of critique. *Archives de Psychologie*, 59, 31–53.

Brown, G. and Desforges, C. (1977). Piagetian psychology and education: time for revision. *British Journal of Educational Psychology*, 47, 7–17.

Bryant, P. (1974). *Perception and Understanding in Young Children*. London: Methuen.

Bryant, P. (1995). Children and arithmetic. *Journal of Child Psychology and Psychiatry*, 36, 1, 3–32.

Chalmers, M. and McGonigle, B. (1984). Are children any more logical than monkeys on the five-term series problem? *Journal of Experimental Child Psychology*, 37, 355–77.

Hamel, B. R. (1974). *Children from 5–7*. Rotterdam: University Press.

Inhelder, B. (1989). Bärbel Inhelder. In G. Lindsey (ed.) *A History of Psychology in Autobiography*, vol. 8, pp. 208–43. Stanford: Stanford University Press.

McGonigle, B. and Chalmers, M. (1977). Are monkeys logical? *Nature*, 267, 694–6.

McGonigle, B. and Chalmers, M. (1992). Monkeys are rational! *The Quarterly Journal of Experimental Psychology*, 45B, 3, 189–228.

McGonigle, B. and Chalmers, M. (1996). The ontology of order. In L. Smith (ed.) *Critical Readings on Piaget*, pp. 279–311. London: Routledge.

National Council of Teachers of Mathematics (1989). *Standards for School Mathematics*. Reston, Virginia: NCTM.

Neimark, E. D. (1975). Longitudinal development of formal operations thought. *Genetic Psychology Monographs*, 91, 171–225.

Pascual-Leone, J. (1970). A mathematical model for the transition rule in Piaget's developmental stages. *Acta Psychologica*, 32, 301–45.

Ridgway, J. and Passey, D. (1993). An international view of mathematics assessment: through a glass, darkly. In M. Niss (ed.) *Investigations into Assessment in Mathematics Education*, pp. 55–72. London: Kluwer.

Ridgway, J. and Schoenfeld, A. (1994). *Balanced Assessment: Designing Assessment Schemes to Promote Desirable Change in Mathematics Education*. Keynote paper for the EARLI Email Conference on Assessment.

Vygotsky, L. S. (1981). The genesis of higher mental functions. In Wertsh, J. (ed.), *The Concept of Activity in Soviet Psychology*, pp. 144–88. New York: Sharpe.

Wason, P. C. and Johnson-Laird, P. M. (1972). *Psychology of Reasoning: Structure and Content*. London: Batsford.

Wylam, H. and Shayer, M. (1978). *CSMS Science Reasoning Tasks*. Windsor: NFER.

Part 5

Development of modal understanding

13 Children's understanding of permission and obligation[1]

Paul Harris and María Núñez

INTRODUCTION

Key modal terms in English straddle two different types of modality. Consider the following two sentences:

1 If Sally rides her bicycle, she *must* wear her helmet.
2 If Sally is riding her bicycle, she *must* be almost home by now.

As these sentences illustrate, the modal *must* can be used in either a deontic sense (sentence 1) or an epistemic sense (sentence 2). Deontic *must* (and related terms such as *have to*) denote obligations in the real world. Epistemic *must* and *have to* denote a certainty – or near-certainty – that is supplied by inference or reasoning. It is interesting to note that this polysemy is not confined to English. As Sweetser (1990) points out, it can be found in many unrelated languages (including Indo-European, Semitic and Finnish). Indeed, there is evidence that, historically, the English deontic modals were established first and the epistemic modals were a later extension.

Such diachronic linguistic evidence must be used cautiously in the study of children. Still, the evidence raises the interesting possibility that children first embark on an understanding of modal terms such as *must* and *have to* by focusing on their deontic meanings. Only later – possibly via a process of extension – do they begin to understand their epistemic meanings. More generally, the linguistic evidence raises the possibility that children might have an early understanding of the modal terms *must* and *have to* when they are used in deontic contexts even if they do not fully appreciate their epistemic force in other contexts. In this paper, we examine children's early comprehension of deontic modals. First, we consider how such terms are incorporated into rules of permission and obligation and present evidence showing that pre-school children have a remarkable grasp of such rules. In reviewing our findings, we consider the ways in which Piaget and Vygotsky approached children's understanding of deontic rules.

PERMISSION, OBLIGATION AND REASONING

Peter Wason (1966) reported how adults perform on the so-called selection task. In his original version of the task, participants are invited to specify which of four cases need to be selected for further examination in order to check the truth or falsity of a descriptive, conditional rule. For example, participants might be given the following rule: 'If there is a vowel on one side of a card, then there is an even number on the other side' (or, more generally, *if p then q*). They are then shown four cards, each having a letter on one side and a number on the other and asked to decide which of the four cards (showing on their visible face respectively, a vowel, a consonant, an odd number and an even number) they should turn over to check if the rule is true or false. Although adults typically realise that they should turn over the card with a vowel (often referred to as the *p* card) in order to check if it has an odd rather than an even number (i.e. *not-q* rather than *q*) on the other side, they often omit to turn over the card with an odd number (*not-q*) to see if it has a vowel (*p*) on the other side. Wason's conclusion was that adults are surprisingly poor at seeking out cases that would violate simple if-then rules.

Research that followed up Wason's initial findings with adults showed that performance sometimes improved with more concrete material, but the variable nature of this improvement meant that no coherent theoretical account emerged. Investigators contented themselves with the fairly prosaic claim that reasoning by adults is prone to context effects: adults do not possess a logical capacity that is applied uniformly across all relevant contexts. Theoretical interest in the task was re-awakened by two different investigations, each pointing to a more principled account of the role of context. In these investigations, adults were not presented with descriptive conditional rules, but with permission rules – deontic rules specifying that the performance of some action (*p*) is only allowed if a condition (*q*) has been fulfilled. An example of this type of rule, echoing sentence (1) above, would be: 'If someone rides a bicycle, he or she must wear a helmet.' When asked to seek out potential violations of such rules, adults perform quite accurately (Cheng and Holyoak, 1985; Cosmides, 1989). Not only do they examine the card displaying the action (*p*) in order to check whether the condition is not being met but they also examine the card displaying the condition not being met (*not-q*) in order to check whether the action is being taken. Some of the earlier anomalies now fell into place. It became apparent that the fluctuating improvement on concrete rather than abstract rules was almost certainly due to the presence of a deontic element in those concrete rules that led to successful performance. Indeed, Cheng and Holyoak (1985) were able to show that adults performed well even on an abstract rule, provided that it included a deontic element.

Why should adults be particularly adroit at spotting potential violations of a permission rule? In their theoretical analyses, Cheng and Holyoak

(1985) and Cosmides (1989) disagreed on several fundamental issues. Nevertheless, they agreed on the proposal that adults possess a specialised ability, be it a schema or a module, that helps them to process the implications of a conditional permission rule. In particular, adults appreciate that engaging in the action without fulfilling the condition amounts to a breach of the rule and they can readily apply this understanding to novel rules.

RESEARCH WITH CHILDREN

Identifying breaches of a permission rule

Subsequent research with adults has mainly sought to identify the critical features of the hypothesised schema or module. In particular, investigators have asked whether adults are particularly sensitive to 'social exchange' rules involving a contract between two parties, as proposed by Cosmides (1989) and Cosmides and Tooby (1992), or alternatively whether adults have a more encompassing sensitivity to deontic rules, irrespective of any clear-cut contract or exchange, as proposed by Cheng and Holyoak (1985).

Surprisingly, little research has been carried out with young children. Yet adults often try to structure children's behaviour by insisting that a condition be fulfilled before a particular action is taken. Children are told that they must wear an apron if they want to do some painting, or wash their hands before they eat. Accordingly, it might be expected that young children would be alert to breaches of conditional permission rules. In line with this expectation, Girotto and his colleagues found that seven year olds performed quite accurately in variants of the selection task so long as deontic rules were used (Girotto *et al.* 1989; Girotto *et al.* 1988; Light *et al.* 1989). In our own research, we have used an evaluation task based on the classic selection task but adapted for use with very young children, namely three and four year olds. We begin by describing three initial experiments using this evaluation task (Harris and Núñez, 1996b, Experiments 2–4).

In the first study to be described, children listened to six stories in which the mother of the protagonist stated a familiar rule. For example, in one story about a little girl children were told: 'Her Mum says that if she does some painting she must put her apron on.' The children were then shown four picture choices depicting the protagonist engaged in the desired target activity (e.g. painting) or some neutral activity (e.g. doing a puzzle) while either meeting or not meeting the specified condition (e.g. wearing an apron or not). Thus, the four pictures showed the protagonist: doing a puzzle with an apron; painting with an apron; doing a puzzle without an apron; and painting without an apron. Children were asked to indicate the picture where the protagonist was being 'naughty and not doing what she (or he) was told'. A correct choice involved selection of the picture showing the protagonist engaged in the target activity but not meeting the specified condition (e.g. painting without an apron). We found that three and four year olds made this choice very accurately. Figure 20 shows the percentage of choices directed at each of the four pictures. Analysis confirmed what is clear from inspection of Figure 20: although the pattern of choice is somewhat more sharply differentiated among the older children, both age groups mainly chose the correct picture – the picture showing the target act being undertaken (+Act) without the condition having been met (–Condition).

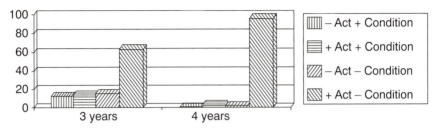

Figure 20 Percentage of choices for each picture by age

Reasoning about unfamiliar rules

Cheng and Holyoak (1985) and Cosmides (1989) invoke the notion of a schema or module in order to explain the fact that adults readily understand the implications not just of familiar permission rules but also of novel rules. Familiar rules – such as the rule about wearing an apron when painting – often include a pragmatic element. They are intended to minimise the consequences of a mishap. Nevertheless, children also have to contend with novel and arbitrary permission rules. For example, adults often strike up a bargain with a young child to elicit compliance – 'If you watch TV, you should first finish your cereal/homework/chores etc.' In such cases, the adult imposes the condition not to reduce any potential dangers associated with the target action of watching television but as a negotiating ploy to ensure that children do something that, in their eyes at any rate, probably has low priority. If children grasp makeshift bargains of this type, which adults introduce to deal with a particular caretaking situation, then children probably understand arbitrary or novel permission rules, with no pragmatic element. This was the issue we explored in our next study. Children were asked about two different types of rule: a familiar, pragmatic rule such as the one about wearing an apron while painting, and a novel, arbitrary rule (e.g. 'Her Mum says if she does some painting she should put her *helmet* on'). Figure 21 shows that although accuracy was slightly reduced for the arbitrary rules, the choices of three and four year olds combined were again mainly directed at the correct picture for both pragmatic and arbitrary rules – the picture displaying the target act being undertaken without fulfilment of the specified condition.

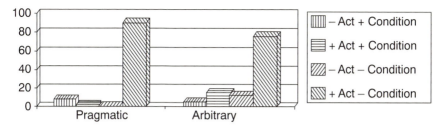

Figure 21 Percentage of choices for each picture by type of rule

Deontic versus descriptive rules

Up until now we have reported children's performance on tasks involving deontic rules. However, as described earlier, a key finding with adults is their superior performance on tasks that include deontic rather than descriptive rules. In the next study, we asked whether pre-school children also display this differential performance. Children were tested with arbitrary, deontic rules, as used in the previous study. These were introduced as prescriptions by the mother directed at the protagonist, for example: 'Her Mum says if she does some painting she should put her helmet on.' In addition, they were tested on arbitrary, descriptive rules that contained the same elements but were announced by the protagonist as a description of his or her behaviour, for example: 'Carol says that if she does some painting she always puts her helmet on.' The test question was suitably adapted to the type of rule. In the case of the prescriptive rules, children were asked, as in previous experiments, to indicate the picture showing the protagonist doing something 'naughty'. In the case of the descriptive rules, they were asked to indicate the picture showing the protagonist doing something 'different'. Figure 22 shows that performance on these two tasks was not equivalent. As expected, children mainly selected the correct picture when asked to indicate a 'naughty' breach of a prescriptive rule but they were much less accurate when asked to indicate a 'different' action from a descriptive rule. Indeed, most children chose at random on this latter task.

Taken together, the pattern of results obtained with pre-school children

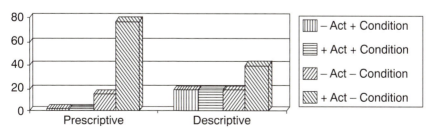

Figure 22 Percentage of choices for each picture by type of rule

fits the pattern obtained among adults. First, like adults, pre-school children readily pick out violations of a conditional permission rule; second, they are sensitive to violations of familiar, pragmatic rules but also to violations of novel rules with no pragmatic element; third, they are less accurate when asked to identify a departure from descriptive rules even when those rules include the same acts and conditions as the prescriptive rules. These findings suggest a remarkable continuity in the understanding of conditional obligations, a continuity that is reinforced by the fact that there was very little difference between the responses of the three year olds as compared to the four year olds.

Two additional features of children's performance are worth stressing. First, children did not construe the rules as *unconditional* obligations. Had they interpreted the rules as a blanket prescription to meet the specified condition – whether or not the target action was being taken – the pattern of choices would have been quite different. Specifically, they would have chosen either (or both) of the two cards where the protagonist was not meeting the condition, irrespective of whether he or she was concurrently carrying out the target action. Inspection of Figures 20–22 shows however, that children chose the forbidden combination +Act –Condition much more often than the neutral combination of –Act –Condition. Thus children clearly understood that the condition was only prescribed if the target action was being carried out (+Act). Second, children did not construe the rules as unconditional proscriptions against taking the target action. Had they interpreted the rules in this way, they would have chosen either (or both) of the two cards where the protagonist was engaged in the target action. Again, inspection of Figures 20–22 shows that children chose the forbidden combination +Act –Condition much more often than the permitted combination +Act +Condition. Third, we found that children could sensibly back up their choice of picture with an appropriate justification. In all three studies, when children were asked to say what was naughty about what the protagonist was doing in the chosen picture, they typically explained that the protagonist was *not* meeting the specified condition, for example: 'She hasn't got her apron on' or 'He should be wearing his helmet.' By implication, the protagonist's actual behaviour was judged relative to a prescribed behaviour that s/he had *not* carried out. Children's sensitivity to such prescribed alternatives was displayed not simply on rules that they were likely to be familiar with but also on novel rules. Nevertheless, it did not extend to the task with descriptive rules. A plausible implication, therefore, is that when children are asked to make a judgement of naughtiness within a deontic framework they readily engage in counterfactual thinking. The course of action that is identified as naughty is compared to an alternative course of action that the protagonist could and indeed should have adopted but did not; the judgement that the protagonist is 'naughty' flows from the discrepancy between the actual course of action and this counterfactual alternative.

Deliberate versus accidental violations

An implication of the above analysis is that children might withhold their judgement that the protagonist has been naughty if it is clear that the protagonist did not have an alternative course of action. To test this idea, children in the next two studies were presented with a more demanding set of picture choices (Núñez and Harris, 1996a, experiments 1–2). The four pictures showed the protagonist engaged in the desired target action or a neutral action while either deliberately flouting the specified condition or accidentally breaching it. For example, the pictures might show the protagonist riding a bicycle (target action) or walking along (neutral action) while either deliberately removing a bicycle helmet or accidentally losing it because it had caught in an overhanging branch. Thus two of the four pictures showed the protagonist engaged in the target action while not meeting the condition – one depicted a deliberate breach and the other an accidental breach. If children base their judgements of naughtiness simply on the forbidden combination of engaging in the target action while not meeting the specified condition, they ought to divide their choices between these two pictures. However, if they are alert to whether an alternative course of action is available to the protagonist they ought to direct most of their choices at the picture showing the condition deliberately being flouted – where the protagonist could have acted differently – and not to the accidental breach – where the protagonist had no obvious alternative. Figure 23 shows the percentage of choices directed at each picture by three and four year olds in the United Kingdom and by three and four year olds in Colombia.

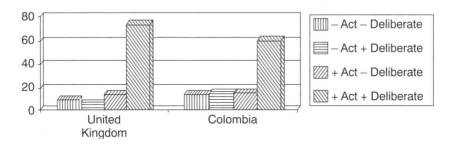

Figure 23 Percentage of choices for each picture by country

Figure 23 shows that in each setting children concentrated their choices on the deliberate breach (+Act +Deliberate); few choices were directed at the accidental breach (+Act –Deliberate). Thus judgements of naughtiness are guided by a consideration of what alternative course of action is available to a protagonist.

Violation of peer agreement

The permission rules that we have described so far have involved rules likely to be associated with an adult authority figure. Indeed, in some of the stories the rule was explicitly introduced in this fashion because it was announced by the protagonist's mother. However, some conditional obligations operate between one child and another, and they may be negotiated by children themselves. For example, agreements to exchange toys, marbles or other treasures are sometimes negotiated by young children. Such agreements have the structure of a conditional obligation, in that each party to the exchange must hand over an agreed item, if they are offered an item by the other party. The obligation, being conditional, only arises for one party if the other party is prepared to carry out their part of the bargain. Given the reciprocal nature of such agreements, a violation can be perpetrated by either party. Thus either party can violate the agreement by accepting or taking an agreed item without offering anything in exchange. In the final two studies to be described, we explored three and four year olds' understanding of such reciprocal agreements (Harris and Núñez, 1996a). As usual, they listened to six stories. Each story involved a boy and a girl who agreed on a swap. For example, in one story, the two children each had different coloured pencils that they agreed to swap. Children were then shown four pictures. Each picture showed the boy and the girl seated at a table – but the pictures varied in terms of the fate of the pencils. They depicted respectively: the two pencils still in the possession of their original owners; the girl with both pencils (and the boy with nothing); the boy with both pencils (and the girl with nothing); and the two pencils duly exchanged. Children were asked to indicate the picture where one of the two children was being naughty. To check whether children could shift flexibly between the two story characters, for half of the stories they were asked to indicate where the little girl was being naughty, and for the other half to indicate where the little boy was being naughty. Figure 24 shows the pattern of choices averaged across three and four year olds. Children appropriately pointed to the picture of the girl in possession of both pencils when asked to say where the girl was being naughty, and to the boy in possession of both pencils when asked to say where the boy was being naughty.

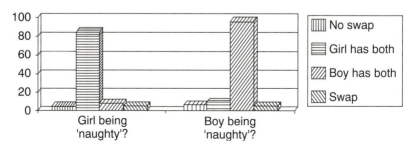

Figure 24 Percentage of choices for each picture by identity of wrongdoer

These results strongly suggest that children understand that both parties to the agreement could violate it – children shifted their choice appropriately depending on whether they were asked about one party or the other. Still, we were concerned that they might be following a simple heuristic. The correct picture always depicted the relevant protagonist with both items in his or her possession and the other protagonist with nothing. Maybe children simply thought it was naughty for one protagonist to have more than the other without really understanding that such a discrepancy violated the agreement to swap. Accordingly, in a final study, we posed a different question. The nature of the stories and the pictures was very similar but we asked three year olds to indicate the picture showing the two protagonists being 'good' and doing what they had agreed. A simple heuristic of checking on the number of items possessed by each protagonist would not allow children to distinguish between the No Swap picture and the Swap picture. Figure 25 shows the pattern of results. The children performed very well. They mostly chose the picture where the swap had indeed taken place.

Reviewing the various studies, we find that three and four year olds readily understand rules in which a condition must be met if a particular action is to be taken. Their understanding extends to novel as well as familiar rules of this type. In judging that it is wrong or naughty to breach such rules, children do not focus simply on the missing condition. They take into account the manner in which that omission came about: they are more likely to condemn a deliberate breach than an accidental one. In addition, the obligation to fulfil the condition need not be imposed by an adult authority figure. Children display the same pattern of judgement, whether the condition is prescribed by an authority figure or part of an agreement between two children. Finally, children are not always accurate in picking out a deviation from a conditional rule. When they are asked to pick out a departure from a descriptive, conditional rule they do not perform as accurately as they do in identifying a breach of a deontic, conditional rule. In offering an account of these findings, we now place them in the broader

Figure 25 Percentage of choices for each picture

context of children's rule understanding, as explored by Piaget and Vygotsky.

PIAGET AND VYGOTSKY

As Piaget (1932) acknowledges, far from seeking out any stable feature of the concept of deontic obligation, he looked for and analysed developmental change in that concept. Inspired by the socio-historical analyses of Brunschvicg (1927), he focused on the alleged developmental shift from the morality of constraint to the morality of respect. He identified two key features of this shift: children's increasing acknowledgement of the role of intentions, and their increasing recognition that obligation flows from reciprocal agreement among equals rather than external authority. Our findings lead us to a different perspective. First, we find that it is not just older children but also pre-school children who differentiate between accidental and intentional violations. We also find that pre-school children condemn a failure to meet an obligation whether that obligation is imposed by an external authority or arises in the context of an agreement between two children.

Accordingly, we want to emphasise the continuity in children's conception of obligation rather than a shift from heteronomous to autonomous obligation. More specifically, we propose that there is an invariant developmental component to the concept of deontic obligation – one that cross-cuts Piaget's distinction between the two modes of moral judgement. We hypothesise that children rapidly acquire – in the third or fourth year of life – an understanding of the way in which certain actions are constrained by norms and agreements whereas others may be undertaken simply on the basis of desire.[2] Recent research on the child's theory of mind has revealed the central importance of the concept of desire. Thus two and three year olds readily predict action and emotion by reference to desires (Wellman and Woolley, 1990) and they frequently talk about what an agent *wants* (Bartsch and Wellman, 1995). Our hypothesis is that their understanding of desire-based action serves as only one anchor for their naïve interpretation of action. A second anchor is their understanding of the norms and agreements that constrain action. In line with this proposal, children start to use deontic modals such as 'must' and 'have to' at two– three years (Shatz and Wilcox, 1991). Moreover, detailed analysis of the spontaneous use of 'hafta' by three year olds reveals that they use that term in a distinct fashion, showing little overlap with 'wanna': they use 'wanna' in connection with actions that are regulated by internal volition, but they use 'hafta' in connection with actions that are, or should be, guided by normative constraints (Gerhardt, 1991). Thus, they use 'hafta' to refer to pre-existing norms ('You hafta put them (i.e. cookies) on a plate') or to introduce a norm ('You hafta get a red, red triangles').

An important question for future research is how young children view the relationship between normative constraints and desires. At first sight, it is tempting to assume that children necessarily think of them as perpetually in conflict with one another. Thus they conceive of agents as either doing what they must or what they want. To the extent that young children's desires and impulses are frequently constrained by externally imposed norms, this expectation is not implausible.

However, Vygotsky (1978) provides an interesting analysis of situations in which such an opposition is absent. He acknowledges that rules are often imposed on the child from the outside, and constrain his or her desires: 'Ordinarily a child experiences subordination to rules in the renunciation of something he wants' (Vygotsky, 1978, p. 99). Nevertheless, he goes on to point out that there are certain pleasurable contexts in which children impose rules on themselves. A key example of this type of self-regulation is play. In the course of their play, children respect certain rituals or norms not because they are obliged to do so by an external authority but because they elect to do so. Thus, on Vygotsky's view, we would expect young children to use the language of obligation, i.e. terms such as 'must' and 'hafta' not just when they are referring to externally-imposed obligations or constraints but also to procedures or rules that they themselves adopt in the context of play. The data reported by Gerhardt (1991) confirm this expectation. In her analysis of the spontaneous utterances of two three year olds engaged in play, she observed that 'hafta' was used to refer to constraints imposed by an adult (e.g. cookies must be eaten from a plate) but it was also used in the context of playful but novel routines that the children invented themselves. Vygotsky's acute observations remind us that it is a mistake to conclude that children always see constraints as conflicting with their desires or as externally imposed. They also recognise obligations even when they are self-selected and self-imposed.

We conclude that young children are engaged in the construction of two distinct interpretations of human action – one focused on the psychology of the agent, notably his or her desires – and the other focused on the norms that constrain his or her actions. Although it is tempting to assume that these two springs for action are in opposition to one another, it is more accurate to think of them as separate. Sometimes desire and normative constraints are in conflict but sometimes, happily, they fuse, even in the eyes of young children.

NOTES

1 P.L.H. was supported by a research grant from the Economic and Social Research Council, United Kingdom (R000 22 1174). M.N. was supported by a post-doctoral fellowship (Ex95 03442629) from the Spanish Ministry of Education.

222 *Paul Harris and María Núñez*

2 The distinction that we make between desires and obligations echoes a distinction made by Piaget (1995) between values on the one hand and normative constraints on the other. However, Piaget developed this distinction in the context of a sociological essay many years after his research on children's moral judgement.

REFERENCES

Bartsch, K. and Wellman, H. M. (1995). *Children Talk About the Mind*. New York: Oxford University Press.

Brunschvicg, L. (1927). *Le progres de la conscience dans la philosophie occidentale*. Paris: F. Alcan.

Cheng, P. W. and Holyoak, K. J. (1985). Pragmatic reasoning schemas. *Cognitive Psychology*, 17, 391–416.

Cosmides, L. (1989). The logic of social exchange: has natural selection shaped how humans reason? Studies with the Wason selection task. *Cognition*, 31, 187–276.

Cosmides, L. and Tooby, J. (1992). Cognitive adaptations for social exchange. In J. H. Barkow, L. Cosmides and J. Tooby (eds), *The Adapted Mind: Evolutionary Psychology and the Generation of Culture*, pp. 163–228. Oxford: Oxford University Press.

Gerhardt, J. (1991). The meaning and use of the modals *hafta*, *needta* and *wanna* in children's speech. *Journal of Pragmatics*, 16, 531–90.

Girotto, V., Light, P. and Colbourn, C. J. (1988). Pragmatic schemas and conditional reasoning in children. *Quarterly Journal of Experimental Psychology*, 40, 469–82.

Girotto, V., Blaye, M. and Farioli, F. (1989). A reason to reason: pragmatic basis of children's search for counterexamples. *European Bulletin of Cognitive Psychology*, 9, 297–321.

Harris, P. L. and Núñez, M. (1996a). Understanding of exchange agreements by pre-school children. Unpublished paper, Department of Experimental Psychology, University of Oxford.

Harris, P. L. and Núñez, M. (1996b). Understanding of permission rules by pre-school children. *Child Development*.

Light, P., Blaye, A., Gilly, M. and Girotto, V. (1989). Pragmatic schemas and logical reasoning in 6- to 8-year-old children. *Cognitive Development*, 4, 49–64.

Núñez, M. and Harris, P. L. (1996). Young children's understanding of intention and reciprocal obligation. Paper presented at Developmental Section Conference of the British Psychological Society, Oxford.

Piaget, J. (1932). *The Moral Judgement of the Child*. London: Routledge and Kegan Paul.

Piaget, J. (1995). Essay on the theory of qualitative values in static ('synchronic') sociology. In J. Piaget, *Sociological Studies*. London: Routledge.

Shatz, M. and Wilcox, S. A. (1991). Constraints on the acquisition of English modals. In S. A. Gelman and J. Byrnes (eds), *Perspectives on Thought and Language: Interrelations in Development*, pp. 319–53. New York: Cambridge University Press.

Sweetser, E. (1990). *From Etymology to Pragmatics: Metaphorical and Cultural Aspects of Semantic Structure*. Cambridge: Cambridge University Press.

Vygotsky, L. (1978). *Mind in Society*. Cambridge, MA: Harvard University Press.

Wason, P. C. (1966). Reasoning. In B. Foss (ed.), *New Horizons in Psychology*, vol. I, pp. 135–51. Harmondsworth: Penguin.

Wellman, H. M. and Woolley, J. D. (1990). From simple desires to ordinary beliefs: the early development of everyday psychology. *Cognition*, 35, 245–75.

14 Necessary knowledge and its assessment in intellectual development

Leslie Smith

> But if something cannot not happen it is impossible for it not to happen; and if it is impossible for something not to happen it is necessary for it to happen.
>
> Aristotle

Truth is deservedly held in high esteem as a rational value. Although truth is important, it is not the only rational value since there are others as well. Modality is one such equally important rational value. And Piaget (1950, translated in Smith, 1993, p. 1) made it clear that the development of modal knowledge is a principal problem in his account. In this context, the terms *modality* and *modal* have nothing to do with modal values in statistics, nor with sensory modalities, nor with cross-modal transfer, nor with social modes and fashions, but rather with modal logic and so modal knowledge.

In modal logic, there is a standard definition of necessity, outlined by Aristotle (1987, sect. 18b) in the *De Interpretatione*, and elaborated in recent texts (Forbes, 1985; Haack, 1978; Sainsbury, 1991):

(1) $\Box p = -\Diamond -p$

Take any proposition p, then that proposition is necessary (symbolised by the box) just in case its negation $-p$ is not possible (symbolised by the negated diamond). Now (1) amounts to

(2) A proposition is necessary just in case its negation is impossible.

Quite simply, necessity is that which could not be otherwise. Similarly,

(3) $\Diamond p = -\Box -p$

Take any proposition p, then that proposition is possible (symbolised by the diamond) just in case its negation $-p$ is not necessary (symbolised by the negated box). And (3) amounts to

(4) A proposition is possible just in case its negation is not necessary.

Quite simply, possibility is that which does not have to be otherwise. It is clear from these definitions that either modal notion (necessity, possibility) can be defined in terms of the other.

The central point is that modal knowledge in line with (1)–(4) is importantly different from non-modal knowledge. Non-modal knowledge is important in psychological investigations where correct responses are distinguished from error. But modal knowledge is distinctive for two important classes of understanding, namely mathematical knowledge and deductive reasoning.

To see why, consider the sceptical proposal that psychologists can simply bypass modal knowledge. Thus it has been contended that modal logic cannot be used in psychology (Johnson-Laird, 1978), and that modal knowledge as a phenomenon is in fact not a 'quintessential' aspect of developmental theory (Karmiloff-Smith, 1994). But the first contention is invalid in that modal logic is already in use in psychological research (Overton, 1990; Piéraut-Le Bonniec, 1980). The second contention is false in fact, since modal phenomena are palpably present in the work of Karmiloff-Smith (see Figure 29). In general, modal knowledge is central to intellectual development in two ways. First, all mathematical truths are necessities. Any mathematical truth such as 7+5 = 12 has to be so, and could not be otherwise (Kant, 1953). Thus if mathematical knowledge is important, then so is modal knowledge. What would you think of a child who could count but who did not realise that any natural number (n) has, and has to have, one and only one successor ($n+1$)? Second, all deductive inferences are necessities. A deductive inference is 'valid only if it *couldn't* have, not just *doesn't* have, true premises and false conclusion' (Haack, 1978, p. 22). It is one thing to make a correct inference from the information available, by ruling out what is not the case. It is quite something else to realise that a valid inference could not be otherwise, i.e. by ruling out what could not be the case. Modal knowledge is ubiquitous, and central to, mathematical understanding and deductive reasoning.

Here are four examples of modal understanding taken from Piaget's work. The first example (Figure 26) concerns pseudo-necessity. This example of modal misunderstanding really is *modal* since it captures the spirit of Aristotle's subtle definition – and this in the untutored response of a five year old!

The next examples (see Figure 27) are taken from two studies of conservation initially published fifty years ago. As Piaget (1952, ch. 1) noted, conservation is successful (at his level three) as *necessary conservation*. Conservation is a paradigm example of necessary knowledge (Smith, 1993, sect. 16).

The third example (Figure 28) concerns modal reasoning leading to necessary knowledge the reasons for which are observationally identified through physical activity together with the subject's commentary.

The final example (see Figure 29) provides an example of the transition (in younger children, such as Nel) from means-end necessity (you have to turn the map upside down) to the realisation (in older children, such as Pie) of a modal proposition (the inverse relation between the map and the route always has to be like this).

Task: a three dimensional, box-shaped figure whose five visible sides are white, leading to the question 'What is the colour of the back which you can't see?'

Phi   White
Adult Are you sure?
Phi   Yes
Adult Could there be any other colour?
Phi   No
Adult Why?
Phi   Because the box is all white and so *the back can't be another colour.*

Figure 26   The white box and pseudo-necessary knowledge (Piaget, 1987, p. 31)

A. Task: clay moulded into different shapes and sizes, leading to the question 'Is there the same now?'

   Giv There *is always the same* clay, so *there can't be* more or less.

B. Task: children are presented with glasses such that A1 is two-thirds and A2 is half-full, or where A1 and A2 are equal but where all of the liquid in A1 is poured into several smaller glasses B1, B2, etc., leading to the question 'Are they the same now?'

   Eus No, you've poured it out of the same glass: like that, *you can never make them the same.*
   Eus *It's always the same*, because it comes from the same glass.

Figure 27   Conservation and necessary knowledge (A: Piaget and Inhelder, 1974, p. 13; B: Piaget, 1952, p. 18)

Task: twelve pictures showing different geometrical shapes such that only one matches the target picture which is hidden behind a set of twenty covers arranged in 5×4 array in a rectangular frame, leading to the question 'Which covers have to be removed to identify the hidden picture?

Fra   (after removing three covers) It could be (indicating seven out of eight possibilities).
Adult Are there any that it can't be?
Fra   Yes (indicating four possibilities) . . .
Fra   (after removing four more covers) G – *it can't be any of the others.*
Adult You don't have to check all the boxes to be sure?
Fra   No.

Figure 28   Activity guided by necessary knowledge (Piaget, 1987b, p. 114)

Task: a route is laid out on a long sheet of wall-paper leading from a forest to a beach with bends and turn-offs in between. A map, presented back-to-front, is available showing this route, leading to navigation questions in travel along the route.

Pie When it is like this (front-back reversal), it's a little more complicated (than left-right reversal), but it *always has to be* the opposite.

Figure 29 Map-reading and modal knowledge (Piaget and Karmiloff-Smith, 1992, p. 117)

Modal phenomena are real enough and are manifest as 'what must be the case' and 'what cannot be otherwise' rather than merely as 'what is the case' in children's reasoning.

The question that I want to address in this paper concerns the response-criteria relevant to modal knowledge. There is insufficient agreement about the criteria to use in assessing such knowledge. This is evident in two ways. One is the ample scope for psychologists to generate 'false positives' and 'false negatives' in their conclusions about intellectual development. The other is that several assessment criteria are used in available studies. This plurality is sign of their incompleteness. I plan to review both tendencies. Finally I will review a modally appropriate assessment-criterion.

ASSESSING MODAL KNOWLEDGE: 'FALSE POSITIVES' AND 'FALSE NEGATIVES'

There is a well-known dilemma in psychological diagnostics in that valid assessment requires the joint avoidance of 'false positives' and 'false negatives' (Flavell *et al.*, 1993). Recent research on modal knowledge is caught on this dilemma.

'False negatives'

Distinct intellectual norms are distinct, definable through their own criteria. Since modality and truth are distinct, each has its own defining criteria. Yet there is ample scope for psychologists to generate 'false negatives' by disregarding cases of modal knowledge where such knowledge is evident. Keil's study of natural kinds is exemplary. A natural kind is defined through its essential (defining) properties, and not through its accidental (character-istic) properties. In his study, Keil presented incompatible information using both types of property about animals which have the observational properties of horses but which are really cows. Asked whether one such instance is a cow, one kindergartener declared that it is a horse in that 'a horse *could never* raise a cow,' whilst another kindergartener argued that 'if it was a cow, if it had a baby, then it *has to be* a cow' (Keil, 1989, pp. 167–8, 171; my emphasis). These are clear manifestations of necessary knowledge, unwittingly shown to be present in a study which was not designed to elicit them. The first example shows a modal error, unlike the second which is modally appropriate. Yet this is ignored in Keil's interpretation which is exclusively concerned with the truth-value (correctness) of the children's inferences, leaving their modal knowledge out of account. This 'false negative' is indicative of modal reduction by default in that these children display modal knowledge which is ignored in favour of an alternative interpretation.

It will be protested: what about the 'division of labour'? Keil's interpretation ignores modality and so does not reduce modality to truth-value. And no study can be expected to deal with everything. True enough. But modality is central to this study since natural kinds are defined by their essential properties, i.e. the properties which any instance must have (Kripke, 1980). It is not necessary for any horse to exist. But it is necessary that any horse has the essential properties of this kind. If it has them, it *must* be a horse; otherwise it *could not* be a horse. These are modal characteristics which are ignored in Keil's own interpretation – but not by his children!

'False positives'

The converse error is also apparent in that children are credited with modal knowledge the case for which has not been made good. Research on infants' knowledge of possibility-impossibility (Baillargeon, 1995) is exemplary. In a typical task, infants were shown events which are 'presented' as being possible (an obstacle blocking movement of a screen) or impossible (a screen completing a 180 degrees movement despite an obstacle). The infants spent longer looking at the latter event and this was interpreted as evidence of modal knowledge. Analogous studies of infants' understanding of mathematical necessity are reported by Wynn (1992) who is well aware that necessity is a modal concept.

These studies suffer from three defects. First, they merge the distinction between the characteristic and defining criteria of a concept. Keil (1989) has shown that the characteristic-defining distinction causes problems for older children. But the so-called 'impossible' event is not definitionally impossible – after all, there is an event for the infants to observe. Rather, the 'impossible' event has characteristic properties of an impossibility (it is unexpected). But it is not definitionally impossible. The infants are presented with two actual events. And anything that can be observed actually exists and so is a possible event. Thus there could be no impossible event for the infants to observe in the first place. Secondly, the study merges the distinction between actuality and possibility, between what is not the case and what could not be the case. This distinction is not well understood by young children (Moshman, 1990). Why should infants have a better understanding? Thirdly, the study merges the distinction between physical and logical impossibility. This distinction is problematic in the minds of children (Miller, 1986). No doubt this is because an event can be physically impossible and yet logically possible, and so absent in fact. How exactly do infants understand this distinction?

It will be said: such studies are psychologically interesting due to their pre-occupation with recognitive abilities rather than with representational understanding of modality. But this misses the point. Exactly what do the infants recognise? Their recognitive abilities are interpreted to bear on a modal distinction. Yet there is no necessity in the actual world, nor possibility likewise (Wittgenstein, 1961, sect. 6.37). These infancy studies are 'false positives', and so are indeterminate, about infants' modal knowledge.

MODALLY INCOMPLETE ASSESSMENT CRITERIA

Five criteria are appropriate for the assessment of modal knowledge of necessity and yet are incomplete: certainty, physical necessity, modal intuition, modal propositions, modal realism.

Certainty

If necessity is such an intractable phenomenon, does certainty provide a way forward? Such is the position accepted by Miller (1986) on the grounds that logical concepts such as conservation and transitivity appear in the mind as 'certainty or necessity'. In his studies, children were invited to express the certainty of their beliefs about logical tasks which embody necessities. Miller's conclusion is that necessary knowledge can be measured through judgments about certainty. This conclusion is open to objection on two counts in that certainty is not necessity and certainty is a modal concept which raises problems analogous to those of necessity.

Firstly, certainty and necessity are independent. They can, but don't have to, co-occur. Thus a belief can be held with certainty, even when it is not a belief in a necessity.

Jean I'm certain I'll win tonight with these six numbers: 1, 2, 3, 4, 5, 6.
Sean You do know that National Lottery numbers are generated randomly?

Jean is certain that her sextet of numbers will win the prize. Thus Jean's belief is accepted with certainty. But there is no necessity that this sextet will be the winning sequence which is random and so not necessary. Further, a belief can be necessary even if it is held without certainty.

Jean What's the sum of the angles of this triangle?
Sean 180 degrees, I think. I measured them as carefully as I could.

It is a Euclidean theorem, i.e. a necessity, that the internal angles of a triangle equal 180 degrees. It is not merely a fact to be verified through careful measurement. A long line of philosophers, from Plato in *The Republic* (1941) in his 'ladder' view of development to recent discussion of modal semantics (Kripke, 1980), have pointed out that necessities may be learned empirically. If certainty and necessity are independent in this way, the former could not be a criterion of the latter.

Secondly, there are at least three distinct families of modal concepts each of which have isomorphic properties (von Wright, 1951; cf. Smith, 1993, sect. 25.2). But isomorphism is not identity. So there is a clear distinction to draw between them. The alethic modalities are necessity, possibility and impossibility. The epistemic modalities are certainty, supposition and doubt. The deontic modalities are obligation, permission and proscription. If the assessment-criteria relevant to one modal family are problematic, switching to a distinct modal family simply pushes the diagnostic problem one step back. If alethic modality poses a problem in psychological research, both epistemic and deontic modalities do too.

It could be objected that there is no conflation in psychological investigation but rather a focus on the co-variation of inter-dependent phenomena. Certainty can be investigated in the same context as necessity so as to establish whether either is in fact linked with the other (Acredolo and O'Connor, 1991; Byrnes and Beilin, 1991; Foltz *et al.*, 1995). Now there may well be co-variation between certainty and necessity – true enough. But this is to postpone substantive problems such as how any form of modal knowledge can be validly assessed, or how any one form of modal knowledge is generated in the first place. It is for these reasons that certainty is an incomplete criterion of necessary knowledge.

Physical necessity

Physical necessity has been used as a criterion of logical necessity, for example by Miller (1986) who asked children about the possibility of dis-confirming evidence against, or about future change to, a logical necessity. A comparable use occurs in the study due to Murray and Armstrong (1976) where the children were asked about whether a logical necessity was always or merely sometimes correct.

This criterion merges the distinction drawn by Goodman (1979) between an accidentally true generalisation such as 'All the coins in my pocket are made of silver' and a physical necessity such as 'All butter melts at 150 degrees F' based on laws of nature. Even if the generalisation is true in fact, it is possible for it to be false. By contrast, there is no set of physi-cal circumstances that could run counter to a physical law. Thus physical necessity is distinct from factual generalisation. And this conclusion can in turn be generalised since physical possibility is itself distinct from logical possibility. Even if a natural law is true as a matter of physical necessity, from a logical point of view things could have been otherwise – perhaps not in the actual world but certainly in any of the unlimited number of logically possible worlds.

The understanding of causality and physical necessity merits its own study (White, 1995). But causal explanation directed upon physical necessities presupposes deductive knowledge relevant to the 'covering law' model (Hempel, 1965). Thus physical necessity could not serve as a complete criterion of modal knowledge.

Modal intuition

Modal intuitions are real enough, occurring just in case someone is obliged to draw the alethically right conclusion from a set of relevant premises, for example in a valid argument. Such rational compulsion is manifest as a 'feeling of necessity' (Piaget, 1980a, p. 40), which 'constitutes evidence of the overall structures which characterise our stages' (Piaget, 1971a, p. 5). Other studies of reasoning are reliant upon subjects' intuition, marked by the capacity to distinguish the validity of an argument from its other extrinsic properties, evident in the realisation that 'the conclusion *must* be true provided the premises were true' (Moshman and Franks, 1986, p. 156; my emphasis). This criterion reflects the modal properties of validity since all valid deductions are necessities.

But this criterion runs into problems. Is modal intuition due to a modal feeling? Any such feeling is important (Brown, 1996). What is in doubt is its public verification as more than a 'lived experience' (Piaget, 1995a, p. 24). By what criteria is a feeling which is phenomenally present to the subject *objectively* shown to be present for the rest of us? There is major problem in reconciling any personal view of the world, i.e. the view from my point of view, with scientific objectivity, i.e. the view from nowhere (Nagel, 1986).

Is a modal intuition due to tacit knowledge, available neither to consciousness nor to linguistic expression (Polanyi, 1969; cf. Karmiloff-Smith, 1994)? This suggestion raises the problem as to whether any such intuition is authentically modal. In children's minds, exactly what is the difference *in tacit inference* between (i) a truth-functionally correct intuition, (ii) a deviantly modal intuition, (iii) an incomplete modal intuition and (iv) an appropriate modal intuition? There is simply no way to tell other than by recourse to children's modal reasoning. Thus modal intuitions are, of course, interesting. But they are also incomplete.

Modal propositions

Is modality related to language? Linguistic contexts no doubt provide paradigm examples for the display of modal knowledge. Preschoolers have been shown to understand modal language (Byrnes and Duff, 1989;

Scholnick and Wing, 1995). Further, children are capable of discriminating the properties of modally distinct propositions, such as necessities from contradictions (Osherson and Markman, 1975; Russell, 1982). This is welcome evidence. Even so, there are two limitations.

One is that the identification of the modal status of propositions is one thing and modal reasoning is something else. Modal reasoning is not confined to the identification of necessary, or contradictory, propositions. Indeed, the individual propositions in a valid argument are typically non-necessities – yet every deductive inference is necessary for all that (Smith, 1993, sect. 4.1). A second limitation is that, if there is a logic of action, it can be manifest outside of language, for example in exhaustively selecting the covers to remove so as to identify a hidden shape (see Figure 28), or knowing exactly how to read a map upside down (see Figure 29). Studies of the modality of propositions do too little to clarify the development of modal reasoning (Piéraut-Le Bonniec, 1980).

Modal realism

The actual world is merely one of an unlimited number of logically possible worlds (Piaget, 1986; Smith, 1995b). How do children understand a 'possible world'?

This question arises in studies of reasoning in fantasy contexts, which are interpreted as showing that children can make deductive (logically necessary) inferences just because they can think through the alternative possibilities in fantasy worlds. It is at any rate clear that children are sensitive to the distinction between actual and fantasy events, shown by their deductive capacities in these two distinct contexts (Hawkins *et al.*, 1984; Markovits, 1995). Yet there is a dilemma in the interpretation of such studies. All depends on what the children have in mind in one and the same train of thought.

Suppose the children imagine a fantasy world *concurrently*, realising that it is not the actual world, i.e. they have one belief with these joint elements. Now according to Putnam (1972), fantasy contexts are not extensional and so the rules of extensional logic cannot be expected to apply to the fantasy world, even though they can be expected to apply to the actual world. Quine (1963) has shown that epistemic and modal contexts are non-extensional (see Sainsbury, 1991, for clarification of this distinction). Adapting Putnam's argument that fantasy contexts are analogous (i.e. they are non-extensional), it is arguable that *modus placens* (this is the whimsical rule 'anything goes' in that any proposition entails itself or its negation: $p => p \lor -p$) can as easily apply as *modus ponens* (the extensional rule that a conditional together with the antecedent of that conditional entail its consequent: $p \rightarrow q \ \& \ p => q$). Presented with the premises in a fantasy context from which some conclusion is to be inferrred, the rational response is 'Who can say?' Yet extensionality is simply assumed to fit all reasoning in fantasy contexts in these studies. (See Smith, 1996a for further discussion.)

Suppose, now, that children imagine the fantasy world by 'bracketing off' the actual world, i.e. they have *consecutive* beliefs about the actual and fantasy worlds. In this case, the children may see the events in the fantasy world as events in the actual world. In virtue of a lively imagination, it is one thing to 'bracket off' the actual world so as make inferences about events in a fantasy world – seen as the actual world – whilst the actual world has been temporally suspended. It is quite something else to do this concurrently with countervailing observational evidence about the actual world. Children may well have the imaginative capacity to do the former but not the latter. At any event, the conflation of *one possible* with *the actual* world has to be avoided. Even though any actual event is also a possible event, the converse is invalid since it is a modal error to infer that any possible event is an actual event. It is not clear that studies of fantasy reasoning keep secure this modal distinction.

AN ASSESSMENT-CRITERION OF MODAL KNOWLEDGE

Competing evaluations about the adequacy of Piaget's work continue to appear. One central issue concerns the extent to which Piagetian theory still offers a productive research-programme or whether there are more promising programmes elsewhere in cognitive-developmental research (Beilin, 1992; Halford, 1989). Clearly, there is a choice here. Equally, neither choice need be exclusive, even if making good an inclusively joint interpretation is as difficult as it is apparently welcome (Flavell, 1992; Piaget, 1987c, quoted in Smith, 1996a, p. vi). My choice is to focus on a specified interpretation which runs through the whole of Piaget's work about the development of modal knowledge.

If 'childhood is the sleep of reason' (Rousseau 1974), how do we wake up? The answer due to Moshman (1994) is that reasoning based on reasons leads to reason. This answer can be adapted to fit an interpretation of Piaget's account.

Modal knowledge develops in line with some account

Not all reasoning is maximally rational since rationality can be minimal or even deviant (Cherniak, 1986). Thus a working hypothesis is that development in an individual's modal knowledge occurs as that individual's own reasoning about modality. What is required is some account of the development of modal reasoning. There is such an account in Piaget's work.

In his first book, Piaget (1918, p. 163) signalled his interest in the development of logical knowledge, making clear that this included necessary knowledge (Piaget, 1928, p. 234). The main problem is stark, concerning the development of necessary knowledge from knowledge based on (physical, social, cultural) experience which is not necessary. But how can necessary knowledge which is true throughout time have an origin in psychological operations which are constructed in time (Piaget, 1950, quoted in Smith, 1993, p. 1)? How can an atemporal necessity develop from a temporal construction (Piaget, 1967)? This same problem is evident in Piaget's (1971a) biological account: what is the mechanism responsible for progress from reflex behaviour to logical demonstrations. Or Piaget's (1995a) socio-logical account: how does autonomous, rational knowledge develop from culturally transmitted knowledge? Or in Piaget and Garcia's (1989) account of development in the history of ideas: why does it take centuries for the best minds to make an intellectual advance which is then routinely under-stood by children in school?

Doubtless there are other empircal accounts. Indeed, the formation of modal knowledge is a substantive question and this is well recognised in debates as to the age of onset of modal knowledge during infancy (Wynn, 1992), early childhood (Piéraut-Le Bonniec, 1980), late childhood (Moshman, 1990) or adolesence (Markman, 1978). However, there are both rational (Haack, 1978; Sainsbury, 1991) and empirical (Murray, 1990; Piéraut-Le Bonniec, 1990) problems in abundance. Even if Piaget's account is incomplete, it is arguably the most developed account to hand.

Modality is independent of truth-value

Distinct intellectual norms are distinct, definable through their own criteria. Since modality and truth are distinct, each has its own, non-reducible defining criteria. It is one thing to make an inference leading to a correct understanding and quite something else to base that inference on logical necessity. Thus it needs to be shown that a correct response which is compatible with some modal principle is also due to it in any subject's own reasoning.

Modal concepts are inter-definable within the same modal family

It is a strict consequence of the standard definition of necessity that any member of a modal family is defined through another member of the same family. Thus necessity is defined as a negation which is not possible, where both *necessity* and *possibility* are members of the same family of alethic modality. Further, possibility is defined as a negation which is not necessary. Although other modal concepts, such as certainty-supposition or obliga-tion-permission, are important phenomena in their own right, the use of a concept from one modal family to resolve a diagnostic problem about its analogue in another modal family simply pushes the initial problem one step back due to the isomorphic properties shared by all modal concepts. If the valid assessment of (alethic) necessity is a problem, (epistemic) certainty and (deontic) obligation pose analogous problems.

Modal knowledge is due to modal reasoning, not to observation, nor to experience

Kant (1953, sect. 14) pointed out that experience teaches us what is the case, *not* what must be the case. Wittgenstein (1961, sect. 6.37) issued the reminder that there is no necessity in the actual world. The general point was not lost on Piaget (1987a, p. 3; 1987b, p. 3) who expressly denied that possibility or necessity are observable. Thus modal knowledge is due neither to observation nor to experience. For Piaget (1918; cf. Smith, 1997), the source of modal knowledge lies in the general logic of action and is manifest in modal reasoning.

Reasoning as what an individual knows how to do

There is a distinction between reasoning in the sense of what a subject consciously thinks and reasoning in the sense of what that subject knows how to do (Piaget, 1967, 1983). Studies of reasoning in the latter sense should meet two requirements. One is for the subject's *own* reasoning to be made public, i.e. the subject should do this and not merely be responsive to an experimenter. The other is for the subject's reasoning to be made *public*, i.e. the subject's performance should be comprehensive enough to reveal both judgements and justifications ('Don't just give your answer – show your working out,' as school-teachers say). Thus a criterion relevant to modal knowledge should bear on activities which reveal the individual's own capacities to engage in modal reasoning, where that reasoning is made public together with the subject's reasons. The argument for both judgments and justifications as 'response-criteria' for modal knowledge is set out elsewhere (Smith, 1993, sect. 13).

Reasoning as a way of knowing something to be so

There is a venerable distinction between *ratio essendi* and *ratio cognoscendi*, between the reason for something being so and the reason for our knowing it to be so. Take transitivity: if $A = B$ and $B = C$, then $A = C$. The equality $A = C$ is really due to the equality of the units. But in virtue of the equality of both A and C with B, we may get to know that $A = C$. If this is so, the way we get to know $A = C$ is not the reason that $A = C$ (Joseph, 1916). This distinction was cited with approval by Piaget (1980b) in his comments on Spinoza's (1959) thought-experiment and the invitation to think of two ideas. First, think of a semi-circle now at rest, now in motion. Second, think of a semi-circle revolving on its centre as a sphere. The two ideas are different. The first is deviant, even false in that motion is not a defining property of semi-circularity. The second exactly captures the defining property of a sphere. The example is instructive, argued Piaget, in that it identifies the developmental problem, namely how to form the second idea from the first one. This is the problem of intellectual transformation. It leads to a focus on activities which generate transformations in reasoning. Taking a different example about the necessity of class inclusion relations, how does actual reasoning based on part-part subordinate class comparison become *transformed* into better reasoning, closed under necessity, about part-whole comparison under a superordinate class (cf. Smith, 1993, sect. 24)? The diagnostic implication is that the individual should be placed in situations which provide the opportunity for the intellectual transformation of one mode of reasoning into a better successor. Any such transformation is the proper unit of analysis.

Modal reasoning is based on reasons

The standard view about rationality is that reasoning is based on reasons, where these are reasons for beliefs or for actions (Sainsbury, 1991). This view does not fit reasoning in animals nor during infancy. However, it does fit modal reasoning, since the only way to gain modal knowledge – as opposed to truth-functionally correct knowledge – is through the subject's own reasons. A *correct* response due to ruling out what *is not the case* is not the same as a *necessary* understanding due to ruling out what *could not be the case*. This distinction could not be drawn other than by reasoning based on reasons. The implication is that a modal judgement must have a justification, where that justification is based on reasons which makes sense to that subject and which also match modal norms. Although modal reasons are not required as a condition of a display of modal reasoning, the capacity to offer modally relevant reasons is so required.

With novel knowledge in mind, this conclusion has an attractive consequence in that a subject's reasons forge connections between otherwise disconnected intellectual states.

Spontaneous reasons for actual reasoning

There are two sources by which new ideas arise, from within the individual mind and from common culture. One source lies within the mind, namely in human intelligence and imagination which is a prodigious fund of ideas and images. Yet a fertile imagination is as likely to generate fantasy as fact. Descartes (1931) specifically contrasted the imagination with the intellect and Kant (1953) contrasted objective knowledge in science with human subjectivity whose reality is less even than a dream. As Pareto (1963, sect. 972) put it, we have a propensity to be satisfied by 'pseudo-logic as well as by rigorous logic'. The other source is common culture, whose contribution is as considerable as it is indispensable (Piaget, 1995a, 1995b; Smith, 1996b). Common culture is available through transmission by parents, teachers and peers. Cultural knowledge may be widely available. It can be liberating. It can just as easily become restricting. Cultural capital can, and does, constrain the mind just as easily as it empowers new modes of thought.

So connections have to be made between ideas within the mind and between culturally available ideas. Piaget refers to this as equilibration (1985), or coordination and integration (1987b). Transformations reveal the mind in action, whether coordinating the subject's own ideas from human imagination or cultural capital available generally. It is in this sense that transformation is spontaneous, reflecting neither the absurd notion of a 'solitary knower' (Smith, 1995a) nor the bankrupt notion of development as a process from 'absence-to-presence' (Smith, 1991) but rather the subject as an autonomous agent and the source of novelty. 'Each individual is called upon to think and rethink the system of collective notions on his own account and by means of his own logic' (Piaget, 1995a, p. 138).

Actual reasons can lead to good reason

Common sense is not always good sense (Descartes, 1931). So too actual reasons are not always good reasons. Piaget (1985) captures this point by defining the mind as in all cases a mind in assimilating action, whilst denying that mental activity as such is successful. Mental activity is a search for, not a guarantee of, coherence. Reasoning is one way in which commonly accepted reasons can be converted into a better reason. Modal reasoning requires the reasons actually at the individual's disposal to match some relevant standard through the serial reduction in both pseudo-modal knowledge and modal blindspots. Piaget (1971b) denied that there could be a general theory of the removal of time-lags in intellectual development and this denial would extend to time-lags in the development of modal reasoning.

Modal reasoning confers universal knowledge

Modal reasoning requires knowledge of universals. This is because necessity is defined across 'possible worlds', and not merely the actual world. Any 'possible world' is an abstract object, i.e. a universal.

What exactly is a 'possible world'? There are three views on offer. One is modal realism, according to which there is an infinite number of possible worlds which exist in much the way that the actual world exists (Lewis, 1986). The second is modal nominalism, according to which possible worlds are fictions in much the way that the characters in fairy-tales are fictions (Rosen, 1990). The third view is modal constructivism, according to which possible worlds are constructions. This view, in turn, splits since there are several proposals as to what sort of construction this is, including logical (Carnap, 1956) or phenomonological (Husserl, 1970). Each of these positions has a standard defect. Realism leads to an ontological slum (Quine, 1963). Nominalism leads to relativism (Putnam, 1972). Constructivism leads to fallibilism (Haack, 1978). No doubt it is for such reasons that problems about abstract objects are intractable (Hale, 1987; Lowe, 1995). Yet they are fundamental, since they bear upon what reality is like. To suppose that reality is just the actual world is to court nominalism and so one answer to this outstanding problem.

Such metaphysical problems have epistemological counterparts (Katz, 1995). The epistemological problem concerns how anyone could get to know a universal. Although epistemology is standardly investigated rationally by philosophers, empirical investigation has a place as well. It has been argued that the Kantian dictum that 'ought' implies 'can' applies not merely in moral contexts but in intellectual contexts as well (Kornblith, 1985). That is, (rational) claims about how knowledge 'ought' to arise presuppose (empirical) claims about how knowledge 'can' arise. Some version of this argument is widely presupposed in cognitive science (Leiser and Gilliéron, 1990). It is a central argument in Piaget's genetic – that is, developmental or empirical – epistemology (see Smith, 1993, p. 7).

Adapting Kant's (1953) dictum that necessity and universality are interdependent properties, there is a promising interpretation of Piaget's work, evident from his first book *Recherche* (1918). Specifically, *universal knowledge* is ambiguous. On this interpretation (Smith, 1995b), necessary knowledge is a knowledge of a universal. It is not thereby knowledge which transfers on possession. So characterised, universal knowledge is marked by problems of access, not by common assent. Modal knowledge is required for the successful communicative exchange of ideas whereby one and the same idea remains self-identical through one and the same train of thought, whether in one mind or between two people (Piaget, 1928, 1995a).

REFERENCES

Acredolo, C. and O'Connor, J. (1991). On the difficulty of detecting cognitive uncertainty. *Human Development*, 34, 204–23.
Aristotle (1987). *De interpetatione*. In J. Ackrill (ed.) *A New Aristotle Reader*. Oxford: Oxford University Press.
Baillargeon, R. (1995). A model of physical reasoning in infancy. In C. Rovee-Collier and L. Lipsitt (eds) *Advances in Infancy Research*, vol. 9. Norwood, NJ: Ablex.
Beilin, H. (1992). Piaget's enduring contribution to developmental psychology. *Developmental Psychology*, 28, 191–204.
Brown, T. (1996). Values knowledge and Piaget. In L. Smith (ed.) *Critical Readings on Piaget*. London: Routledge.
Byrnes, J. and Beilin, H. (1991). The cognitive basis of uncertainty. *Human Development*, 34, 189–203.
Byrnes, J. and Duff, M. (1989). Young children's comprehension of modal expressions. *Cognitive Development*, 4, 369–87.
Carnap, R. (1956). *Meaning and Necessity*, 2nd edition. Chicago: University of Chicago Press.
Cherniak, C. (1986). *Minimal Rationality*. Cambridge, MA: MIT Press.
Descartes, R. (1931). *Discourse on Method*. In G. Haldane and G. Ross (eds) *The Philosophical works of Descartes*, vol. 1. New York: Dover.
Flavell, J. (1992). Cognitive development: past, present and future. *Developmental Psychology*, 28, 998–1005.

Flavell, J., Miller, P. and Miller, S. (1993) *Cognitive Development*, 3rd edition. Engelwood Cliffs, NJ: Prentice-Hall.

Foltz, C., Overton, W. and Ricco, R. (1995). Proof construction: adolescent development from inductive to deductive problem-solving strategiees. *Journal of Experimental Child Psychology*, 59, 179–95. Reprinted in L. Smith (ed.) *Critical readings on Piaget*. London: Routledge.

Forbes, G. (1985). *The Metaphysics of Modality*. Oxford: Oxford University Press.

Goodman, N. (1979). *Fact, Fiction and Forecast*, 3rd edition. Hassocks: Harvester Press.

Haack, S. (1978). *Philosophy of Logics*. Cambridge: Cambridge University Press.

Hale, B. (1987). *Abstract Objects* Oxford: Blackwell.

Halford, G. (1989). Reflections on 25 years of Piagetian cognitive-developmental psychology, 1963–1988. *Human Development*, 32, 325–57.

Hawkins, J., Pea, R., Glick, J. and Scribner, S. (1984). Merds that laugh don't like mushrooms: evidence for deductive reasoning by preschoolers. *Developmental Psychology*, 20, 584–94.

Hempel, C. (1965). *Aspects of Scientific Explanation*. New York: The Free Press.

Husserl, E. (1970). *Logical Investigations*, 2 vols. London: Routledge and Kegan Paul.

Johnson-Laird, P. N. (1978). The meaning of modality. *Cognitive Science*, 2, 17–26.

Joseph, H. (1916). *An Introduction to Logic*, 2nd edition. Oxford: Oxford University Press.

Kant, I. (1953). *Prolegomena*. Manchester: Manchester University Press.

Karmiloff-Smith, A. (1994). Précis of *Beyond Modularity*. Author's response. *Behavioural and Brain Sciences*, 17, 732–45.

Katz, J. (1995). What mathematical knowledge could be. *Mind*, 104, 491–522.

Keil, F. (1989). *Concepts, Kinds and Cognitive Development*. Cambridge, MA: MIT Press.

Kornblith, H. (1985). *Naturalizing Epistemology*. Cambridge, MA: MIT Press.

Kripke, S. (1980). *Naming and Necessity*. Oxford: Blackwell.

Leiser, D. and Gilliéron, C. (1990). *Cognitive Science and Genetic Epistemology*. New York: Plenum Press.

Lewis, D. (1986). *On the Plurality of Possible Worlds*. Oxford: Blackwell.

Lowe, E. (1995). The metaphysics of abstract objects. *The Journal of Philosophy*, 92, 509–24.

Markman, E. (1978). Empirical versus logical solutions to part-whole comparison problems concerning classes and collections. *Child Development*, 49, 168–77.

Markovits, H. (1995). Conditional reasoning with false premises: fantasy and information retrieval. *British Journal of Developmental Psychology*, 13, 1–11. Reprinted in L. Smith (ed.) *Critical Readings on Piaget*. London: Routledge.

Miller, S. (1986). Certainty and necessity in the understanding of Piagetian concepts. *Developmental Psychology*, 22, 3–18.

Moshman, D. (1990). The development of metalogical understanding. In W. Overton (ed.) *Reasoning, Necessity and Logic*. Hillsdale, NJ: Erlbaum.

Moshman, D. (1994). Reason, reasons and reasoning. *Theory and Psychology*, 4, 245–60.

Moshman, D. and Franks, B. (1986). Development of the concept of inferential validity. *Child Development*, 57, 153–65.

Murray, F. (1990). The conversion of truth into necessity. In W. Overton (ed.) *Reasoning, Necessity and Logic*. Hillsdale, NJ: Erlbaum.

Murray, F. and Armstrong, S. (1976). Necessity in conservation and non-conservation. *Developmental Psychology*, 12, 483–4.

Nagel, T. (1986). *The View from Nowhere*. New York: Oxford University Press.

Osherson, D. and Markman, E. (1975). Language and the ability to evaluate contradictions and tautologies. *Cognition*, 3, 213–26.

Overton, W. (1990). Competence and procedures: constraints on the development of logical reasoning. In W. Overton (ed.) *Reasoning, Necessity and Logic*. Hillsdale, NJ: Erlbaum.

Pareto, W. (1963). *The Mind in Society: A Treatise on General Sociology*. New York: Dover.

Piaget, J. (1918). *Recherche*. Lausanne: La Concorde.

Piaget, J. (1928). *Judgment and Reasoning in the Child*. London: Routledge and Kegan Paul.

Piaget, J. (1950). *Introduction à l'épistémologie génétique*, vol. 1. *La pensée mathématique*. Paris: Presses Universitaires de France.

Piaget, J. (1952). *The Child's Conception of Number*. London: Routledge and Kegan Paul.

Piaget, J. (1967). *Logique et connaissance scientifique*. Paris: Gallimard.

Piaget, J. (1971a). *Biology and Knowledge*. Edinburgh: Edinburgh University Press.

Piaget, J. (1971b). The theory of stages in cognitive development. In D. Green, M. Ford and G. Flamer (eds) *Measurement and Piaget*. New York: McGraw-Hill.

Piaget, J. (1980a). Fifth conversation. In J. C. Bringuier, *Conversations with Jean Piaget*. Chicago: University of Chicago Press.

Piaget, J. (1980b). La raison en tant qu'objectif de la compréhension. Unpublished paper.

Piaget, J. (1983). Piaget's theory. In P. Mussen (ed.) *Handbook of Child Psychology*. New York: Wiley.

Piaget, J. (1985). *Equilibration of Cognitive Structures*. Chicago: University of Chicago Press.

Piaget, J. (1986). Essay on necessity. *Human Development*, 29, 301–14.

Piaget, J. (1987a). *Possibility and Necessity*, vol. 1. Minneapolis: University of Minnesota Press.

Piaget, J. (1987b). *Possibility and Necessity*, vol. 2. Minneapolis: University of Minnesota Press.

Piaget, J. (1987c). *Psychologie*. Paris: Gallimard.

Piaget, J. (1995a). *Sociological Studies*. London: Routledge.

Piaget, J. (1995b). Commentary on Vygotsky's criticisms. *New Ideas in Psychology*, 13, 325–40.

Piaget, J. and Garcia, R. (1989). *Psychogenesis and the History of Science*. New York: Columbia University Press.

Piaget, J. and Garcia, J. (1991). *Toward a Logic of Meanings*. Hillsdale, NJ: Erlbaum Associates.

Piaget, J. and Inhelder, B. (1974). *The child's construction of quantities*. London: Routledge and Kegan Paul.

Piaget, J. and Karmiloff-Smith, A. (1992). A special case of inferential symmetry. In J. Piaget, G. Henriques and E. Ascher (eds) *Morphisms and Categories: Comparing and Transforming*. Hillsdale, NJ: Erlbaum Associates.

Piaget, J., Henriques, G. and Ascher, E. (eds) (1992) *Morphisms and Categories*. Hillsdale, NJ: Erlbaum.

Piéraut-Le Bonniec, G. (1980). *The Development of Modal Reasoning*. New York: Academic Press.

Plato (1941). *The Republic*. Oxford: Oxford University Press.

Polanyi, M. (1969). The logic of tacit inference. In M. Grene (ed.) *Knowing and Being: Essays by Michael Polanyi*. London: Routledge and Kegan Paul.

Putnam H. (1972). *The Philosophy of Logic*. London: George Allen and Unwin.

Quine, W. (1963). *From a Logical Point of View*. New York: Harper and Row.

Rosen, G. (1990). Modal fictionalism. *Mind*, 99, 327–54.

Rousseau, J.-J. (1974). *Emile*, London: Dent.

Russell, J. (1982). The child's appreciation of the necessary truth and necessary falseness of propositions. *British Journal of Psychology*, 73, 253–66.

Sainsbury, M. (1991). *Logical Forms*. Oxford: Blackwell.

Scholnick, E. and Wing, C. (1995). Logic in conversation: comparative studies of deduction in children and adults. *Cognitive Development*, 10, 319–45.

Smith, L. (1991). Age, ability and intellectual development in developmental theory. In M. Chandler and M. Chapman (eds) *Criteria for Competence*. Hillsdale, NJ: Erlbaum.

Smith, L. (1993). *Necessary Knowledge*. Hove: Erlbaum.

Smith, L. (1995a). Introduction to *Sociological Studies*. In J. Piaget, *Sociological Studies*. London: Routlege.

Smith, L. (1995b). Universal knowledge. Paper presented at the 25th Annual Symposium, Jean Piaget Society, Berkeley, June.

Smith, L. (1996a). Piaget's epistemology: psychological and educational assessment. In L. Smith (ed.) *Critical Readings on Piaget*. London: Routledge.

Smith, L. (1996b). With knowledge in mind. *Human Development*, 39, 257–63.

Smith, L. (1997). Jean Piaget. In N. Sheehy and T. Chapman (eds) *Biographical Dictionary of Psychology*. London: Routledge.

Spinoza, B. (1959). *Treatise on the Development of the Understanding*. In A. Boyle (ed.) *Spinoza's ethics*. London: Dent.

White, P. (1995). *The Understanding of Causation and the Production of Action*. Hove: Erlbaum.

Wittgenstein, L. (1961) *Tractatus Logico-Philosophicus*. London: Routledge and Kegan Paul.

von Wright, G. H. (1951). *An Essay in Modal Logic*. Amsterdam: North-Holland.

Wynn, K. (1992). Evidence against empiricist accounts of the origins of numerical knowledge. *Mind and Language*, 7, 315–32.

15 Modality and modal reasoning

Peter Tomlinson

MODALITY: WHAT WE MEAN AND HOW WE TELL

I have long thought that psychologists tend to pay too little attention to distinctions such as that between defining (what we mean by) something and understanding it (seeing/saying how it works, what goes on), or between either of these and assessing (how you tell) when something is present. Ignoring such distinctions can be problematic enough in what used to be called 'pure' psychology, where psychologists are selecting their own topic of interest and working within a well-established theoretical tradition. But in applied areas such as education it has often tended to be mislead-ing and counter-productive, since here not only does the field decide the priorities for the applied psychologist to elucidate, but often has no clear and agreed meaning for the terms it uses. When 'operational definitions' are introduced in lieu of theoretical conceptualisation, then we all know the consequences.

The importance of getting clear in these respects about the nature of model reasoning can surely not be overstated. As Les Smith argues, modal necessity is a key aspect of logical reasoning and its development. And even for those of the most relativist post-modern bent (cf. Chaiklin, 1992), the other modal families are no less important in real-world psychology: the deontic mode featuring in Paul Harris's studies of young children is at the root of the psychology of values and decision-making, and issues of possibility and likelihood must be central to attributional aspects of self-appraisal and action generally.

The sorts of distinctions I referred to in the first paragraph above are of course not only subtle and closely inter-connected, but to attempt to elucidate them, as Les Smith does in the case of the already subtle second-order concept of logical necessity, really is to grasp an intellectual nettle!

Whilst admitting uncertainty as to whether I have assimilated every relevant aspect of his treatment, his critiques of the limitations of certain 'appropriate ... yet ... incomplete' criteria (certainty, physical necessity, modal intuition, modal propositions, modal realism) seem to me well taken. Collectively and, in particular, considered in relation to each other but avoiding any sort of circularity, they surely point towards systematic limitations in the power of empirical methods to gain access to others' minds. That is, indicators, particularly in this area of cognitive psychology, can only ever be partial and probabilistic.

However, he then goes on in a later section of his paper ('An assessment-criterion of modal knowledge') to make a number of recommendations concerning criteria of modal reasoning and its development. It seems to me that the combination of criteria he states or implies in that section are reasonable when seen as indicators of a relatively full version of capability for modal necessity reasoning. However, although his emphasis on the provision of explicit rationales particularly the sub-sections on pp. 233–8 accords with his prior account of modal reasoning as involving a second-order treatment of first-order reasons, I think that that when the 'classical view' of reasoning as always being 'based on reasons' is seen as meaning 'consciously articulatable reasons', we have a questionable psychological assumption (as opposed to a conceptual definition) whose adoption might occasion false negatives. One may, in other words, draw a distinction between what we might call cognitive level and consciousness level. A meta-cognitive process is here defined as a process that deals with, involves information about, another cognitive process, in which sense it is at a level 'beyond' that of the targeted process. There may be various definitions of and corresponding criteria for consciousness, but in terms of such traditional features as verbal articulation of process or of product, a meta-cognitive process surely need not be reflective in the sense of conscious.

There is of course a considerable literature on the role of justification in establishing cognitive capability and Les Smith is right to make the point repeatedly that understanding of correctness is not the same as understanding necessity, which is a meta-level insight. However, as argued above, in principle the requisite cognitive processes could presumably occur unconsciously: I've always wondered about the tension between the Piagetians' welcome refusal to be railroaded into identifying thought with verbalisation, on the one hand, and their tendency to insist on verbal justifications on the other. The availability of such justification, especially when spontaneous, doubtless constitutes stronger evidence of modal capability (when allied with a correct pattern of responding, that is). On the other hand, a correct response pattern in the absence of modal justification should leave us with a 'not proven' verdict on modal insight, not a firm negative, even in the case of older children and adults, let alone very young children whose verbal articulation capacities may lag behind their actual information-processing.

Many moons ago, Herbert Klausmaier and his colleagues (1974) pointed out that one can have a *classificatory* capability in the case of a concept, without having the *formal* capability to give an explicit definition and justification of the inclusion/exclusion of exemplars. Applying this to the second-order issues of modality, is it impossible that a person's consistent correct first-order responding might be dependent on 'second-order' processes which they nevertheless could not verbally articulate? After all, to suppose that second-order processes must be consciously accessible is surely to buy into a particular sort of model of mental processing, known variously as rationalism or dualism. One aspect of Mike Oaksford and Nick Chater's recent work (1995a and b) on the Wason selection task seems to indicate pretty clearly that people's actual probability-based strategies are not consciously and reflexively held and, more broadly, as I read it, much of Diane Berry and Zoltan Dienes' (1993) book on implicit learning is compatible with the 'unconscious' alternative just sketched.

Thus we seem, as I indicated earlier, to be between a rock and a hard place as regards empirical study in this area. In such circumstances we naturally reach for other indicators, such as surprise. My view is that whilst Leslie Smith is right to point to their inconclusiveness, an indicator such as surprise isn't *nothing*. At the very least, we do have a problem and cannot *insist* on the verbal articulation side as a necessary indicator of modal comprehension.

It may of course also be the case that modal insights in a given domain are actually componentially complex, with some décalage not only between judgement and justification on any particular component, but also between components. The work reported in the paper by Maggie Chalmers and Brendan McGonigle is surely of relevance here.

CHILDREN'S DEONTIC UNDERSTANDING

Although I am more struck by the actual findings cited by Paul Harris and María Núñez concerning the young age at which children master obligation and permission concepts, their work also illustrates something comparable to what I was suggesting above regarding necessity. What I have in mind here is that deontic modality is, as it were, built into the meaning of words like 'must' and 'have to', so that to characterise or at least pick out some-one who 'doesn't' (fit the condition) as naughty is already some degree of indication of grasp of this kind of modality. Further aspects of this meaning are evidenced when to this are added indications that intentionality is part of the criterion for such deontic failure. When as in the Harris and Núñez work there are also patterns contrasting such performances with atypicality judgements and showing that the children's censures are not unconditional, then we surely have a pretty clear indication of the grasp of this kind of modality, though further reflexive comment and spontaneous definitions might lend still further support.

Whether this very early emergence in children of relative mastery of social permission over other comparably patterned schemata owes more to the sort of innate 'cheater-detection module' argued for by Cosmides and Tooby (Cosmides, 1989; Cosmides and Tooby, 1994) or to a broader pre-eminence of value/motive together with persistent parental social framing, is something Paul Harris and María Núñez perhaps wisely refrain from pursuing at this point. In either case, the contrast with age-norms emerging from traditional Piagetian work on use of intentionality in judging naughtiness is interesting (cf. Tomlinson, 1980). On the one hand capability can be highly specific, on the other, both a 'cheater detection module' or an early sensitising to intentional violation of social prescriptions would surely be expected to be general enough to apply to the Piagetian stories' scenario. An obvious extension here would be to involve both kinds of measure in the same study.

REFERENCES

Berry, D. C. and Dienes, Z. (1993) *Implicit Learning: Theoretical and Empirical Issues*. Hove: Lawrence Erlbaum Associates.

Chaiklin, S. (1992) From theory to practice and back again: What does postmodern philosophy contribute to psychological science? In Kvale, S. (ed.) *Psychology and Postmodernism*. London: SAGE Publications, pp. 194–208.

Cosmides, L. (1989) The logic of social exchange: has natural selection shaped how humans reason? Studies with the Wason selection task. *Cognition*, 31, 187–276.

Cosmides, L. and Tooby, J. L. (1994) Origins of domain specificity: the evolution of functional organization. In L. A. Hirschfeld and S. A. Gelman (eds) *Mapping the Mind: Domain Specificity in Cognition and Culture*. Cambridge: Cambridge University Press, pp. 85–116.

Klausmaier, H. J., Ghatala, E. S. and Frayer, D. A. (1974) *Concept Learning and Development: A Cognitive View*. New York: Academic Press.

Oaksford, M. and Chater, N. (1995a) Information gain explains relevance which explains the selection task. *Cognition*, 57, 97–108.

Oaksford, M. and Chater, N. (1995b) Theories of reasoning and the computational explanation of everyday inference. *Thinking and Reasoning*, 1, 2, 121–52.

Tomlinson, P. D. (1980) Moral development and moral psychology: Piaget, Kohlberg and beyond. In S. Modgil, and C. Modgil (eds) *Towards a Theory of Psychological Development*. Windsor: NFER, pp. 303–66.

Postface

16 The view from giants' shoulders

Deanna Kuhn

Although it was not apparent at the time, 1896 was an auspicious year for developmental psychology, a field that at the time did not even have the firm identity that it does today. During their lifetimes, so disparate in length and circumstances, Piaget and Vygotsky each contributed to our understanding of learning and development in ways that we now appreciate as revolutionary. Yet these two men of the same age developed their respective visions within very separate cultural and intellectual communities. Although aware of one another's work, they never met, and, with a few isolated exceptions, did not profit from a dialectical interchange of ideas. Today, we have that advantage.

Thanks in large part to Vygotsky's influence, we have become aware of the need to understand phenomena in their sociohistorical context, and this applies certainly to the assimilation of first Piaget and then Vygotsky by English-speaking psychologists. Widespread attention to either theorist's contributions by the English-speaking community was delayed many years beyond the original appearance of their work. Why do events happen when they do? The burst of attention to Vygotsky over the past decade occurred in the historical context of our perceiving the need for a 'corrective' to what appeared to many as the missing social element in Piaget's theory. The time was clearly conducive. How would things have gone differently if we had 'discovered' Vygotsky first? Might Vygotsky's theories by now have been demonstrated to be wrong in as many respects as researchers of the last several decades have demonstrated Piaget's theories to be wrong? And how would things be different today if Piaget and Vygotsky had themselves engaged in a dialectical interchange during their lifetimes?

But none of this is what happened. In the 1960s and into the 70s, the antithesis that opposed Piaget's constructivist thesis in American developmental psychology was social learning theory. In the minds of Piagetians, the concept of internalization was firmly located on the opponent's turf. The time was not right for Vygotsky, whose ideas could only have muddied the conceptual waters that defined these opposing camps. Several decades later, we are in a better position to appreciate Vygotsky's vision. Internalization is no longer a dirty word.

It is also striking to note in 1996 that although both Piaget's and Vygotsky's visions were revolutionary in their time, how different again is our current conception of development. This is particularly the case if we contrast the current picture to the picture one comes away with, from a surface reading at least, of the classic Piagetian opus – a picture of discontinuous change from one singular, all-encompassing stage to another, with the entire explanatory burden borne by these monolithic structures. Today, we have much evidence to support a view of development as quite the opposite of singular, discontinuous and uniform across time and place. The picture we now have is one of a socially embedded process of transition, extended in time, encompassing multiple interwoven but at least partially independent strands, and exhibiting significant temporal and contextual variability.

How is it that we gather now to commemorate the birth and life of a figure whose ideas have been so thoroughly discredited? But this is not the case, of course. It is a testament, perhaps, to the richness and power of Piaget's vision that we have found him to be wrong in so many ways and yet there remain so many ways in which we recognize him to be right. A number of the topics that figure prominently in examining Piaget's or Vygotsky's work remain at the forefront of current discussion and debate. The issues they involve are clearly fundamental ones. I will focus here on three topics that are very much at the centre of attention in the field today – microgenesis, metacognition and social collaboration. In the case of each of these topics, I believe, both Piaget's and Vygotsky's insights continue to have key roles to play in advancing our understanding.

The first topic is *microgenesis* and the microgenetic method as a key to studying the phenomenon of prime concern to developmentalists – change (Kuhn, 1995; Siegler and Crowley, 1991). Vygotsky's ideas from the beginning were centered on dynamic rather than static assessment of intellectual capability, reflected most explicitly in his concept of zone of proximal development, and these ideas continue to have much to offer us in conceptualizing the change process theoretically and examining it empirically. Inhelder's work on procedures lay useful groundwork for some of the methodological developments we have seen in recent years in the use of a microgenetic method to better understand the process of change.

Recent microgenetic research by Fischer, Siegler, myself and others has made it clear that in general people – both adults and children – don't have just one way of doing things. Instead, they have developed a repertory of multiple strategies that they apply to the same or similar situations in ways that are not perfectly consistent. This variability is a key factor in understanding change. One reason we know this is that when we engage children or adults in repeated encounters with the same or similar situation, the distribution of strategies they exhibit is likely to shift, rather than remain constant. It is this gradual shift, of course, that provides researchers with a very valuable window on the change process. Microgenetic methods are powerful enough that they can even breathe new life into well-worn topics, such as conservation acquisition (Siegler, 1995).

But in order to fully appreciate the relevance of the microgenetic approach we need to turn to my second topic, one that to an equal extent has been the focus of current interest – *metacognition*. If different strategies are applied in repeated encounters with the same or similar tasks, we need to invoke some mechanism to explain strategy selection. And unless we are satisfied with initial concepts such as associative strength (Siegler and Jenkins, 1989), we need to invoke some executive – that is, metacognitive – component that explains strategy choice.

Both Vygotsky's and Piaget's work prefigures the current attention being given to metacognition. Metacognitive awareness is a key element in both of their theories, and they both saw it as having a directing, even determining, influence on cognition. For both of them, to know means to know that you know. Yet in the interpretive efforts of English-speaking psychologists, the role of metacognitive elements of thought have for a long time tended to be subordinated to strategic or operational ones. In one of his last papers, Michael Chapman (1991) revisited the old judgments vs. explanations controversy (Brainerd, 1978). He questions the widely accepted interpretation of this controversy – the interpretation that in contrasting judgements and explanations we are debating the merits of two alternative methods of assessing a single competence. Instead, he suggests, we are dealing with two alternative kinds of competence, each deserving of attention in its own right. One is the more traditional operational competence, and the other is a form of metacognitive competence, one that has a communicative aspect – the ability to communicate and justify what you know, to yourself and others. This latter mode of competence has been curiously neglected in American cognitive psychology, which has focused its attention on modelling processes that occur inside an individual head and on problem-solving, rather than argument, as the prototypical cognitive activity.

In my own recent work, focused on scientific and argumentive reasoning – which I see as closely connected in core respects – I have identified metacognitive phenomena of three different types, and each I believe plays a crucial role. One is the *metastrategic* selection and monitoring of strategies that I have already referred to. It entails knowing about the strategies available in one's repertory – what they buy you and don't buy you cognitively speaking. The significance of metastrategic knowing is underscored by the fact that it is metastrategic, rather than strategic, knowledge that determines which of the alternative behaviours that exist in a repertory will actually appear.

The distinction between the metastrategic component and the second meta-component, which I call *metacognitive*, roughly parallels the distinction between procedural and declarative knowledge, but in this case at a second-order, reflective level. It refers to the *content* of one's knowledge, in contrast to the strategies one uses to operate on this knowledge. This universe of things one knows needs higher-order management, just as does the universe of strategies that can be applied to it. I shall provide some examples shortly.

Finally, an *epistemological* component of knowing connects metastrategic and metacognitive competencies to the broader social context in which knowledge and knowledge acquisition are situated. How does anyone know? What role does knowledge play in our social life? Before discussing these various meta-competencies further, let me say something more about the domains in which I have investigated them – scientific and argumentive reasoning.

A serious limitation in the study of scientific reasoning and its development, and one that has become increasingly apparent in approaches to science education, is the narrow, specialized status we have assigned it. The scientific reasoning we study in children and adolescents may well be a developmental precursor to the reasoning of professional scientists, but a form of thinking may be fundamental to science, without being particular to it. In my own work, I have focused on science as argument and treated both scientific and more familiar, everyday argumentive thinking as broad, strategically critical forms of thought involving the coordination of theories with evidence.

The major developmental dimension I believe is at stake in the development of both scientific and argumentive reasoning is the attainment of increasing control over this process of theory-evidence coordination. Although even very young children use theories as vehicles for understanding the world, they have scant awareness of these theories and little cognitive control over their revision in the face of new evidence. In other words, they lack both metacognitive and metastrategic control. Like so many developmental attainments, attainment of this control has been found to be a multi-faceted acquisition taking place over an extended period of years, with the paradox of early competence and later incompetence very much in evidence. Like cognition, metacognition is not a zero-one phenomenon that enjoys what Siegler (1995) has dubbed an 'immaculate transition'.

A close although not often noted connection exists between the earliest origins of metacognitive awareness critical to scientific and argumentive reasoning and the early competencies studied by researchers whose work focuses on theory of mind. Fundamental to scientific thinking is the understanding of assertions as belief states. It is a critical precursor to recognizing the role of evidence in supporting assertions, and, conversely, in falsifying assertions. It also serves as a fundamental foundation for both epistemological understanding (of the nature of knowledge and of inquiry) and strategic development (of the skills required in supporting assertions).

Somewhere in the age range of three to five years – the exact age being a matter of debate – children acquire the insight that assertions are expressions of someone's belief (Olson and Astington, 1993). As such, they are subject to verification and potentially disconfirmable. Prior to attainment of this insight – the significance of which rivals other milestones in cognitive development – assertions remain descriptive of and isomorphic to an external reality. An account of an event differs from the event itself only in that one exists on a representational plane while the other is perceived directly. In other words, the world is a simple one in which things happen and we can tell about them. There are no inaccurate renderings of events.

Understanding assertions as belief states carries the implication that they could be false. Accordingly, assertions are subject to disconfirmation by evidence – the same potential for disconfirmation that has long been a hallmark of science. Even very young children have some awareness of assertions as disconfirmable claims – that opening the closet door will disprove the claim that a ghost is inside. Still, they have a long developmental course to negotiate in attaining full metacognitive awareness of their own belief states as hypotheses to be coordinated with evidence.

This attainment has several aspects to it. Recognizing correspondences between a theory and evidence is a skill for which we can readily identify early precursors. Piaget's baby who moves his legs and observes the resulting movement of the rattles to which they are connected manifests the most primitive awareness of correspondence between a thesis (in this case expressed only as a sensorimotor scheme) and the external sense data that support it. Later, children will be able to understand correspondences between propositions and evidence bearing on them even to the extent of identifying the more informative of two kinds of evidence, as Sodian *et al.* (1991) have shown. And contrary to Piaget's claim that children cannot deal with the counterfactual, the young child even shows some facility in identifying these correspondences when the theories are contrary-to-fact or contrary to the child's own belief (Ruffman *et al.*, 1993). As interesting as these early precursors are, the greater challenge is in understanding how development proceeds from them, in particular how and why it does not proceed to a more accomplished level in most adolescents and adults.

But even as rudimentary skills, they do not tell the whole story. In addition to recognizing *correspondences* between theories and evidence, there stands a more subtle competence that has not received as much attention, although I think it deserves a great deal, and that is the *differentiation* of theory and evidence from one another, as entities having different epistemological status. In none of the situations I've just referred to is the distinction between what is the proposition and what is the evidence in question. Even in its most rudimentary forms, it is a metacognitive skill, par excellence, that is involved in maintaining this distinction.

We see the developmental challenge most vividly in the at best fragile awareness that children, and in many cases adults as well, have of the source of their own beliefs: How do I know what I know? In our microgenetic studies of subjects coordinating their theories with an accumulating evidence base, we observed both children and adults gradually become more convinced of the correctness of some of their theories but less metacognitively aware of the source of this certainty. Theory-based justifications were frequently offered in response to questions about the implications of evidence, and in the most difficult situations in which theory and evidence supported the same conclusion, theory- and evidence-based justifcation merged in the service of a common end, leaving the subject certain of the conclusion but not metacognitively aware with regard to its source. Although seductive to all of us, for these subjects the temptation was unsurmountable to use evidence simply to *illustrate* what from their perspective they knew to be true. Evidence, for them, did not have a status epistemologically distinct from that of theory.

The metacognitive skills involved here develop, to be sure, and we can see rudimentary forms of them in childhood. Yet studies of such skills differ from the more typical studies of early competence devoted to documenting the impressive competencies already in place in early childhood. Instead their picture is one of early lack of competence and gradual development. Gopnik and Graf (1988), for example, found preschool children insensitive to the source of their knowledge – they were unable to indicate whether they had just learned the contents of a drawer from seeing them or being told about them. Similarly, Taylor *et al.* (1994) reported preschoolers showing little ability to distinguish *when* they had acquired knowledge – whether it had just been taught to them or it was something they had 'always known' (as most of them claimed regarding a newly learned fact). Flavell's (Flavell *et al.*, 1995) numerous studies are also informative here.

In some of my own current work, we focus on the more difficult challenge of understanding the source of one's own *inferences* (as opposed to simple factual knowledge). Children see a sequence of pictures in which two runners compete in a race. Certain cues may suggest a theory as to why one will win, e.g. one is clearly overweight. The final picture in the sequence may leave the outcome unspecified or it may indicate the outcome in various ways – one of the two runners holding a trophy or exhibiting a wide grin – and the outcome might be either theory-congruent (the expected winner runs) or theory-discrepant. The questions children are asked following their viewing of the final picture are designed to assess their ability to distinguish two kinds of justification – 'How do you know?' and 'Why is it so?' – in other words, the source of their knowledge versus their explanation for this knowledge. They are also asked to make these distinctions for others who will view the pictures. Without going into further detail here, let me merely stress, again following Chapman, that children's difficulties here are not attributable to semantic confusions that mask their true competence. We may find more facilitative ways to ask these questions

– ways that will serve to scaffold the competencies in question – but the ability to think and communicate about sources of knowledge *is* the ability of interest to us here. It is not merely an imperfect conduit to some deeper or more 'genuine' conceptual competence.

How might we facilitate the development of these kinds of metacognitive competence? The broad answer, I believe, is by seeking to make children from their earliest years more aware of knowledge acquisition as a process that occurs in themselves and others. And it is here that Vygotsky has the most important insights to offer us, for knowledge acquisition is widely regarded as a solitary and private process that goes on inside an individual, with both process and product hidden from external view. We can with benefit seek to make children more aware of their own knowledge acquisition efforts from this individualist perspective. But there is much to gain from making them aware of knowledge acquisition as a social process, particularly one that has tangible products in the form of a knowledge base available to and shared within a community. This is Popper's (1972) 'World 3' that Bereiter (1994) advocates the need to highlight in the educational arena, by emphasizing the creating and maintaining of collective knowledge, rather than only the improvement of individual minds (Popper's 'World 2'). Knowledge is indeed an entity that has identity and permanence beyond the individual. It does not remain hidden inside people's heads. This idea of knowledge as an entity beyond the individual that is maintained and transmitted across generations is of course central to Vygotsky's thinking and indeed to his conception of what makes development possible.

How do children become aware of knowledge in this sense? The most apparent means is by participating in the acquisition and creation of knowledge with others. This brings me to my third topic, one that, like the first two, is the object of much current attention – *social collaboration*. In moving on to this topic, let me begin by rejecting the simplistic opposition that has characterized much discussion of Piaget and Vygotsky on this front. Are new forms of thought constructed anew by individuals or are they internalized from the culture? Clearly, this is one of those either/ ors that deserves to be put finally to rest. Development must proceed simultaneously from the inside out and from the outside in. It is well to think of exactly what we mean by this.

One of Piaget's earliest and most persistent theses was that social influence on the individual is never direct. Accommodation is 'doubly directed by assimilation' – it both directs attention to the external and registers its results. The social must be assimilated, interpreted and indeed 'reconstructed' by the individual. One of Piaget's earliest American interpreters, Furth, makes the point that this bidirectional process – from inside out and from outside in – originates in the earliest months of life. The infant who first constructs and later symbolizes the permanent object in so doing creates an understanding of it as an object and a symbol shared by others. This accomplishment Furth links to the human 'capacity for society' – a social 'frame' that, once emerged, puts children in a position to assimilate the specific features of their own societies. Consequently, Furth (1996, p. 267) says, 'far from neglecting societal features, Piaget's theory of development can be appreciated as clarifying, at least from a logical perspective, how humans became empowered to construct societies and culture in the first place'.

Today we have the social theorists versus the cognitivists or computationalists, one emphasizing direct participation in the culture as not just the source but the essence of development and the other focusing on the individual's rational constructive enterprise (Astington and Olson, 1995; Bruner, 1995; Feldman, 1995; Leadbeater and Raver, 1995; Olson and Astington, 1995). Although this debate goes on, increasingly we hear voiced the recognition that it is not an either/or matter. It needs to be specified what culture consists of and how it shapes human experience, but doing so is not sufficient to explain the process by which the child constructs meaning through participation in it. In the words of Astington and Olson, 'Social understanding cannot . . . proceed via "participation" without appeal to concepts (p. 187).'

Analysis must thus go beyond the structure inherent in the culture and the structure of social interactions among individuals, to include the meaning-making activity of individuals who participate in this collective experience. Although he didn't give it the attention Piaget did, Vygotsky appeared to recognize the role of this meaning-making component. Internalization, he said, is an internal *reconstruction* of an external operation. What agent can accomplish this reconstruction except an individual psyche? The conclusion, I believe, that we are left with is that Piaget's efforts to map processes of individual mental construction – the essence of his constructivist enterprise – must be incorporated along with Vygotsky's emphasis on the powerful mediating role played by culture. We need to develop our understanding of both ends of the process, and we need to draw on both theorists' insights to do so.

Piaget, to be sure, ignored specificity. Children grow up in very specific and variable social worlds. Whether these environments are 'enriched' or 'deprived', as we've come to regard these concepts from a Western perspective, they are rich in opportunities for cultural learning. The specificities as well as the general dimensions of social interaction provide raw material that makes development possible. But they also channel it in particular directions. And it is here that Vygotsky has much to teach us.

Yet socioculturalists inspired by Vygotsky's thinking need to go beyond the recognition that specific (situated) experience is powerful, as impressive as the demonstrations of its role have been. And they even need to go beyond studies focused on observing the process of cultural transmission, as central as this work is. In addition, their efforts need to embrace the fact that there are general directions and dimensions in terms of which development proceeds – this was of course Piaget's insight – and that these need not be ignored in order to recognize the powerful role of specific experience. Development is characterizable in terms of dimensions that transcend the totally particular. Elaborating and refining such characterizations I believe remains a central task for the future. And I believe the explanatory power claimed by socioculturalists would be enhanced if they included this task in their agenda.

Socioculturalists are fond of claiming that the appropriate unit of analysis is the episode of social transaction, rather than the competencies of an individual. But I think that they go further than they need to here in casting the matter in either/or terms. To say that there is no possibility of examining development at the level of analysis of the individual is to overstate the case. Individuals do change, sometimes in idiosyncratic ways and directions but also in ways likely to be common across populations, phases of the life cycle and periods of history. We need not abandon analysis at this level, nor discard the accrued insights it has produced, in order to be sensitive to the ways that individual and culture interact.

One development in neo-Piagetian theory aids the needed integration: the idea that cognition has structure and organization is no longer tied to claims of universality as it was in orthodox Piagetian theory. We can now postulate highly organized cognitive structures that are powerful in their implications and yet, because they depend on the particularities of individual experience for their formation, vary across individuals (Case, in press; Lewis, 1994). Still, they are not entirely idiosyncratic.

My quibble, then, with the socioculturalists is that despite the rich attention they have paid to process – or perhaps because of it – they have paid too little attention to what it is that they are observing the development of, at a level of abstraction above the particular. Yes, with careful work we can observe the assimilation of new 'ways of being' through participation in the culture. But these 'ways of being' are more than just content subordinated to a focus on process – a stance quite reminiscent of the dismissal of content as irrelevant and subordinated to structure observable in much early work in the Piagetian tradition. These ways of being are contextualized and situated, to be sure, but they are also amenable to description in terms of at least some categories that have at least some generality across contexts, across content and across individuals. In other words, there are products of development that are identifiable within the individual, as the unit of analysis, and that are not entirely specific to the particular contexts in which they occur. If we wish to describe and to explain development, we need to engage in the conceptual abstracting that will allow us to identify its dimensions. Although a process of social appropriation may indeed be critical to the occurrence of this development, describing the process is not the same thing as describing the development.

In the time remaining, I would like to say a few words about my own current research involving peer collaboration, in which we have sought a dual focus on individual and social processes. We have observed dyads of both preadolescents and adults collaborating on the kinds of scientific inquiry tasks mentioned earlier in which subjects reconcile their existing theories with an accumulating data base of evidence that they access over repeated occasions. In other work, we have observed pairs of early adolescents and adults engage in dialogues with one another regarding the pros and cons of capital punishment. Again, the observation is microgenetic, involving repeated sessions over a period of weeks, in this case with a changing series of partners. In both these settings we observe change over time – in the scientific inquiry setting, in the knowledge of the microworld being investigated and in the strategies of investigation; in the case of the capital punishment dialogues, we observe it in the range and quality of argumentation.

In this microgenetic work, we have also turned to social collaboration as a vehicle for developing ways to empirically assess metacognition and metacognitive development, which have largely been regarded as internal and unobservable and hence remained in the realm of theoretical constructs. We do so by externalizing the normally interior mental processes involved in understanding how to approach a task. Specifically, in the scientific reasoning paradigm, we ask subjects to explain to a new peer 'what is going on here' – what the task is and how best to do it – once near the beginning of repeated encounters with the task and once at the end. In this way, we obtain an index of how the subject's own metastrategic understanding has evolved in the course of engagement with the task.

The argumentive dialogues, in particular, we have examined as offering us a methodological window on the social appropriation process of assimilating and transforming another person's ways of thinking. Analyses of these data, we believe, allow us to maintain the dual focus I've argued is necessary – on the social process of development from the outside in and the constructive process of development from the inside out. Our subjects acquire new ideas from their partners in the dyads, to be sure, and even new strategies or ways of thinking, and we can trace the emergence and course of these new elements across the sequence of dialogues.

But we also see growth from the inside out, as the exercise of investigative or inference strategies or argumentive sequences strengthens and consolidates their use. And in the domain of argumentive reasoning the experience of expressing one's ideas, and having them interpreted and reacted to by another, shapes the ideas themselves – allowing me to mean something I didn't mean before because of the way another has reacted to what I have said. All of these outcomes are measurable as products that reside within the individual. Studying and measuring them does not diminish our awareness of the fundamental role played by processes that are social in nature.

In our empirical work, we have accordingly conducted analyses at both social and individual levels – social analyses of dyadic process and individual analyses of change from pre-test to post-test assessments of skill. In the work on argumentive reasoning, an initial and formidable task was to develop an analytic framework for assessing the quality of arguments about capital punishment – requiring essentially a typology of all of the possible reasons that might be offered for and against capital punishment, which we were then able to organize into categories based on adequacy according to several criteria. At both age levels (early adolescent and adult), we observed significant pre- to post-test change (following five dialogue sessions) in the range of arguments voiced. Almost all subjects showed this improvement. But in addition we were able to identify change of ten different structural types (i.e. having to do with the structure of the overall argument, rather than only the number of different argument elements included). These changes, for example, involve a shift from a one-sided to a two-sided argument, from a non-comparative to a comparative argument (one in which the topic is considered in a framework of alternatives), from absence to presence of evidence and, at the lowest level, from no opinion to opinion and from no argument to argument.

In analyses of social process, an initial question we focused on was this: When and how did the new argument elements absent at a subject's pre-test and present at the post-test appear in the course of the dialogues? In each of the cases examined, these elements did indeed appear in the dialogues. There were no instances of a new element appearing for the initial time at the post-test. We identified the first appearance of new arguments, distinguishing whether the argument was first exhibited by the focal subject, in the course of justifying or critiquing a claim that arose in the discussion, or whether the argument was first exhibited by a partner and only subsequently adopted by the subject. In addition we traced the appearance of other argumentive dimensions such as the use of evidence and two-sided argument.

We also identified all of the preceding occurrences as a function of whether the dialogue in question was between two partners who agreed (both pro or both con at the pre-test) or disagreed (one pro and one con). In examining these data, we came to agree with the view expressed by Kruger (1993) that the tendency to contrast 'conflict' and 'cooperation' models of peer interaction – a contrast often connected to one between Piaget and Vygotsky – is a vast oversimplification of what is in fact a complex array of different forms of interaction each having many possible outcomes. The major contribution we have to offer based on our case studies is to highlight dialogues between agreeing (as well as disagreeing) partners as contexts for change. Especially in the case of argumentive reasoning, it has been implicitly assumed that the power of dialogue stems from the discrepancy between viewpoints, forcing members of the pair to justify their own and challenge the other's view. Yet all of the forms of advancement identified in our work can occur as readily in interaction with an agreeing partner as a disagreeing one, including in particular those forms we found most prevalent. Agreeing partners have the potential to reason in a framework of alternatives and can express two-sided as well as one-sided arguments. And all dialogues between agreeing partners, our case studies revealed, are far from alike. A few are limited to simple reiteration and reinforcement of one another's views, but more often the partners differ in their functional roles, with one doing more of the structure-imposing dialogue work than the other, with the outcome that claims may be examined, elaborated and critiqued, and alternatives generated, even though the partners share the same basic opinion. Thus one partner performs metastrategic scaffolding for the other. This functional role of dyadic interaction – and externalization of metacognitive components of thought – we also observed in our microgenetic studies of scientific inquiry, as, for example, when one partner cautioned,'We don't know that,' in response to the other's claim.

Although our case study analysis is based on a small and incomplete sampling that makes precise quantification inappropriate, among the cases we examined the advancements evident at the post-test most often first occurred in the context of an agreeing dyad, with the partner first expressing the new element and the subject subsequently adopting it, either later in the dialogue in a new context or in a subsequent dialogue with a different partner. But we observed the remaining patterns as well – a new element initiated by a disagreeing partner and subsequently adopted by the subject and a new element initiated by the subject in justifying or critiquing a claim voiced during the dialogue.

Moreover, it may well be that dialogues among disagreeing partners have unique functions to perform that dialogues between agreeing partners do not accomplish. Our case studies contain some indication of such a possibility. Some subjects, for example, may need the stimulation of an opposing partner, even to articulate a justification of their own position. One of our subjects began a dialogue by expressing her position, with little supporting argument, and then stopped, leading her partner to inquire, 'What arguments would you use to persuade me?' She responded, 'Well, it depends on what you come and contradict me with, you know.' Again, partners are providing metastrategic scaffolding for one another, in this case in the routines of argumentive reasoning.

These dyadic interactions make it easy to appreciate the close relation between dialogic and individual (rhetorical) argument (Billig, 1987; Kuhn, 1991) – a relation that both Piaget and Vygotsky would be sympathetic to, despite their differences on issues of process. And the development of argumentive reasoning skill is clearly a dual process – again, from the outside in (as forms originating in social interaction become interiorized) as well as from the inside out (as newly constructed forms are consolidated and applied in social interactions).

And thus the power of the social is not in question here – the majority of newly appearing argument elements in our research could be traced to a partner's influence – but the claim made earlier that is well supported by our data is that this social influence does not operate in any automatic way. Why, of all of the possible argument elements they might have adopted from their series of partners, did a subject adopt the particular two or three that typically appeared as new elements at the post-tests, and not any of the others to which they received equal exposure? To find an answer to this question we must look within the individual – to the various competencies and understandings the individual brings to the situation – as well as examining the social process that occurs between individuals. In conclusion, again, we need not choose between one level of analysis and the other.

Anyone who questions the power of the social need look no further than Geil and Moshman's (1994) intriguing study of college students working in small groups on Wason's four-card problem. The correct solution was the consensus response for 75% of the groups, although only 9% of individuals had given that response when assessed individually prior to the group interaction. Moreover, in three out of eight correctly responding groups, no individual had initially exhibited the correct response. Similarly, in our microgenetic studies of scientific inquiry, our dyads often showed superior inquiry and inference skills working together than either member did while working on equivalent tasks individually over the same period of time.

In seeking to explain the power of the social – why and how two minds in interaction are better than one – we must not overlook the affective dimension. The desire to share knowing with another human being is a fundamental one. It is at heart a desire to make your thoughts known to the other and to learn whether they are understood, even shared – always with the chance that I will mean more than I meant before because of the way the other has understood what I have said. The process is one that truly works from both the inside out and the outside in, as we each become different persons through our interaction with one another. I propose this collaborative process as one worthy focus of attention in our efforts to build on the substantial foundations laid by Piaget and Vygotsky.

REFERENCES

Astington, J. and Olson, D. (1995). The cognitive revolution in children's understanding of mind. *Human Development*, 38 (4–5), 179–89.
Bereiter, C. (1994). Constructivism, socioculturalism, and Popper's World 3. *Educational Researcher*, 23 (7), 21–3.
Billig, M. (1987). *Arguing and Thinking: A Rhetorical Approach to Social Psychology*. Cambridge: Cambridge University Press.
Brainerd, C. (1978). The stage question in cognitive-developmental theory. *Behavioral and Brain Sciences*, 78 (2), 173–213.
Bruner, J. (1995). Commentary. *Human Development*, 38 (4–5), 203–13.
Case, R. (in press). The development of conceptual structures. In D. Kuhn and R. Siegler (eds), *Handbook of child psychology*, vol. 2. *Cognition, Perception, and Language*. (5th edn). New York: Wiley.

Case, R. and Edelstein, W. (eds) (1993). *The New Structuralism in Cognitive Development: Theory and Research on Individual Pathways. Contributions to Human Development*, vol. 23. Basel: Karger.

Chapman, M. (1991). The epistemic triangle: operative and communicative components of cognitive competence. In M. Chandler and M. Chapman (eds), *Criteria for Competence: Controversies in the Conceptualization and Assessment of Children's Abilities*. Hillsdale, NJ: Erlbaum.

Feldman, C. F. (1995). Commentary. *Human Development*, 38 (4–5), 194–202.

Flavell, J., Green, F. and Flavell, E. (1995). *Young Children's Knowledge about Thinking. Monographs of the Society for Research in Child Development*, 60 (2), Serial no. 243.

Furth, H. (1996). Human mind in human society. *Human Development*, 39, 264–8.

Geil, M. and Moshman, D. (1994). Scientific reasoning and social interaction: the four-card task in five-person groups. Paper presented at the meeting of the Jean Piaget Society, Chicago.

Gopnik, A. and Graf, P. (1988). Knowing how you know: young children's ability to identify and remember the sources of their beliefs. *Child Development*, 59, 1, 366–71.

Kruger, A. (1993). Peer collaboration: conflict, cooperation, or both? *Social Development*, 2/3, 165–80.

Kuhn, D. (1991). *The Skills of Argument*. New York: Cambridge University Press.

Kuhn, D. (1995). Microgenetic study of change: What has it told us? *Psychological Science*, 6, 133–9.

Kuhn, D., Garcia-Mila, M., Zohar, A. and Andersen, C. (1995). *Strategies of Knowledge Acquisition. Monographs of the Society for Research in Child Development*, 60 (4), Serial no. 245.

Leadbeater, B. and Raver, C. (1995) Commentary. *Human Development*, 38 (4–5), 190–3.

Lewis, M. (1994). Reconciling stage and specificity in Neo-Piagetian theory: self-organizing conceptual structures. *Human Development*, 37 (3), 143–69.

Olson, D. and Astington, J. (1993). Thinking about thinking: learning how to take statements and hold beliefs. *Educational Psychologist*, 28 (1), 7–23.

Olson, D. and Astington, J. (1995). Reply. *Human Development*, 38 (4–5), 214–16.

Popper, K. (1972). *Objective knowledge: An Evolutionary Approach*. Oxford: Clarendon Press.

Ruffman, T., Perner, J., Olson, D. and Doherty, M. (1993). Reflecting on scientific thinking: children's understanding of the hypothesis-evidence relation. *Child Development*, 64, 1, 617–36.

Siegler, R. (1995). How does change occur? A microgenetic study of number conservation. *Cognitive Psychology*, 28 (3), 225–73.

Siegler, R. and Crowley, K. (1991). The microgenetic method: a direct means for studying cognitive developments. *American Psychologist*, 46, 606–20.

Siegler, R. and Jenkins, E. (1989). *How Children Discover New Strategies*. Hillsdale, NJ: Erlbaum.

Sodian, B., Zaitchik, D. and Carey, S. (1991). Young children's differentiation of hypothetical beliefs from evidence. *Child Development*, 62, 753–66.

Taylor, M., Esbensen, B. and Bennett, R. (1994). Children's understanding of knowledge acquisition: the tendency for children to report they have always known what they have just learned. *Child Development*, 65 (6), 1,581–1,604.

Vygotsky, L. (1978). *Mind in Society: The Development of Higher Psychological Processes*. Cambridge, MA: Harvard University Press.

Name index

Subject index